Memoirs *of a* Revolutionist

Vera Figner.

Moscow, 1925

Vera Figner

Memoirs *of a* Revolutionist

Authorized Translation from the Russian

Introduction by Richard Stites

NORTHERN ILLINOIS UNIVERSITY PRESS

DeKalb   1991

© 1991 by Northern Illinois University Press
This copyright covers the material written expressly for this edition by
the editor as well as the compilation itself. Figner's work is copyright
1927, renewed 1955 by International Publishers Co., Inc., and
reprinted here with permission.
Published by the Northern Illinois University Press, DeKalb, Illinois
60115
Manufactured in the United States using acid-free paper ∞
Cover design by Julia Fauci

Library of Congress Cataloging-in-Publication Data
Figner, Vera, 1852–1925.
    [Zapechatlennyĭ trud. English]
    Memoirs of a revolutionist / Vera Figner ; authorised translation
from the Russian ; new introduction by Richard Stites.
      p. cm.
    Translation of: Zapechatlennyĭ trud.
    ISBN 0-87580-552-3
    1. Figner, Vera, 1852–1942.   2. Women socialists—Soviet Union
—Biography. 3. Women revolutionists—Soviet Union—Biography.
I. Title.
HX313.8.F54A3   1991
335.83′092—dc20
  [B]   90-28720
                            CIP

CONTENTS

CONTENTS

LIST OF ILLUSTRATIONS

INTRODUCTION

A Study in Rebellion

Richard Stites

VERA NIKOLAEVNA FIGNER (1852–1942) lived a revolution for forty-five of her ninety years and was an icon of that revolution in her last twenty-five years. I began reading about this remarkable woman three decades ago and had my closest contact with her memory when I spoke to her niece, Margarita Nikolaevna Figner (now deceased), in Leningrad on a frosty sunny day in January 1968.[1] On that day, Margarita Nikolaevna voiced the hope and the belief that her aunt would be soon honored by renaming after her the little street that links Perovskaya and Zhelyabov streets not far from the Church on the Blood—the site of the assassination of Tsar Alexander II on March 1, 1881. When I met her again a few years later, she was still nurturing that hope. The streets and squares of Leningrad (formerly St. Petersburg) bear the names of many famous revolutionaries of the age of populism: Chernyshevsky, Kropotkin, Bakunin, Khalturin, Lavrov, and the two mentioned above who were central in organizing the assassination and were hanged for their act. There were even plans to turn the Church on the Blood, built in 1907, into a museum devoted to the memory of the heroes of the People's Will, the party to which Vera Figner linked her destiny.

At the present moment, it is more likely that the church will revert to its earlier intention—to commemorate the murdered tsar and not the revolutionaries. Leningrad is likely to be renamed St. Petersburg by the time this book goes to press. The reputation of Russian revolutionaries of any stripe has never been lower than it is now among the general population, from the working class and peasants to the urban intelligentsia. In line with the whole rethinking of the past, the history of the revolutionary movement is being rewritten, and for many people the heroes and martyrs of yesterday now seem more like dark and evil villains. The revulsion against Stalin—villain number one—is working its way rapidly backward to Lenin, the Bolsheviks, the other radical parties of 1917, and thence to the entire phenomenon of radical protest and political violence that occupied several generations of men and women through much of the nineteenth century. This is a natural and understandable reaction against Soviet mythology and historiography, which for years exalted its own saints and prophets and vilified the old regime. Many Russians now want to bend the historical record back the other way, to rediscover the charms of tsarism, the empire, conservatism, religion, and even fashion and styles of life. A tremendous wave of nostalgic revivalism is sweeping the cities of Russia at this moment, and it is putting a negative stamp on everything that smacks of the Revolution, its makers, or its precursors. Thus the author of this book and her fellow revolutionaries seem destined for at least temporary oblivion in Russia. All the more reason then to reissue these once famous memoirs at a moment when the flame of memory seems about to be extinguished—just as Figner's own revolutionary life was extinguished when, in 1883, she was placed behind bars for twenty-two years and, for her, "the clock of life stood still."

Figner's memoir is one of those books that can best be read by starting in the middle, that is at Book Two which describes her years in prison. Here we find the essence of the woman, the deepest layer of her personality, her character, one may even say her soul. In her narrow cell in the forbidding Schlüsselburg Fortress, fifty miles upriver from St. Petersburg, built on a rocky island at the point where the vast Lake Ladoga pours its waters into the Neva River, Vera Figner confronted her life and painfully sought its meaning. Prison literature, rooted in the murky themes of Dante's *Inferno* and the lives of Christian martyrs, has seized the fancy of generations of readers who have found in it the ultimate meaning of sacrifice for an ideal. From the dungeons of Naples, the death rows of Malaga and Barcelona, the Moabit under the Nazis, and the Lubyanka under the Communists have risen the voices of political prisoners to tell us not only of the horrors of unfreedom and wrenching fear but also of the process of rehumanization that men and women can experience in the depth of despair.

During the long years of incarceration, Figner codified the moral rules of her life as a revolutionary: assume blame for one's own actions, suit the action to the word, and make one's own decisions and adhere to them until they appear clearly unworkable or counterproductive. She had applied these principles in the revolutionary movement by insisting on being directly involved in the terrorist acts she approved. In prison she was a beacon for other prisoners by insisting on facing punishment, demanding equal punishment for herself, and participating in acts of rebellion such as hunger strikes. Through a telegraphic system of tapping on pipes or walls (devised earlier in the century by prisoners in Europe and described graphically in Arthur Koestler's *Darkness at Noon*), the Schlüsselburg inmates kept each other informed, exchanged personal information, and struggled furiously over moral issues of accommodation and resistance. In the endless chain of dilemmas over solidarity and personal conscience, Figner was as quick to judge herself as she was her comrades. Through it all she and the others created a collective ethical community in which the welfare of the group exceeded in priority that of the individual—a familiar Russian tradition long before the dawn of Marxism.

The prison section of the book also presents a number of miniature epics of fellow revolutionaries caught up in the dragnet of the imperial police and buried alive in the fortress to end their days in a hopeless cul-de-sac. In the intense relationship of these prisoners with each other—especially Figner and Lyudmila Volkenstein—one may read better than in the programs and manifestos of their parties what it meant to be a revolutionary and what utter dedication and uncompromising zeal—a zeal that hostile historians have called "fanaticism"—motivated their actions and sustained their lives. Vera Figner became a prison legend in her lifetime, and upon release in 1904, devoted herself to public work on behalf of Russian political prisoners. The anonymous preface to this book, first published in 1927 by International Publishers, a New York house specializing in radical literature, struck the right note for the times by calling Figner's memoirs "a rare document of human loveliness, force and grandeur, rising above sordid reality, and proclaim[ing] the possibility of a heroic life even at this un-romantic age of ours" (p. 3).

Now let us trace the path of Vera Figner to her title as most wanted criminal in imperial Russia in the years prior to her arrest. She was born in 1852—nine years before the emancipation of the serfs—in a family of the noble class in the province of Kazan on the middle Volga. Until entry into maturity, Vera's life was similar in almost every way to that of other little girls of her class and station: a childhood of privilege and freedom from want, a comfortable home, and a happy family. Though, like some other radical women, she would form very strong ties with her mother, this bonding was not the result of a reaction against a despotic father.[2] Indeed Vera Figner's path to radicalism was very slow and by no means pre-determined by something in her character. Everything in her auto-biography points to a sober and sane person who was driven into revolt by her perception of the world around her and by the re-pressive policy of the regime. This needs to be emphasized in view of the attempts by some historians to depict the populist generation of rebels as abnormal misfits and hysterics. The daydreams of Vera as a child presented no conflict or contradiction to her: to marry a tsar when she grew up (rather than helping to kill one); and to help the poor, the persecuted, and the weak. Nor did her early and sin-cere Christianity conflict with the militant humanitarian faith that she later acquired. Indeed the two merged into one as she suggests in a remarkable passage on page 205 and in her dream (p. 296) which seems to combine the Christian vision of heaven with that of Chernyshevsky in his famous utopian scenes in *What Is To Be Done?*

After private tutoring at home, Vera attended what was prac-tically the only type of school open to girls of her rank in society at that time, a private *institut* or boarding school. These schools were modelled on the famous Smolny Institute in Petersburg, founded in the eighteenth century by Catherine the Great for daughters of the upper classes. At her school in Kazan, Figner developed—or had confirmed—a sense of discipline that would serve her well later in underground activities; an air of self-confidence and good-manners that continued to impress her captors during the years of incarcera-tion; and, as she put it, a burning need for deep comradeship that

went beyond the casual relations among schoolmates. The comradeship she found in full measure in the revolutionary movement
and in the Schlüsselburg Fortress. What she did not get, she
claims with perhaps some exaggeration, was spiritual or educational enrichment. "In regard to scientific knowledge and especially mental development, my school years not only gave me precious little but even retarded my spiritual growth to say nothing
of the harm done to me by the unnatural isolation from life and
people."[3] But how was one to achieve more? There is no hint, at
this point in her life, that Figner was an enemy of the tsarist system
or even politically conscious. But like hundreds of Russian women
who came of age in the 1860s, she was clearly dissatisfied with the
map of life drawn in advance for her by society: marriage to a social
equal, children, and only enough knowledge of the world to make
her a good companion and hostess.

Vera Figner's emergence into adulthood coincided with a mo-
mentous social and cultural movement in nineteenth-century Russia: the emergence of the "woman question" and the struggle for
female higher education.[4] Women's dissatisfaction with the gender
structure of their society—an impatience shared by women all over
the western world at the time, though seldom with such intensity as
in Russia—led them to seek release through a variety of solutions.
One was simply to acquire more and better knowledge in order to
take up a useful role in society beyond that of the ascribed function
of housewife; this aspiration helped to feed the feminist mentality
that was just then taking hold of educated women. Another was
sexual revolt in the form of "nihilism," a generalized rebellion by
men and women against the established conventions of midcentury
Russian upper- and middle-class norms, a rejection of marriage
and parental authority. After graduation from the institute in 1869,
Figner became infected by both of these currents but never became
a feminist or a nihilist in the true sense of those terms. Her initial
rebellion was fueled by endless reading, intellectual curiosity, and
a thirst for more learning. She was electrified by the writings of the
journalists of the early sixties which had fed the radical movement[5]; and by the exploits of Nadezhda Suslova, a Russian who
had become one of the first women physicians in Europe by enrolling in medical school in Switzerland.

Figner's marriage to a young local lawyer, Alexei Filippov

(spelled Philipov in this edition), is recounted in a wholly offhand manner; her husband and his place in Figner's life would remain shadowy throughout all versions of her memoirs. But a symptom of the coming separation is revealed in her discomfort at his occupation as an investigative magistrate. Like the later prophet of Bolshevik feminism Alexandra Kollontai,[6] Figner could not abide in her spouse what she took to be an exploitative occupation. She persuaded him to give it up and go with her to Zurich. After preparatory study of medicine in Kazan, she, her husband, and her sister Lidiya left for Zurich. Figner's primary concern was to study medicine in order to bring her skills back to Russia and in some way ease the suffering of the diseased and impoverished masses there, an eminently practical and humanitarian goal in a nation where medical talent was in very short supply and largely congregated in the cities around the wealthier clientele. In Zurich she at first evinced no burning interest in politics but devoted herself to study and, apparently, to domestic concerns. But it was difficult to remain aloof in a town that was aflame with émigré revolutionaries, their ideas, and their followers.

Her younger sister, Lidiya, who was unmarried, soon became embroiled in the heady debates between the disciples of Peter Lavrov, who taught gradual propagandism among the Russian people, and those of Michael Bakunin who preached a maximalist tactic of peasant revolt; between Marxists of various persuasions; and among the veterans and postmortem analysts of the recently suppressed Paris Commune.[7] Lidiya was pulled into the radical vortex and joined a circle of female students residing at Frau Frietsch's pension. This became the nucleus of a new organization of women— later joined by a few males—who wrenched themselves free of avocational pursuits and burned their bridges in order to return to Russia and engage directly in revolutionary propaganda. The fruit of this decision was the All-Russia Social-Revolutionary Organization. The immediate impetus for this drastic decision to break the current of their studious life, to risk their freedom and their careers by becoming underground agitators, was an insulting decree issued by the Russian government in 1874, ordering all Russian women studying in Zurich to leave that city or risk future penalties. The reason?—the official belief that the young women had fallen under

the influence of treacherous ideas and personalities and that some
of them were studying medicine in order to perform abortions on
each other since they were living in immoral liaisons with men.
The Frietschi women found this allegation unbearable and were
thus impelled to make the final breech with "respectable" profes-
sional life. But Vera Figner remained in Switzerland and continued
at Berne for a year after the expulsions from Zurich.

Reassembled in Moscow as the All-Russian Social-Revolutionary Organization—a tiny and fragile group in all its phases—the
women and men from Zurich went into the factories to propagan-
dize among the workers for a socialist order. Their amateurish
efforts and their upper-class backgrounds soon betrayed them, and
they fell into the hands of the police.[8] The few survivors entreated
Vera Figner to return to Russia and take up the struggle. This was
the real turning point in Figner's life. In the abbreviated version of
the memoirs here presented, this part of her story is severely trun-
cated, probably reflecting a belief at the time of publication (1926)
that the preparatory stage of Figner's revolutionary activity was less
interesting than the years of struggle in Russia. But Figner, on the
verge of writing her doctorate and then becoming a licenced physician, faced a cruel dilemma, and her solution reveals a tremendous
sacrifice: she would have to throw away her medical career, a
dream that had already once compelled her to break with a traditional past, and plunge into the unknown void of illegal activity for
which she had no preparation whatsoever. That she and dozens like
her were willing to make sacrifices such as this illustrates more
clearly than anything else the tremendous force of social conscience that had grown within them during the early 1870s and
shows also the enormous gulf that was now yawning between the
government and large segments of the educated youth. No revi-
sionism, no exposure of the maladies of the revolutionary movement can weaken this fact.

After much soul searching, Figner broke with her husband, her
studies, and her entire former way of life, packed her bags, sat
down in the Russian ritual of farewell, and departed in 1876 for an
uncertain destiny to her native land. At this point in the memoirs,
the narrative becomes sufficiently detailed again and the reader
may follow the saga of Vera Figner in her own words. Only a few

comments are needed for clarification. One is about her "discovery" of the people. In childhood, as she herself confesses, she had almost no contact with the peasants (p. 20) and thus in the mid-1870s found herself in an entirely new milieu—the remote world of a Volga village. From the works of recent scholarship[9] we know much about the daily lives of peasants in the late nineteenth century—folk medicine, education, and the round of life; but for Figner, this world seemed alien indeed—as if being on another planet. The combination of rural poverty, her own relative helplessness in allaying it, and the petty persecutions of local authorities drove her further and further into the mortal struggle against the autocracy that took the final form of terrorism and assassination. Figner here relates the dramatic events from the inside—the formation of the People's Will party, the various failed attempts against the life of the tsar, the successful assassination in March 1881, and Figner's role in holding the party together in the aftermath until her arrest in 1883.[10]

While prison was thought by the Russian underground fighters to be a "diploma of decency," their trial was considered the final tribunal of history, the venue where one's "last duty" to society was performed: the *apologia pro vita sua*. It was also a theatrical stage upon which the accused could engage in political communication with part of the public—an opportunity denied to them by the nature of their subterranean existence. Previous arrestees—especially women—had availed themselves of this forum to exonerate themselves and their movement and to win sympathy from the educated public, often with brilliant success. Indeed, Figner called her own trial "the last, conclusive act of the revolutionary drama." This self-conscious theatricality of Russian radicals ought not to surprise us or be taken as a sign of false pathos or histrionics. It was a mode of expression deeply connected with moral conscience and the need to explain their motivations to a state that rarely listened. Figner was condemned to death for her role in preparing the assassination and for other terrorist acts, but the death sentence was commuted to life imprisonment.

Figner had become, at the end of her career, one of the major female figures of Russian radicalism at midcentury. Two others are Vera Zasulich,[11] whose notoriety came when she fired point blank at a prison governor, was exonerated in a famous jury trial, and then fled abroad, later to assist in the founding of Russian Marxism; and Sofia Perovskaya, daughter of a former governor general, and agent of the tsar's assassination.

Figner was released in 1904 but was required to reside for some time in provincial settings.[12] During a visit to her native Kazan province an incident occurred that ironically illustrated the tremendous gulf between the revolutionary intelligentsia, with its exalted sense of dedication to the people, and the people themselves. The peasants on her ancestral estate burned the manor house to the ground. When Figner was finally allowed to visit Moscow, she was politically disoriented but feted by liberals, socialists, the newly founded groups of Russian suffragists, and female students. Throughout her subsequent years of self-imposed exile in Europe (1907–1917), Figner maintained friendly relations with the feminist movement in her native land, though she had rejected feminism as such in her younger years and never really became an activist. In 1908, she joined the Socialist Revolutionary party—the commonly accepted heir of populist traditions—but resigned over differences with the leadership. She spent the remainder of the emigration years wandering from city to city, writing and speaking on the revolutionary movement and prison conditions in Russia.

In 1917, after the tsar fell from power in the midst of war and a "free Russia" was proclaimed, Figner returned to the capital, Petrograd. But new faces and new forces had reshaped the political arena, and Figner became one of many "old revolutionaries" confronting an unexpected sort of revolution. She was treated deferentially as an ancient icon of the radical movement, a heroine of terror; she adorned the rostra and stages of revolutionary spectacles and performances. But there was no real place for her in the power structure of this revolution, and she could settle upon no party. She was coopted by her old feminist friends and used as an emblem of the oppression of women under the old regime and as a freedom fighter of the past.

When the Bolsheviks took over, Figner did not know what to make of the event. "The overturn of October 25," she wrote, "from which our great social revolution began, was a great shock for me.

I was not prepared for it." But unlike some other figures of the past—Kropotkin, Plekhanov, Breshkovskaya—she did not stand against the new regime. Nor did she join the Bolshevik party, though she was actively courted by it. She did remain in Russia performing prodigious works of personal charity for the poor and hungry—in a sense reverting to the days of her sojourn in the countryside in the 1870s—did literary work for the Society of Political Exiles, and even tried to recruit émigré revolutionaries back to Russia. When all the institutions connected with the old populists were abolished by Stalin in the 1930s, Figner retreated further from active life. We have no record of her knowledge or opinions of the terrible massacres carried out by the Stalinist regime in those years. She was living in Moscow when the Germans invaded on June 22, 1941. In the autumn, as enemy forces were approaching the capital, the authorities evacuated certain key figures, groups, and institutions; when they sought to evacuate this great symbolic figure, the feeble old heroine refused, saying "concern yourselves with the living." She died the following year on June 15, 1942, at the age of ninety and was buried with honor at the Novodevichy Cemetery. Her grave can still be seen there.

At this fateful juncture in Russian history, when the people of that long-suffering country are constantly invoking the need for a moral and spiritual renewal, for personal courage and sacrifice, for universal human values, for selfless devotion, it may be worthwhile for them to contemplate some of the bright examples of these values as personified in the life of Vera Figner. They may well disagree with her political views, her turn to violence, her commitment to revolution. But if they peer closely at her testimony, they will perceive in her the kind of profound devotion that was so characteristic of the best exemplars of the revolutionary movement of the nineteenth century.

This book is not a scholarly edition of Figner's memoirs. Such a book would require several volumes of newly translated and fully annotated material for the use of specialists.[13] As a reprint of a revolutionary classic, it is meant to be read by students and the general public interested in entering the convoluted emotional world of Russian revolutionaries via the life—as filtered through memory—of one of its most outstanding figures. The translation is on the whole very good, even elegant, though it contains a few errors that are listed at the end of this introduction. It would be pedantic to try to modernize this translation by replacing "men" with the more accurate "people" (for the word *liudy*); the editors may have had feminist sympathies but did not possess the linguistic gender style that prevails today. A more serious flaw is the amount of material left out of the original translation, which gives a telescoped account of Figner's life in Switzerland and thus misleadingly condenses the pace of her revolutionary development to consciousness which was agonizingly slow. I have tried to fill in a bit of that story in the previous pages.

Figner's account of the revolutionary movement is full of flat judgements and personal opinions that modern scholars would dispute. Her vision of an active alliance between revolutionaries and peasant masses in the aftermath of the assassination of the tsar did not come to pass; and the bloody and bestial massacre of the gentry in the manner of Pugachëv or "the extirpation of the Roman patricians by the Lombards" (p. 114) did not even occur in the rural revolutions of 1905 and 1917–18. Her evocation of violence contradicts other passages where she fully admits its corrupting role— not only of the government but of the revolutionaries as well. There are also whole sections of the memoirs excised by the translators that reflect Figner's ambivalence on many issues; this helps quicken the tempo of the narrative but of course weakens that narrative as a source for the history of the movement.

The importance of this work is not in its historical accuracy or the nuances of its assessments, but in its function as moral witness and personal testimony. Furthermore, larger truths are often lodged inside offhand remarks. Figner's claim that a terrorist machine could help infuse life into a "liberal" movement may puzzle modern students who identify liberalism with moderation, compromise, and a rejection of terror. But in its original early nineteenth-century form—in Spain, Italy, Latin America, Poland, and elsewhere—liberalism, along with nationalism, was considered revolutionary by conservatives who deployed barbarous methods against it, and this justified to the rebels their own resort to violence. Russian socialism was even more radical than European liberalism and was repressed with force. Through the eyes of Vera Figner we witness the tragedy of this collision and better understand what makes people rebel against perceived despotism.

NOTES

1. I want to thank Iain Elliot of the School of Slavonic and East European Studies in London who first introduced me to M. F. Figner and assisted in the interview at a time when my spoken Russian was very weak.

2. For this important theme, see Barbara Engel, *Mothers and Daughters; Women of the Intelligentsia in Nineteenth Century Russia* (Cambridge, England, 1983).

3. V. N. Figner, *Zapechatlënnyi trud; vospominaniya*, 2v. (Moscow, 1964), I, 86.

4. On this broad subject see Engel, *Mothers and Daughters*; Richard Stites, *The Women's Liberation Movement in Russia: Feminism, Nihilism, and Bolshevism 1860–1930* (Princeton, 1978); G. A. Tishkin, *Zhenskii vopros v Rossii 50-60-e gody XIX v.* (Leningrad, 1984); Christine Johanson, *Women's Struggle for Higher Education in Russia, 1855–1900* (Montreal, 1987); Jeannette Tuve, *The First Russian Women Physicians* (Newtonville, 1984); Ann Hibner Koblitz, *A Convergence of Lives: Sofia Kovalevskaia* (Boston, 1983); and E. A. Pavlyuchenko, *Zhenshchiny v russkom osvoboditelnom dvizhenii: ot Marii Volkonskoi do Very Figner* (Moscow, 1988).

5. A fine introduction to the radical traditions and the youth movement is Abbott Gleason, *Young Russia: The Genesis of Russian Radicalism in the 1860s* (New York, 1980).

6. On this crucial figure in Russian women's history, see Barbara Clements, *Bolshevik Feminist: The Life of Alexandra Kollontai* (Bloomington, 1979); and Beatrice Farnsworth, *Aleksandra Kollontai: Socialism, Feminism, and the Bolshevik Revolution* (Stanford, 1980).

7. For the radical atmosphere in Zurich from various perspectives, see: J. M. Meijer, *Knowledge and Revolution: The Russian Colony in Zuerich (1870–1873)* (Assen, 1955); Philip Pomper, *Peter Lavrov and the Russian Revolutionary Movement* (Chicago, 1972); and Amy Knight, "The Fritschi: a Study of Female Radicals in the Russian Populist Movement," *Canadian-American Slavic Studies*, IX/1 (Spring, 1975), 1–17.

8. For a brief account of this group, see Richard Stites, "All-Russian Socialist-Revolutionary Organization," *Modern Encyclopedia of Russian and Soviet History*, I.

9. Two handy collections in English are Wayne Vucinich, ed., *The Peasant in Nineteenth-Century Russia* (Stanford, 1968); and Ben Eklof and Stephen Frank, eds., *The World of the Russian Peasant* (Boston, 1990).

10. For an up-to-date historical treatment of these events, see Norman Naimark, *Terrorists and Social Democrats: The Russian Revolutionary Movement under Alexander III* (Cambridge, Mass., 1983); and Derek Offord, *The Russian Revolutionary Movement in the 1880s* (Cambridge, Eng., 1986).

11. On Zasulich, see Jay Bergman, *Vera Zasulich: A Biography* (Stanford, 1983).

12. For Figner's subsequent activities, see V. N. Figner, *V borbe*, ed. M. N. Figner (Leningrad, 1966), pp. 183–227; Stites, *Women's Liberation Movement*; and Linda Edmondson, *Feminism in Russia 1900–1917* (London, 1984).

13. In addition to the works cited in notes 3 and 11 above, see the further works of V. N. Figner: *Polnoe sobranie sochinenii*, 6v. (Moscow, 1929); "Studencheskie gody (1872–1873)," *Golos minuvshego*, X (October, 1922), 165–181; *Shlisselburgskaya uznitsa Lyudmila Aleksandrovna Volkenshtein* (Moscow, 1906); *Posle Shlisselburga* (Leningrad, 1925); and *Les prisons russes* (Lausanne, 1911). Barbara Engel and Clifford Rosenthal, eds., *Five Sisters: Women against the Tsar* (New York, 1975) contains excellent translations of Figner (pp. 1–58) and other women. Figner's poetry is found in *Poety-demokraty 1870-1880-kh godov* (Moscow, 1962), pp. 495–531.

NOTES TO THE TEXT

21/2   N. A. Demert, popular Russian journalist for *Notes of the Fatherland* in the 1860s.

24/1   "Knize" should probably be "Kniesse," a German name.

30/9   "P. H. Kupriyanov" would now be rendered as "P. Kh. Kupriyanov"

44/9B and passim   "assistant physician" (*feldsher*) should be rendered "surgeon's assistant"

61n   This note confuses the Soloviev attempt of 1879 with the more famous Karakozov attempt of 1866; on the latter and Komissarov, see Gleason, *Young Russia*, p. 333.

188/3   Simon Meyer, French-Jewish National Guard captain during the Paris Commune whose memoirs were a classic of prison literature.

229/8   The introduction of a work regime by the new warden (properly spelled Gangardt) is missing from this text and therefore comes to the reader as a surprise. See n. 50 on p. 230.

303/20   S. Ya. Nadson (1862–1887), a civic poet whose work was admired by radicals but was suffused with impotence.

Memoirs *of a* Revolutionist

INTRODUCTION TO 1927 VOLUME

At the age of seventy-five, the author of these Memoirs displays the same nobility of spirit, the same fortitude of character and convictions, the same personal magnetism that have distinguished her revolutionary leadership half a century ago. Neither the strenuous experiences of terroristic activity, nor the deadening years—twenty years of confinement in the Schlüsselburg Fortress—have dimmed the flaming faith of Vera Figner in humanity, in the worth of heroic efforts for the betterment of life. Indeed, the one manifest effect of the prison term was to soften somewhat the austerity of her outlook, to instill more charity into her intransigency. The Memoirs present a rare document of human loveliness, force and grandeur, rising above sordid reality, and proclaim the possibility of a heroic life even at this unromantic age of ours.

At the completion of the second part of her Memoirs, "When the Clock of Life Stopped," Vera Figner wrote somewhat apologetically:

" 'Sufficient unto the day the evil thereof.' New times require new songs, whereas my book is a song of what is past, finished, and will never come back.

"Yet though my book speaks of the past and contributes nothing to the practical life of the present moment, a time will come when it will be of use. The dead do not rise, but there is resurrection in books. Silvio Pellico's *My Prisons,* or De Coster's *Eulenspiegel,* are alive for us, even though the one was written a hundred years ago, and the other describes events of the sixteenth century.

" 'Write!' admonished me the great tragedian, Eleanora Duse, when we met abroad. 'Write: you *must* write; your experience *must not* be lost.'

"Let then my experience of the time 'When the Clock of Life Stopped' not be lost for those who are going to live under conditions of ceaseless movement on the part of the clock's hand, a movement in the ever forward direction toward genuine equality and freedom, for the happiness of Russia and all humanity."

Vera Figner has authorised this abridged translation, and has written a special foreword for the American edition. The bulk of the translation has been done by Miss Camilla Chapin Daniels; Mrs. G. A. Davidson translated the latter portion of Book Two. Professor George R. Noyes, of the Department of Slavic Languages at the University of California, has revised the manuscript, jointly with his colleague, Alexander Kaun, who is responsible for the general editing of the text. The editor acknowledges his gratitude to his collaborators.

AUTHOR'S FOREWORD TO THE AMERICAN EDITION

MORE than one hundred years ago the advanced portion of Russian society became imbued with the idea of the necessity of overthrowing the Autocracy, and replacing it by a representative government. But from the military conspiracy of the Decembrists (1825) to the seventies, only individual persons or small isolated groups figured as the opponents of absolutism, and they were swiftly crushed by the repressive measures of the government. Only with the liberation of the serfs (1861) and the inauguration of reforms during the early years of the reign of Alexander II (1818-1881) was Russian life rejuvenated, and social forces received a chance for a broader activity. However, the land and court reforms, and the introduction of county (zemstvo) and city self-government, could not satisfy the progressive men of Russia, as long as the obsolete political order remained. Despite the abolition of serfdom the economic condition of the people was quite unsatisfactory; the long-expected "freedom" failed to fulfil the hopes of the peasantry. On the other hand, the educated class, now increased in numbers, demanded a wider field of activity, and this was impossible in the absence of civil liberties.

These were the two causes of the incessant turmoil which reigned in the internal life of Russia and generated a revolutionary movement with the permanent slogan of *Land and Freedom*. At first the social-revolutionary movement was directed toward the organisation of the peasant masses for an uprising, with the aim of overthrowing the existing economic order. It was expected that this would inevitably result in

the fall of the political order and its replacement by a new one.
Such a formulation of the revolutionary programme implied
no direct struggle against the government. But toward the
end of the seventies, a new tendency ripened, owing to the lack
of response on the part of the peasants, and to the persecutions and intolerable oppression of the unlimited Autocracy:
the overthrow of absolutism was formulated as a definite task.
In 1879 was formed the revolutionary socialist party, The
Will of the People, headed by its Executive Committee. Planning the organisation of a military conspiracy backed by factory workers and by all the discontented, this party resolved to
throw its own forces without delay into a ruthless battle with
the Autocracy, directing its blows against the head of the
state, who personally assumed the responsibility for the rule
of the millions and millions of his people. This battle by means
of violence against violence was waged for three years with
unexampled energy and obstinacy. It culminated on March
1 (14), 1881, when Emperor Alexander II fell on the streets
of St. Petersburg from the bombs hurled by two members of
the party.

The first part of my book comprises the brief period of
1876-1884, describing the consecutive activity of the secret
society, Land and Freedom, and later, of the party, The Will
of the People. I took part in working out the programme of
Land and Freedom, and was the last member of the Executive
Committee of The Will of the People when arrested, in 1883.
I describe the events as an eye-witness and participant.

The Executive Committee perished to the last person, the
party was smashed, but its significance in the history of the
revolutionary movement was extraordinary. After The Will
of the People, political struggle became an essential part of
the programmes of all the subsequent revolutionary generations.
Seventy-two members of the party appeared before court
within five years. Those who were not executed or exiled to
Siberia, were incarcerated in the Fortress of Sts. Peter and
Paul, and from 1884, in the Schlüsselburg Fortress. In the
latter, I, too, was confined. The majority of us died, and I

was freed in 1904, after twenty years of confinement, and sent into exile. Life in Schüsselburg, mine and that of my comrades—this epilogue of our struggle against Autocracy—is described in the second part of my book.

VERA FIGNER.

Moscow, Spring, 1927.

P.S. For those who may be dismayed by the cruel methods employed by The Will of the People in its struggle against Autocracy, I should like to recall the declaration of the Executive Committee of our party, on the occasion of the assassination of President James A. Garfield in 1881:

"Expressing its profound sympathy for the American people, on the occasion of the death of President James Abram Garfield, the Executive Committee regards it as its duty to declare in the name of the Russian revolutionists its protest against such acts of violence as that of Guiteau. In a land where personal freedom gives an opportunity for an honest conflict of ideas, where the free will of the people determines not only the law but also the personality of the ruler, in such a land political murder as a means of struggle presents a manifestation of that despotic spirit which we aim to destroy in Russia. Personal despotism is as condemnable as group despotism, and violence may be justified only when it is directed against violence.

(Signed) "THE EXECUTIVE COMMITTEE."

September 10 (23), 1881.

V. F.

BOOK ONE: A TASK FULFILLED

THE MEMOIRS
OF A REVOLUTIONIST

I

MY FAMILY

I WAS born on the 24th of June, 1852, in the province of Kazan, of a family of prosperous noblemen. My mother, Ekaterina Khristoforovna, had received the usual home education of her time. Her father, Kupriyanov, the judge of the district of Tetyushy, had succeeded in the course of his life in squandering a large fortune. Although he possessed almost seventeen thousand acres in the province of Ufa, besides his land in the Tetyushy district, he left his affairs in such confusion after his death, that his heirs preferred to relinquish their inheritance, inasmuch as the sum of their grandfather's debts could not be estimated.

My father, Nikolai Alexandrovich Figner, was educated in the Forestry Corps, and after the completion of his course served as forester, first in the district of Mamadyshy, and later in Tetyushy. But after the liberation of the serfs he retired in order to become a justice of the peace, and he retained this office until it was abolished.

There were six in our family, besides two boys who died in early childhood. Both my father and mother were very active and energetic people. They were of remarkably robust constitution and strong will. In this respect they gave us a good heritage. I, the eldest, took part in the revolutionary movement during the most desperate period of the struggle against autocracy, was sentenced to the death penalty, and ultimately imprisoned in the Schlüsselburg Fortress. My sister Lydia was a member of a revolutionary organisation which engaged in socialist propaganda among the factory workers. She was condemned to penal servitude, but the Senate commuted the sentence to loss of personal rights and privileges, and exile for life to Eastern Siberia. My brother Pyotr was a prominent mining engineer in the metallurgical plants of the provinces of Perm and Ufa. My brother Nikolai had a brilliant career as an operatic tenor. He was the first to transform the opera, by not only singing but acting his rôles, and he gave esthetic delight to hundreds of thousands of people during his twenty-five years of artistic activity. My sister Evgenia was a defendant in the Kvyatkovsky Trial, in connection with the explosion in the Winter Palace (in 1880), and was deprived of all her rights and privileges, and deported to Siberia. My youngest sister, Olga, a very capable and energetic girl, took little part in the revolutionary movement. She married a doctor, Florovsky, followed him into administrative exile in Siberia, and engaged with him in cultural and educational work in Omsk, later in Yaroslavl, and after the death of her husband, in St. Petersburg. In Siberia, my sisters Lydia and Evgenia married the former political convicts, Stakhevich and Sazhin, men remarkable for their intellect, culture and energy.

I WANT TO BECOME A TSARITSA

According to father, I was a beautiful child. Thanks to this, grown-up visitors always paid especial attention to me, in contrast to our mother and father, who treated all of their children alike. The visitors petted me, gave me little presents, and were amused by my chatter. This contact with older people contributed to my early and rapid development, and sometimes inspired in me such ideas about myself and about the relations of other people to me as are generally foreign to children of that age.

When we went visiting my father's sister at Mamadyshy, her friend, Andrey Andreyevich Katkov, used to spend whole days there. He joked and played with me, often calling me his wife, while I called him my dear husband. Later, when we had moved to the Tetyushy district, and I was not yet seven years old, there came a letter from him which my aunt read aloud. Andrey Andreyevich was going to be married. When I heard that, I felt deeply outraged. How did he dare to get married, when he used to call me his wife! That was treachery, a base affront, when I had considered him bound to me. I did not shed many tears; instinct told me that it was forbidden to talk about it to older people, to express my feelings to them. Why it was forbidden, I did not know, but I simply felt that I must keep silent, and I kept silent.

Something similar to this happened still later, when I was nine years old.

A young girl, my mother's sister, Elizaveta Khristoforovna, who had just graduated from the Rodionovsky Kazan Institute, came to live with us; and from that time, officers of the regiment quartered at Tetyushy began to pay us visits. One of them, Yergolsky, devoted not a little of his time to me, and I imagined that I had especial claims on him. However, my keen, childish eyes quickly observed that he paid still greater attention to my young aunt. I became jealous, and choosing a moment when we were left alone on the terrace leading out onto the garden, I burst into stormy reproaches and made Yergolsky a regular "scene."

Curiously enough, he treated this outburst with utter seriousness, and began to soothe me, instead of ridiculing me for having made a little fool of myself.

If some grown-ups, especially men, by their excessive attentions developed in me the pretentions of a woman, others unconsciously impelled me to seek success in life.

In the district, three miles from town, on the beautiful estate of Lyudogovka, there lived two elderly society women, who had spent all their lives in St. Petersburg, and who only in their declining years had come to live in the solitude of a backwoods district. They amused themselves night and day by playing cards, in which pursuit guests from the neighbourhood joined them, eager to gather around the green table. The younger of the sisters, Natalya Grigoryevna Tselshert, knowing that my parents were thinking of sending me to the Smolny Institute [1]

---

[1] The Smolny Institute was an exclusive boarding school for daughters of the nobility, until 1917, when it became the headquarters of the Bolsheviks.—*Translator.*

in St. Petersburg, would seat me in an armchair beside her every
time we met, and begin to talk about the Institute, and my
future destinies.

"Mind you, you must study as hard as you can," she would
impress upon me, "and don't fail to be the first in your class.
If you are first, you will receive a gold decoration on a ribbon.
Grand dukes, and the Tsar himself come to visit the Institute.
They will notice you, and if you have received the decoration,
they'll make you one of the ladies-in-waiting at court. You
will live in the palace and dance at the court balls," and so
forth.

Until that time I had known nothing beyond the village, and
I listened to the tales of the two sisters as children listen to
stories from "Arabian Nights."

After these conversations, I began to have still grander
dreams.

During those years, mother as a rule rarely read to us aloud.
Yet she did, now and then. Once she was reading to us from
some history, a narrative of the life of the ancient Moscow
tsars, about either Mikhail Fyodorovich or Alexey Mikhailo-
vich—I have forgotten which. Mother read that when the
time came for the Tsar to marry, he issued a proclamation
commanding all the nobles throughout Russia to bring
all their grown daughters to Moscow. There, at Moscow, in
the palace, the Tsar was to view all the assembled maidens, and
choose from them, as wife, the one who seemed to him the most
beautiful. And then it went on to tell how many plots and in-
trigues centred about that choice, and how, with evil intent,
they plaited so tightly the braid of a beautiful maiden who had
pleased the young Tsar, that she sank in a swoon, and, as one
"possessed," lost her chance to become tsaritsa.

"When the Tsar wants to get married, they'll surely take me
to Moscow, too," I reasoned, making no distinction between
the times of the past and the present. "And perhaps of all the
girls there, the Tsar will choose me, me! I'll be a tsaritsa!
. . . Then my nurse will be dressed in silver and gold, and I
shall wear diamonds and rubies."

I do not know what would have happened had I gone to

Smolny, which had the reputation of being a school for the children of wealthy and fashionable families; but this did not happen. While in the Rodionovsky Institute at Kazan, just at the time that they sent me there, a happy change in the general character of education had taken place. And all at once, somehow, in the simple, almost monastic surroundings of this Institute, without any suggestions from an outside source, my childish fantasies of the glitter of court and a golden crown faded away.

However, life eventually fulfilled my immature expectation in quite a peculiar manner, and I received, if not a tsardom, at any rate, a kingdom.

In Schlüsselburg, where among the convicts there were only two women, Volkenstein and myself, our comrades brightening the wretchedness of our life with a touch of tenderness, called us "the queens." To be sure, I wore no royal purple and white ermine, but a grey prison coat, with a yellow diamond-shaped patch on the back.

AT HOME

Save for those influences that I have just mentioned, I was a lively, capable little girl, a mischievous romp and a squabbler, often abusing my brother and sister, who were about my age. When I was engaged in a desperate battle, they would drag me off and say, "Stop fighting!" and I would shriek back, "I want to fight!" and in a rage I would "mop up the floor," to use nurse's expression for describing the convulsive movements peculiar to unruly children at such moments.

Of course, this never took place under my father's eyes, but in nurse's room.

I did not like to play with dolls, but in my play I unconsciously learned to read and write, I do not remember precisely when. I only know that at Khristoforovka, kneeling on a chair in order to reach the table, I produced in large, printed letters a missive, probably the first in my life, to my aunt whom we had left in Mamadyshy. I was scarcely seven.

Up to the time that I entered the Institute, my mother, to whom I owed so much in the later period of my mental develop-

ment, devoted little time to her children. I think that this was
due to the frequency with which children were born to her, who
later had to be nursed at the breast. In fact, I was ten years
old when my youngest sister, Olga, was born, and in that short,
intervening decade, there were six births. Is it to be wondered
at, then, that we knew only the discipline imposed by our
father, while she touched only the outside of our lives? We
realised her presence most strongly at the constant family
gatherings in the morning, the evening, and the general table.
The rest of the time, save when we had committed some high-
handed mischief, we were left to ourselves.

Occasionally we saw in the background of our domestic life
peculiar figures, now appearing, now disappearing, but always
strange to us. At first it was an old man, a German named
Ufers, brought from Mamadyshy for some unknown reason; and
then an absurd companion or housekeeper, whose face was constantly swollen, and who bore the unpleasant surname of Svinyina.[2] And finally another old man, Avtonom Yakovelich,
grandfather's former serf, was summoned to teach us penmanship. He had lived at Khristoforovka with his relatives, and
differed from them only in his dress. Svinyina and Avtonom
Yakovlevich, whom we disliked, had to endure a good deal from
us, especially from that uncontrollable mischief, my brother
Nikolai, who always called the old man "Automaton Yakovlevich," and drove him into a rage by incessantly repeating the
teacher's customary ejaculation, "Fugh! My God!"

Our parents were always distant to us, and did not seek a
closer acquaintance. In our relations there was none of that
intimacy which lends so much charm to childhood. That fell
only to the lot of little Olga, who was eight years old when
father died.

But we loved our mother. My sister and I were constant
rivals for the place next to her. We loved, especially, when
father was away on business connected with his service in the
district, to sleep with mother in the broad, double wooden bed,
which dated from the time of our grandfather. Springing onto
the bed from the bearskin spread on the floor, you would creep

2 Russian for pork.—*Translator.*

down under the warm, knitted quilt, and feel so warm and cosy. In the corner of mother's room was a cabinet of yellow wood, filled with holy images. There were the Christ, and Saint Nicholas, Sergey, the miracle worker, and other saints in silver and gilded chasubles, and the Mother of God, adorned with pearls. A little lamp hung from the ceiling in front of the cabinet, and its small flame, half illuminating the room, glowed tenderly and reassuringly. You lay there, but mother had not yet come to bed; she was standing and praying before the cabinet. There, she sank to her knees, and with her eyes turned toward the ikons, prayed earnestly, almost passionately, whispering some indistinguishable words in her prayer. . . .

What could mother have been praying about so long and so earnestly, those many years ago? Her life flowed along evenly, without great joys or disturbing sorrows. In the village backwoods, one met no outsiders, there were no temptations or allurements; there could have been no infatuations. Life, especially the life of a woman in the provinces, was confined within the narrow boundaries of petty interests, and it seemed as though there were no escape from those boundaries. Then, too, in those times, the human soul was not so complicated, so subtle in its aspirations and experiences, not so exacting, venturesome, eternally aspiring, as it later became.

And, looking at her dear face whose lips offered to heaven their secret whisper, you would fall asleep, bearing into your dreams the touching picture of her as she prayed.

LESSONS

Aside from mother's injunction to tell the truth, I remember a moral lesson which she gave us once at twilight when, contrary to her custom, she called us all into one room, and in an impressive voice said, "Listen: to-day they will bring us a little girl who will stay here to live with us. This little girl is very unfortunate. You can all run about, but ever since she had a fever, she has lost the use of her legs. She cannot walk like other children, but only creep. Be careful! Don't think of laughing at her; you will see for yourselves, how clever and good she is."

This was our little cousin, who all her life remained a cripple.

Not long before this, something had happened to me which left for all time a deep mark upon my soul. I shall call it, the story of the broken lock.

In the broad, low room, called since the time of our grandfather "the maids' room," because the servant girls used to embroider there on frames, there stood a large, iron-bound chest, which was always locked. In it were kept those things which were seldom used: the old table linen, clocked stockings, nurse's handiwork, rolls of silk and woollen cloth awaiting their turn to be used, silver, and so forth. Once mother opened up the chest and began to look through it. Sister and I hovered near, lightly touching the ribbons and laces, admiring the silver salt-cellars and goblets. But the padlock hanging from the chest interested us most of all. It was of an American type, made of brass in the form of a lion, a real lion with a mane and tail, and locked with a little scalloped plate. We passed the lion back and forth, from hand to hand. It was so fine to open it and snap it shut. Finally, when mother began to lock the chest, the key, it appeared, would not shut.

"Who broke the padlock?" asked mother. "Not I—not I!" we both assured her with one voice. "But some one surely has spoiled it," mother insisted. "Lyddy had it last," said I.

Mother quickly seized Lydia and slapped her. She, of course, began to wail, but I was ashamed: it was not pity, but shame, real shame. For perhaps I was guilty, perhaps I had spoiled the lion, while all the blame fell on my sister, and all because I had said that she had the lion last.

Probably, sister soon forgot this dark deed, for we were tots of five and seven years—but I could not forget that shame, the first shame of my life. It gave me a lifelong lesson. That lesson was, *to take the blame on yourself.*

SERFDOM

I could not have grasped the meaning of serfdom, and its abolition could not have deeply impressed me in the conditions under which my childhood was passed. In our family relations, they were reflected mainly by the despotic order of our early domestic life, and by the change in character and conduct of our father, in the period which followed.

The six years in the Forest quite removed us from the life of landowner and peasant, while Khristoforovka with its twenty homesteads, although settled by the serfs of our grandfather, gave no material whatsoever, for judging of the relations between peasant and landowner. I had never heard of the system of forced labour by the peasants, never witnessed any acts of oppression, or heard any complaints. No relations of any kind between the proprietor and his serfs were in my field of vision. The only serfs that I knew were our house servants. Mother was always kind and indulgent towards them. She possessed a splendid, even disposition; patient and humane, she was always loved by those who surrounded her. As for father, he was hot-tempered, exacting and stern to the servants, but he was just as severe in his relations with us. Occasionally he would shout at the cook, when there chanced to be a fly in the soup tureen, or he would fly into a fit of anger when the white bread was poorly baked. During such outbursts, mother was usually silent, and sat with downcast eyes. Never in our presence did she interrupt father, or enter into disputes with him, and so we never beheld a quarrel between them. But if father was blustering, while mother said nothing, we knew without words that her silence was a reproach, and we always agreed with her.

In our relations with the serfs, I remember only one serious incident in the Forest. Every one in the house, from mother and nurse down to the little serf girl, Parasha, went about in a tense atmosphere of alarm. Father was not at home, and they uneasily awaited his arrival. They all talked in a whisper, and my childish ear caught the words, "They are going to thrash Prokofy in the stable." Why, they did not say, or else I do not remember. Perhaps it was the time when Prokofy disappeared from home and was gone for three days. In vain the bell in the courtyard pealed its slow and melancholy notes, calling him home. They said that he had lost himself in the Forest, and that a cow that had strayed away also but had found the road by instinct, had guided him home. Whether or not this was true, or whether he had made an unsuccessful attempt to escape in order to become a free man, and had later returned, I do not know; neither do I remember how this unhappy incident ended. Perhaps the shameful chastisement did not take place after all, for it is improbable that I should so clearly recall the painful atmosphere that ruled over our household while the menace impended, and forget the punishment itself, had it taken place. Perhaps, by a private talk, mother had managed to mollify father's wrath.

The abolition of serfdom was signalised in our home by the fact that, to mother's great indignation, Dunyasha and Katya, both of her maids, who had lived with us for many years, refused to serve us any longer, and preferred to return to their families in Khristoforovka, where they were soon married. Parasha, who was an orphan, remained with us, while Nurse had been freed long ago when grandfather was still alive, and was bound to us by love only.

The great change in the life of the common people, with all its moral and economic consequences, could not have been understood by such a child as I was on that nineteenth of February, in the year 1861; while at the Institute, during all the time I was there, not a word was spoken about serfdom and the emancipation of the serfs; or about land allotments and the redemption of the land.

During vacation times, I often saw throngs of peasants in the corridor of our house, and in father's study I heard his thunderous voice, when, in his capacity as justice of the peace, he carried on various negotiations with the peasants. But what kind of negotiations, I did not ask, nor was I interested in knowing. In the village there were so many enticements— books, companionship with mother, excursions into the forest, bathing and fishing. We were free for only six weeks in the year, and those weeks fled by so swiftly that you did not have time to look about you before they were taking you back to the Institute.

And then, my father did not like to talk about matters connected with his public service, at the family gatherings on summer evenings, or at dinner. Only once, when I was a grown girl, had father surprised me with the memorable words, during the period of enthusiasm over the personality of Garibaldi, and the articles of the publicist Demert, "If the serfs had not been freed, and had revolted, I should have led their rebellion."

I did not understand at all then, the obligations that phrase laid upon the man that spoke it, and he himself scarcely realised it.

At all events, as a justice of the peace, father always acted with the peasants' interests in mind, as I afterwards learned from outsiders. In every way he sought to dissuade them from unprofitable agreements, such as the alternative of the free "beggar's" land grant.[3] Notwithstanding this, Khristoforovka, where we lived, yielded and accepted the free allotment, for which it afterwards repented bitterly. Apropos of this, father used to speak with exasperation of those "mischief-makers," who suggested to the people that the "freedom" described by the manifesto was not real freedom, and that another freedom would come, when all the land of the proprietors would pass on to the peasantry, gratis. These rumours, so father said, injured the essential interests of the peasantry, by disturbing their friendly relations with the proprietors; and delayed the progress of land reform as it was set forth by the manifesto of the nineteenth of February.

[3] An extreme minimum grant of land, for which the government required no redemption.

II

THE INSTITUTE

I ENTERED the Institute in the year 1863. Separation from my family, from the village (Nikiforovo, to which I had not yet become accustomed), was not painful to me, and falling into the midst of a group of little girls, I quickly adjusted myself to my new environment and to the new order of life with its fixed régime.

My first class supervisors were Marya Stepanovna Chernyayevskaya and Mlle. Fournier, who were absolutely unlike each other. Marya Stepanovna was charming. Though her face was plain and of masculine cast, and she was deformed by a large hump on her back, she was enchanting in her manner. Her low, rich voice spoke to your very soul, while her smile and the affectionate glance of her grey eyes invited your confidence. She was a rosy-cheeked young woman with chestnut hair, and rather stout; her little hands were plump and warm, and there was something soft and warm, something maternal, in her very personality. Yet her character was not flabby or colourless. Back of her mildness one sensed a firmness ready for action should necessity demand. Without this she would not have possessed our respect, and we not only loved her but respected her as well. This was partly due to the fact that she was well educated, and could always help us over perplexing problems. At the Institute, we had scant respect for incompetent class supervisors.

Of quite a different type was the other woman, Fournier (or old Fourka, as we called her privately in our childish spite). She was a dried-up old maid, with black eyes and a yellow face, and foreign features which were death-like in their immobility. The smoothly plastered coils of her black hair and the rheumatic, knotted fingers of her ugly hands, were repulsive to us. And her voice, which corresponded to her mummy-like appearance, was dry and devoid of all music or modulation. It seemed as though not only her body, but also her soul had dried up and turned into parchment. We never received, nor could we expect anything save formalism from that old pedant. She did not help us in our studies, but did us injury, and great injury at that, by filling all of our hours which were free from lessons, with French dictation, in which we saw no rime or reason.

RESULTS

What did my six years at the Institute give me? A cultivated manner and a sense and need of comradeship developed in me by living with many others who were in a position identical with my own—the ordinary life of a student, cloistered in a boarding school. Moreover, the regular course of study, and the strict order of the day had accustomed me to a certain kind of discipline. Though I had studied willingly before I attended the Institute, I acquired there in addition the habit of intellectual work. But as for scientific knowledge, or still more, intellectual training, these years at school not only gave me almost nothing, but even retarded my spiritual development, not to mention the harm caused by the unnatural isolation from life and people.

The staff of teachers at the Institute was, generally speaking, unsatisfactory. The best of them was Porfiryev, a professor in the Theological Academy, who lectured on Russian and foreign literature. Porfiryev's course in literature was very good, but it extended only up to the forties. In Russian literature we never heard of Belinsky,[4] not to mention the later critics; and we learned nothing of contemporary fiction and poetry. We were acquainted with Turgenev only through the tale "Mu-Mu," which had once been given to us for analysis.

In history, Znamensky of the same Theological Academy, kept us for a whole year on the dry mythology of the Greeks and Romans, and on the history of Persia and Babylon. For mediæval and modern history we used Ilovaisky's [5] textbook.

4 1810–1848. A celebrated critic and leader of the radical youth during the thirties and forties.—*Translator.*

5 A shallow chauvinist.—*Translator.*

In the upper classes, Knize, the instructor in geography, was good; the other teachers are not even worth mentioning. It is enough to say that Levandovsky, who lectured on zoology and botany, never showed us a skeleton, nor even a stuffed animal, and not a single plant. Never once did we look into a microscope, and we had not the remotest idea what a cell was, or tissue. Chernyayevskaya and Sapozhnikov who taught physics and mineralogy, might have imparted something to us, to be sure; but their classes met only once a week through the year, and the courses were ridiculously meagre.

On the other hand, for four years they tormented us over penmanship. For seven years we had to study drawing, notwithstanding the fact that during all that time not one of us displayed the smallest sign of talent. We did not respect the teacher of drawing; he did not know how to inspire in us the desire to work. No one ever did anything during one of his lessons, but every one received twelve (*i. e.*, perfect grades). Singing and music were not obligatory; a special payment was required for them, and our studies in that direction depended on the desires of our parents.

In the evening, after classes were over, we prepared our lessons for the next day, and much time was spent by some in composing, and by others in copying, notes on various subjects. Save for Ilovaisky's History, there were no textbooks at all. We learned from the words of our teacher, but how? Two or three of the best students were obliged to take notes hurriedly, with all sorts of abbreviations, on what the teacher recounted to us. Then, comparing our notes and filling out omissions, we would puzzle over the meaning of this or that initial of an uncompleted word, and by a mighty strain of memory and imagination, would compose the general text, which the other little girls had to copy into their own notebooks. In addition to this, the priest gave us massive notebooks containing lectures on "Liturgy" and on "Christian Duties," which we also had to copy. History, Russian and foreign literature, botany, zoology, physics, mineralogy, pedagogy—all these were studied from notes written, and for the most part composed, by the pupils themselves. One can imagine how we were overburdened by this utterly useless writing and copying. We were free only during recess periods, one of which lasted for an hour, the other for two hours. To tell the truth, there was no time for us even to be mischievous.

In summer, we occasionally went walking in the Institute garden with its avenue of old linden trees, and a ravine into which we were afraid to peep, while in winter time they took us out of doors only two or three times. We had no warm clothes for winter, and wore rather light, wadded capes. We had no physical exercise at all—unless you count one hour of dancing a week—and we grew up into fragile, anemic creatures.

But if little attention was paid to the physical development of the little girls in the Institute, what then shall I say of the moral education there, of the preparation for life? There was no such education. We never heard of any duties to ourselves, to our families, to society and our native land—no one ever spoke to us about them.

Reading was not encouraged at the Institute, and during all those years no one ever breathed a word of its necessity. Out of all my classmates only three or four little girls besides myself ever took up any book except a notebook. In the evening, when my appointed work was done, I would surreptitiously raise the lid of my desk; behind it a book was hidden from the eyes of the class supervisor. Not satisfied with this, I used to read at night, and in this I was alone. Candles were not allowed. In the spacious dormitory burned a meagre light—a tallow candle set in a tall copper vessel of water. But in the corner of the room where the three oldest classes slept, stood a small table with an ikon of Christ, and before it a little lamp burned in witness of our zeal. We bought the oil for it with our pennies, and when there was not enough, I filled it up with castor oil. At nighttime, the horribly cross Marya Grigoryevna was on duty. She was a small, thin old woman, in a black cap and dress, with fiery black eyes, and traces of great beauty in her regular features. Whether she was doing penance for the sins of her youth, or whether she was naturally pious, I do not know, but she used to pray for whole hours in the room where her bed stood. Making use of the religious devotion of this little fury, I would betake myself to our corner table, and, kneeling, become absorbed in reading.

From time to time, Marya Grigoryevna would interrupt her prayers and make the rounds of all the dormitories. Detecting the sound of her catlike steps, I would kneel and repeatedly beat my forehead on the floor, as long as I felt her standing at my back. And she would stand there and stand there—and go away at last, seeing that there was no end to my devotions. Then I would again take up my book, which was hidden under the table. For the most part I would read English novels which my best friends, Rudanovskaya and Krotkova procured from their relatives who lived in Kazan.

Yet there *was* a library in the Institute, although our eyes never beheld its books. They were kept in a case, the key to which was in the possession of the inspector, Kovalsky, a dean of the University, who rarely called at the Institute. Once, supervisor Chernousova gave me a book by Belinsky, taken from that book-preserve. But I was quite unused to serious reading; moreover, this book contained articles about the theatre, about the acting of Mochalov as Hamlet, while I had never been inside a theatre up to the time of my very graduation. It is not surprising that the articles did not interest me; I had read only novels and tales, and during all the six years of my life at the Institute, not one serious book fell into my hands save this one volume of Belinsky.

LITERARY INFLUENCES

All of my intellectual development during these years was due to the reading to which under my mother's direction I devoted myself during my vacations. But at home, though I read all day, I devoured only novels, stories, and tales such as I read at the Institute; though to be sure they were the best of those in the contemporary magazines.[6] Mother did not offer me articles on serious subjects, and so, as before, my reading

---

[6] Once mother said to me about a certain story, "Don't read it—it's not worth it." This intrigued me. I surreptitiously took the book from the case and read it. It was a worthless, vulgar story. I was ashamed of myself for not having relied upon mother's opinion.

was one-sided, excluding everything save the emotional. During the last two years at the Institute I did not have even this reading. They did not give the older girls vacations; they were afraid of corrupting influences.

I was twelve years old when mother gave me a short novel, long since forgotten, by a writer of minor importance even in his own day—Feoktist Tolstoy's "Diseases of the Will." I read it through and was perplexed. Why had the author given the story such a strange name? Why should he call by the name of disease, the hero's longing for truth, his aversion to lies, which became the source of his sufferings and misfortunes, the rupture of relations with his best friend, his parents, and at last with his sweetheart? He acted just as he should have done, thought I. Where, then, was the "disease of the will"? I went to mother with my perplexity, and she explained to me that of course one should always speak the truth, and require it from others; but in unimportant instances one must not treat digressions from fact with such severity as did the young man in the story. You must not break off relations if people indulge in one trifling, innocent lie; otherwise you risk the possibility of being left solitary, and becoming wretched as did the unfortunate hero of Tolstoy. His inordinate truthfulness, according to mother's words, assumed the dimensions of a disease. This explanation lowered mother in my estimation. I went away dissatisfied and grieved.

A year later, Uncle Kupriyanov let me take to the Institute two thick volumes of a magazine in which were published the romances of Spielhagen, and among others, "One Man in the Field Is No Warrior." This novel made an indelible impression upon me. I understood well both the nature of the characters and the social aspect of the story, the noble aspirations of Sylvia and Leo, and the vulgarity of the bourgeois surroundings from which Leo erroneously sought support and sympathy. No other novel so broadened my horizon as did this one; it portrayed two camps, sharply and definitely opposed to each other. In the one, there were lofty ideals, conflict, and suffering; in the other, sated complacency, emptiness and the golden tinsel of life. My apprisal, made at the age of thirteen, was so just that when I again read the book many years later, I did not need to change it.

Human character is usually built up under the influence of scarcely perceptible contributions made by people, books, and surrounding life. But it happens sometimes that one or another of these elements makes a deep groove in your soul and marks out the foundation of a newly forming character. Nekrasov's "Sasha," which Porfiryev gave us for analysis, laid such a foundation for my development.

The substance of this poem is familiar. The clever, accomplished and sophisticated Agarin drops from the whirl of life in the capital into a lonely country village. There, in the simple, patriarchal family living on the neighbouring estate, he meets a young girl, as yet intellectually undeveloped. He begins to create a new consciousness in her, speaks eloquently and at length of social problems, of work for the welfare of the people. Under the influence of this sermon, idealistic longings and questions arise in Sasha's soul. But a year or two later, on meeting him again, she has cause to become disillusioned with him. In the eyes of Sasha, who has now blossomed forth intellectually and morally, Agarin is revealed as an empty babbler, who "wanders round the world, seeking some gigantic adventure," and strews his eloquent words here and there, confining himself to words only, and contributing absolutely nothing to life itself. Sasha sees that her hero's words do not correspond with his actions, and, disillusioned, she leaves the man who has awakened her mind and seemed to her an ideal.

I pondered over this poem as it had never yet been my lot to ponder in all my fifteen years. It taught me how to live, revealed a goal to which one should aspire. This was what the poem taught me: to make my words coincide with my actions; to demand this consistency from myself and from others. And this became the watchword of my life.

III

MY ENVIRONMENT

In the year 1869 I finished my course at the Institute. I came forth a vivacious, merry, frolicsome girl, frail in appearance, yet healthy both mentally and physically, not starved by the seclusion in which I had spent six years, but with a knowledge of life and people acquired only from the novels and tales which I had read. The facts of reality did not enter the walls of the boarding school; while at home, at Nikiforovo, where my sister and I spent our vacations, we never met any one outside of our own relatives. My parents lived continuously in the country, and, at the end of my term at the Institute, I found myself in the same surroundings in which as a little girl I had spent my vacations. This quiet, simple, and serene country environment disposed one to serious thoughts.

While still in the Institute, I received one impulse in this direction. It is to my class supervisor, the clever and energetic Chernousova that I am indebted for these words which were forever impressed on my mind, and had an immense moral significance in my life. It happened that once, while addressing herself not to me but to another pupil, whom she was reproving for laziness, she said with emphasis, "Do you think that when you leave the Institute, that's the end of your studying? No! you can never stop studying. All your life long, up to the very grave, you must keep on." This truth, apparently so commonplace, I heard then for the first time. It made me reflect, and cast a ray of light into my mind. I could not and did not forget those words, heard by chance.

But first of all, it is to my mother, who had received no school education in her childhood, but who through independent effort had reached heights of spiritual development, and was cultured in the best sense of the word, that I am indebted for the fact that, immediately upon leaving the Institute, I began to work mentally. Mother gave me the best periodical of that time, *Notes of the Fatherland;* in her library also I found *The Contemporary,* and in Uncle's, *The Russian Word, The Word,* and *The Cause.*

The society which surrounded me was the same as of former years. Of landowners and their families we knew practically none; there were no young people at all of my own age and education, and the only people whom we saw frequently were two families of relatives: our uncle, P. H. Kupriyanov and his wife, and the Golovnya couple. These were all. But these people, only four in all, were, to do them justice, a whole head higher than the society of the district residents. They were "thinking realists" (a term which was not then in my vocabulary), and liberal democrats, to use a later term. They were not socialists, and I never heard a word of this teaching from their lips. Never did they mention the names of the most famous founders of the socialist doctrine, Fourier, Saint-Simon and others. I did not even know the name of Lassalle, whose brilliant activity found such a response in Germany in the sixties. When I went abroad, and for the first time attended a workingmen's discussion on this leader, I confused the name of Lassalle with that of Laplace, and, ashamed of my ignorance, could not make up my mind to ask for an explanation. My relatives were not republicans, although they praised the political organisation of Switzerland and the United States, and recommended to me two books by Dixon, "Switzerland and the Swiss," and "America and the Americans," which I read with great enthusiasm. But they never discussed how to attain such an order in Russia, and I was so immature that this question did not occur to me.

Being followers of Pisarev,[7] they attached great importance to natural science, and at their suggestion, I read the works of Darwin, Lyell, Lewes, Vogt, and the popular articles of Pisarev, although, owing to my lack of preparatory work, there was much that I could not understand. Uncle and Golovnya, who were democrats and free from religious, social

[7] 1841–1868. Literary critic and champion of that current of materialism which acquired the name of Nihilism in the Sixties.—*Translator.*

and class prejudices, stood for universal popular education, for universal self-supporting labour, equal rights for women, and a simple mode of life. Uncle, the best educated and most mature of them all, often laughed at the golden trinkets and fashionable clothes which I wore. "Let's count up, Vera dear, how many pounds of rye there are hanging on your ears in the form of those earrings," he would say. The answer came out somewhere in the neighbourhood of eighteen hundred pounds. Or, "How many bushels of oats would that fine woollen cloth make?" and so forth. Assuming that at the Institute they had inspired in me a longing for society polish and wealth, my relatives often said that I should surely marry some wealthy old man. I think, they did not have a very high opinion of me at first. Thus it happened that I heard an unflattering conversation about me, which caused me great grief and bitterness. One night I happened to rouse from my sleep. It was summer; every one was asleep, but two of our kinswomen were still sitting out on the balcony and talking—mother's younger sister, Varenka, and a cousin who had come to visit us from Kazan. They were talking about my sister Lydia and myself. "Lydia will grow into a fine woman; she'll amount to something," said Varenka. "But Vera's a beautiful doll. She is like that pretty, crimson lantern that hangs in the corner of her room. On the near side it is good to look at, but the side that is turned to the wall is empty." Burying my head in my pillow, I cried bitterly. At that time, there was no Leonid Andreyev with his "It is shameful to be good," and with streaming tears I asked myself how to become good. Uncle was an admirer of Chernyshevsky,[8] Dobrolyubov,[9] and Pisarev, but he gave me very little of Pisarev's work to read, and I simply could not understand Chernyshevsky. In the family circle we often talked of various public affairs and questions, and emphasised the idea of a life spent not only for oneself and family, but for society as well. At the time I left the Institute, my mind was entirely free from any social or

[8] 1828–1889. Radical economist and literary critic. Author of the Nihilist novel, *What Is To Be Done?—Translator.*

[9] 1836–1861. Literary critic in the Sixties, collaborator of Chernyshevsky. —*Translator.*

political ideas whatsoever. It was virgin soil, but on it might well grow up respect for science, for knowledge, and an aspiration for the commonweal and social activity. And these grew up from the seeds sown intentionally, and in part unintentionally, by the relatives who surrounded me.

MY MOOD

Several months in all had passed since my graduation from the Institute, and I was already beginning to feel dissatisfied with our quiet village life and its aimlessness. What was I to do? What would become of me now? I pondered. Should I go on the stage, or join the ranks of the schoolteachers? The first career was somewhat vague in my mind. I was entirely unadapted to the second, of which fact I became convinced while teaching my sister Evgenia, whom I prepared for the Institute.

The aspiration among women for a university education was at that time quite new, but Suslova had already received the diploma of a doctor of medicine and surgery at Zurich. News of this in the journal *The Cause*, indicated to me in what direction to turn. Not the thought of my duty to the people, not the conscience of the "repentant nobleman" impelled me to study in preparation for a position as village physician. All such ideas were a later growth, under the influence of literature. My main moving influence was a mood.

An excess of vital forces of which I was unconscious, but which permeated my entire being, excited me; and a joyous sensation of freedom after the four walls of the private school came to the surface. It was this superabundance of joy in my attitude towards life as I first entered it, that formed the real source of my altruistic aspirations. My exalted frame of mind demanded activity, and a life that offered no outward manifestation of my personality was unthinkable. In comparing myself with my friends, I, with or without reason, considered myself most happily situated, both in regard to my physical and spiritual existence. This, and the fact that it seemed to me that I was more beloved than any one else around me, touched me and awakened a tender, but indefinite feeling of gratitude. Gratitude to whom? To my friends who loved me and were not envious of me. To the teachers who had successfully supported me in my claim to first place. To my father and mother, who, after my severe and Spartan childhood, surrounded me with watchful solicitude, and granted me everything that could charm a girl, fresh from school. To the sun, which bathed the field in its golden light. To the stars which shone over the garden at night. . . . It was gratitude for everything in general; not gratitude to some one for some particular thing, but to every one, and for everything. I wanted to give thanks to some one for the blessings of the world, the blessings of life. I wanted to do something good . . . so good that it would benefit both myself and some one else.

One of Eliza Orzeszko's stories tells how the Madonna stood on the top of the temple and stretched out her hands to the world. And from those hands, extended to the unseen tears of the desolate, flowed golden threads which brought light and warmth to all who were in need of love and sympathy. Surely this might be a picture of the happy mood that every healthy young soul experiences as it enters life under joyous auspices. Has not every one passed through such a period, when standing on the top of the temple, one yearns, simply, without philosophising or remorse, to sow about the gold of goodness? When one wishes that all surrounding things be in harmony with him, be healthy, joyous, beautiful and strong?

Around me there was the village. There was dirt and poverty, sickness and ignorance. But the golden thread stretched from Suslova to me, and then it went on, to the village, to its inhabitants, that it might later extend still farther, to the people at large, to our native land and all humanity.

In addition to this mood I was also influenced by the good words of others. From Uncle I heard for the first time the theory of utilitarianism. He gave me an article on the subject. "The greatest good of the greatest number of men," said Uncle, "should be the aim of every person," and I was impressed by this thought. My mind was not encumbered with notions and doubts; it did not contradict what Uncle said. On the contrary, the doctrine of utilitarianism at once appeared to me a manifest truth; Uncle had only formulated in words something of which I was already convinced. It was inconceivable for me not to act upon that which I had acknowledged as true. The true, the desirable, and the morally needful, were for me triune and inseparable; and every truth, once recognised as such, became thereby compulsory for my will. This was the logic of my character.

All these moods and influences were bound to push asunder and break the confines of that tranquil village life in the bosom of my family. I could not bear the thought of a life without activity, without a distant, lofty goal. The copy of the magazine with the news of Suslova determined my future. I began to work for admission to a university, either a foreign university, or the one at Kazan. It made no difference; all I wanted was to study, to become a physician, to bring my knowledge into the village as a protection against sickness, poverty and ignorance. In vain I begged father to let me go abroad —he would not consent. Our parents were afraid at that time to send their daughters out into the open sea of life. The idea was still too new, too untried, and father and mother dreamed of all possible dangers for those who should leave the family nest.

I had one consolation. Once, in my coaxing, I asked father, "Perhaps, though, you think that I will not accomplish my aim, that I have not the strength to do it?"

And he replied, "No, I know that if you undertake a thing, you will finish it."

I do not know what evoked such confidence, but I remember that it greatly strengthened my self-reliance. These seriously spoken words had an immense influence in forming my character; they fortified my will.

But of greater significance still was a later episode which also occurred during that first year after my graduation. I had a serious and vital question to decide. Father was ill. It was evening. He was sitting in an armchair. I was kneeling close to him. I spoke to him, and asked for his advice.

Father turned his face away and said with annoyance: "I do not know."

I rose.

"Why did I speak? Why did I tell him?" I thought, with a feeling of burning shame that I had revealed my soul. And definitely, sharply, the thought was burned in my consciousness: *One must make his great decisions for himself.*

At that moment my soul crystallised.

I GO TO A BALL INSTEAD OF A UNIVERSITY.

I was longing to go to a university, but my parents took me to Kazan, apparently to tempt me with the pleasures of society, and to test my firmness. They were progressive people, but held to the usages of their group in society, that if there was a young girl in the family, she must be "brought out," have a glimpse of people and display herself.

Father had a good acquaintance in the district, an old gentleman, Victor Feodorovich Filipov, a landowner and, like father, a justice of the peace. He lived the year round in the country, in complete solitude, since his wife had remained in Kazan for the education of their children. Having learned that we were preparing to go to Kazan, Filipov invited father to stop at their house. Consequently, when we set forth in December, we availed ourselves of his family's hospitality. Thus it was that I became acquainted in Kazan with the oldest son of Victor Feodorovich—Aleksey Victorovich, a bachelor of laws, at that time working as an investigating magistrate, and met him every day. On our visits to the theatre, which until then I had never once attended, and at balls at the Noblemen's Assembly and in the Commercial Club, Aleksey Victorovich became my constant companion and escort.

I cannot say that it was with pleasure that I made my début at a large ball. Standing before a pier-glass, in a light cloud of white gauze, with white slippers and my hair in ringlets, I displayed considerable restiveness and caprice. When I found myself in the spacious ballroom, glittering with lights, where, to the strains of an orchestra, dozens of handsome, graceful couples were circling about, all of them strange and unknown to me, I felt so utterly lonely that I was ready to burst into tears. But Aleksey Victorovich and several other young men whom he presented to me, straightway surrounded me, and I began to circle around in the throng of the dancers, quickly forgetting my fear and distress. On ensuing occasions, I was much bolder, and little by little began to acquire a taste for society amusements. However, we did not remain long in Kazan, and when we returned to our village quietude, the dizzying excitement passed away as quickly as it had come.

Shortly after this, Aleksey Victorovich was transferred from Kazan to Tetyushy, so that he might have the opportunity of visiting us. He shared my views and sympathised with my plans. We read books together, and were of one mind with respect to my entering a university. The first year of our acquaintance was not yet finished when, on the eighteenth of October, 1870, we were married in the village church of Nikiforovo.

A few weeks later my father died, and before long mother and my two younger sisters went to Kazan, where my brothers, Pyotr and Nikolai, were studying at a boys' preparatory school, while sister Lydia was finishing her work at the Institute. Aleksey Victorovich and I made our home at Nikiforovo, inasmuch as the capital of the district did not attract us in the least.

My life was unchanged after my marriage. My entrance into a university was a definite matter now. It was merely a question of sufficient funds to allow me to make the trip to Zurich. They were not forthcoming for a year and a half. Thanks to Chernousova, I knew the German language tolerably well. Immediately after my graduation, mother procured the works of Schiller and Goethe for me from Kazan, and now, in making my preparations for the university, I improved my knowledge of the language. In addition, under Aleksey Victorovich, I studied geometry, in which I was weak, and also algebra, which they had not offered in the Institute curriculum. I had also persuaded Aleksey Victorovich to give up his office and go to Switzerland with me. I was already convinced that crime proceeds from poverty and ignorance, and regarded the work of an investigating magistrate as horrible. Several times, sitting in an adjacent room, I had heard a cross-examination, with evasions on the one side, and snares on the other, and this procedure moved me to the depths of my soul. I proposed to Aleksey Victorovich that he also become a physician; or that he choose some zemstvo activity, and I was ready to undergo all privations if only that hated office of his might be abandoned. At last I prevailed on Aleksey Victorovich to give up his office, and go abroad with me to study medicine.

At this time I was on the best of terms with my relatives and friends. They all sympathised with my plans and met them with warm wishes for success. On the other hand, I was mature enough to take a critical attitude towards those people who earlier, in one way or another, had aided my development. The zemstvo elections drew near. One of the candidates for president of the district board was Prince Volkonsky, a rather clever but exceedingly lazy man, who said cynically that he served only for the salary, and that it was all the same to him whether he was a swineherd or a justice of the peace. My uncle was angry, knowing the unfitness of Volkonsky for the position, and I expected that he would offer himself as candidate. But he did not do this, and I was sorrowfully obliged to explain it by the fact that the president of the board was obliged to live in the district capital; such a move would disturb Uncle's life and interrupt his farming operations. And at the same time I learned that the husband of my late Aunt Varenka, a former student who had been expelled from the university for a demonstration in the form of a requiem for the peasants who had been shot in Bezdna,[10] was himself oppressing the peasants, imposing exorbitant penalties for damage done to grain on his estate. I, on the other hand, demanded that a person's acts harmonise with his words.

In the meantime, our journey abroad did not materialise quickly, and in the period of waiting while we were gathering together the indispensable funds for our four years' sojourn at the university, I decided to go to Kazan and attempt to enter

10 A mutiny occurred at this place after the publishing of the manifesto of 1861.

the university there, together with my sister **Lydia**, who had already completed her work at the Institute.

At Kazan, we began our studies under Markovnikov, the professor of chemistry, and Leshaft, the professor of anatomy. The former was a good-natured, but rather formal sort of person, who did not take any personal interest in us whatever, and left us entirely to our own devices. But Leshaft, on the contrary, inspired in us an earnest desire to learn; created in all his students an enthusiasm for science equal to his own, and a profound reverence for it. He aroused our warm and hearty admiration and affection, both as a teacher and as an individual. All of his students loved and admired him, and strove to be worthy of him.

His course was in full swing, and we felt that a world of undreamed of wonders was opening up to us, when one morning on arriving at the laboratory, we found that the work-tables were empty, and learned to our amazement and consternation that Leshaft had been dismissed from the faculty. The story went that some professors, resenting Leshaft's uncompromising, straightforward character, had complained to the authorities at St. Petersburg of certain harmful influences which he was supposed to be exercising on the youth of the university. We were all indignant and wretched. We went to see Leshaft before he left, and found him calm and charming as always. We bade him a sad good-bye, and left. After his departure, there was nothing to keep us longer in Kazan. I returned once more to the village in the district of Tetyushy, and in the spring of 1872 the three of us (for my sister **Lydia** had joined us), left **Nikiforovo** and departed for **Zurich.**

IV

IN ZURICH

My one idea on arriving at the University of Zurich was to study medicine, and to devote myself wholeheartedly to this work. Gradually we found friends, and my sister Lydia became especially friendly with a group of Russian girl-students, finally even taking up her quarters with them. There were many new faces, new impressions, and incidents, among them the founding of a new students' library to take the place of the old, meagre, and poorly administered one. The experiment of the women's discussion club also furnished much material for thought. Here such vital and lofty themes were discussed that the students were carried away by their enthusiasm, and the meetings were too stormy to prove productive of any generally accepted platform or doctrine. It lasted for only five or six weeks. The Frichi Club, on the other hand, was of a more sober nature, and there we studied most seriously social and labour problems, and the history of Socialism. Yet we did not neglect our regular courses either. In fact, the professors united in praising the diligence of their Russian women-students. Then came the unexpected and insulting ukase of the Russian government, demanding that we leave the university, giving as a pretext for this order the assertion that our morals were questionable. A meeting was called and a formal protest to the government urged, but the more conservative of us drew back and would not sanction the action. From this time on, the Zurich group was dispersed.

My husband and I had been following gradually diverging paths. He was inclined to be conservative, while I became ever more strongly attracted to the radical group. So it was that I came to see in the practice of medicine only a palliative for an evil which could be cured only by social and political means. I came to believe with others of our student group that the unjust and depraving economic order was the source of all social evils; and that the only way to cure these evils was to change this order through active warfare, with the purpose of overthrowing the tyrannical and privileged classes. In my twenty-first year, while in Switzerland, I joined my sister Lydia's revolutionary student society, a group of young socialists who based their platform and programme on the socialist doctrines prevalent in Europe at that time. We planned to impart these doctrines to the people directly, to live and work with them, and gradually educate them to revolt.

The members of this group gradually dispersed, some returning to Russia, others going to France, Serbia, and other countries. I, however, continued my medical studies at the University of Berne for more than a year, in the hope of being able subsequently to work among the common people as a physician and surgeon.

MY DEPARTURE FOR RUSSIA

Meanwhile our circle was working energetically in Russia. It had worked out a well-arranged plan, as one might judge from its programme which was read at the Trial of the Fifty.[11] In reality, there were no more than twenty or twenty-five members. It had its own periodical, *The Worker*, which was published abroad. Having as its aim the formation of a socialist minority among the people by means of peaceful propaganda, the organisation at the same time approved of agitation, that is, the support of local uprisings, without waiting for a general and victorious outbreak. The plan of the organisation itself remained purely federalist, without any hierarchy or subordination of one group to another. The activity of the intelligentsia members was to be strictly proletarian and democratic. The organisation chose the factory workers as the field of their endeavours, for they were more highly developed mentally, and, moreover, still maintained their connection with the village where they might easily communi-

11 In 1877. Most of the fifty defendants, accused of spreading revolutionary propaganda, were sentenced to hard labour.—*Translator.*

cate new ideas to the peasants when they returned home for
the summer labour. With this in view we worked out our plan
for oral and written propaganda. The members of the organisation distributed themselves among the factory centres:
some entered the factories in Moscow; others became weavers
in Ivanovo-Vosnesensk; the third group worked in the beet-
sugar refineries in Kiev, while the fourth settled in Tula. But
by the autumn of 1875, the organisation was wiped out. All
the members, those who had been affiliated with them, and
many workingmen, were imprisoned. But even after this de-
bacle a few were left, and planned to continue the work.

Then they remembered that there were members of the same
organisation abroad, who had made the vow to stand "all for
one and one for all." Mark Natanson requested Dorothea
Aptekman and myself to come to Moscow to regulate and carry
on the affairs of the circle. I confess that it was only after a
great struggle that I resolved to take this step. My husband
was no longer a hindrance, since I had already written to him
in the spring that I would not accept further financial help
from him, and asked him to discontinue all relations with me.
But the medical diploma? Some five or six months remained
before the end of my course; I had already considered the
theme for my doctor's thesis, which I was to begin to write
within a month or two. The hopes of my mother, the expectations of my friends and relatives, who had looked upon my
attainment of a learned profession as upon some brilliant and
laborious exploit; self-love, vainglory! All these things I had
to shatter with my own hands, when the goal was already
before my eyes. When I had analysed both this side of the
question, and the other, on which were ranged my friends who
had given themselves unreservedly, with all their souls, to the
cause; people who had disregarded these same feelings, these
same blessings, who had not yielded to the egotism of their
relatives, or to their personal ambitions; when I remembered
that these people were suffering in prison, and had already
experienced that hard and grievous lot for which we had all
been mentally preparing ourselves; when I realised that I
already possessed the knowledge necessary for a physician,

lacking only the official stamp of that calling, while people who knew the state of affairs said that I was needed at that very moment, and could be useful in the work for which I had prepared myself, I decided to go, in order that my deeds might not disprove my words. My decision was deliberate and firm, with the result that later I did not look back with regret even once. In December, 1875, I left Switzerland, carrying away with me forever a bright remembrance of the years which had given me scientific knowledge, friends, and a goal so exalted that all sacrifices seemed insignificant before it.

At the very time that I was returning to Russia, my mother was preparing to go to Switzerland in order to regain her health, which had been seriously undermined by Lydia's arrest. My return was unexpected, and I barely succeeded in meeting her in St. Petersburg. It is useless to say how heavily this new blow fell upon her. A few days later she left, taking with her my sister Olga, and little Evgenia.

After my mother's departure, I settled in Moscow, the centre of the defunct organisation. In order not to incur for myself and my comrades the surveillance of the police, I had to forego meeting my sister Lydia, who was imprisoned in one of the Moscow police stations. I easily became reconciled to this, for I had not come to Moscow for her sake; I was full of hope and assurance that the social work before me would present such broad demands on my mental and spiritual resources, that the personal element would be entirely crowded out of my life. The most bitter disillusionments awaited me. The comrades who like myself had heard the call of revolutionary activity, formed a disorganised and undisciplined group, utterly lacking in experience, and with no general plan of action. The best and most capable ones were soon arrested; the local youth had had no preparation whatever for the work, while the workingmen with whom we came in contact, were depraved, and shamelessly abused our pocketbooks. Instead of a far-reaching and fruitful activity, I found only certain shreds, without system or cohesion; in no way could I orient myself in the midst of this chaos.

To me was allotted the task of communicating with our comrades in prison. Whole days I spent in writing code letters, while in the evening I would turn my steps to filthy taverns, there to meet certain questionable characters; or to the boulevards and gloomy Moscow byways, for appointments with gendarmes and policemen. It was repulsive to look at these people, prepared any moment to betray either side. We planned for a few rescues, but nothing resulted save considerable expenditure.

The general situation of the revolutionary party lay like a heavy yoke over all; all the groups up to this time had been destroyed by governmental persecutions. Judging from the report of Count Pahlen, Minister of Justice, about eight hundred people had been indicted; the number of people who had been subjected to inquiry and temporary imprisonment, was much larger; it was as though a pestilence had swept a certain social stratum—every one had lost a friend or relative. A multitude of families were sorrowing, but all these anxieties were nothing in the face of the moral shock caused by the failure of the propagandist movement. The hopes of many crumbled to dust; the programme which had seemed so feasible did not lead to the expected results; faith in the soundness of its theoretical construction, in one's own strength, wavered. The keener the enthusiasm of those who had gone out among the people to spread propaganda, the more bitter was their disillusionment. The old outlook had been destroyed, but new views had not yet evolved.

In vain did individual workers try to rally the scattered ranks—they straightway fell apart, for their leaders built on the old foundations and thoughts to act according to their old routine. The most gifted among them, Mark Natanson, succeeded in uniting the surviving members of the Tchaikovsky Circle with the Lavrists (the group which had centred around Lavrov, and supported the journal *Forward* with money and literary material); but at the end of a month the new society broke up. Later a group of propagandists who had gone to Nizhni Novgorod, were forced to return: police surveillance became so severe, and every new element aroused such suspicion that it was impossible for them to remain in the country.

After these attempts, initiative disappeared. I myself was in such a mood, that I longed to die. Out of all my acquaintances during that period, I remember affectionately Anton Taksis, a Lavrist, who was living under a false passport. He encouraged me in my most despairing moments, and instilled into me a few principles which I never afterwards forgot. He pointed out to me some of the causes for the failure of the revolutionary movement. Like a true Lavrist, he ascribed the cause of the failure to a too theoretical organisation of the work; to the unpreparedness and inefficiency of the workers. He had utmost confidence in the future of the revolutionary cause, and regarded the present situation as a mere transient moment, a period of change, which was inevitable in any movement. Moreover, he constantly impressed upon me the fact that the cause required not momentary outbursts of enthusiasm, but painstaking work, and though the results of this "hard labour" might be insignificant, we must be prepared for this, and not despair. He claimed that every new idea became incorporated into life very slowly, and that under certain historical conditions one was obliged to turn his activity to the one field that lay open to it. He also encouraged me in my desire to leave Moscow, settle in the country, and see for myself what kind of a sphinx this Russian people was.

In the spring I found some one to assume my duties, and departed for Yaroslavl. At the advice of one who had had experience, I concealed the fact of my sojourn abroad and my studies at the University of Zurich—that caused one to be regarded as a suspicious character—and I began to visit the Yaroslavl Zemstvo Hospital. At the end of six weeks I took the examination of the Medical Board for assistant physician. According to the inspector of the Medical Board, I answered the questions "as a man-student," and that I knew my Latin better than he; my diploma stated that I had passed the examination brilliantly.

From Yaroslavl I went to Kazan to wind up my family affairs, for my husband and I had agreed to a legal separation. At the end of a few months, this separation was arranged, and I resumed my maiden name. On my return to St. Peters-

burg, I passed the examination for midwife in the Academy of
Physicians and Surgeons. By November, 1876, all my worldly
accounts were settled. The past was buried resolutely. From
my twenty-fourth year my life was linked exclusively with the
destinies of the Russian revolutionary movement.

V

THE PROGRAMME OF THE NARODNIKI (POPULISTS)

UNTIL the end of 1876, the Russian revolutionary groups were divided into two main branches: the Propagandists and the Insurrectionists. The former prevailed in the north, the latter in the south. The former adhered, more or less, to the views of Lavrov's *Forward*, while the latter professed the revolutionary catechism of Bakunin. Both agreed on one point, namely that all activity should centre among the common people. But the nature of that activity was understood differently by the two factions. The Propagandists regarded the people as a blank sheet of paper, upon which they were to inscribe socialist characters. They proposed to raise the mass morally and mentally to their own level, and prepare a consolidated and intelligent minority in the midst of the people, which would assure, in time of an elemental or organised revolution, the promulgation of socialist principles and ideals. That required, of course, considerable labour and effort, as well as personal qualification. The Insurrectionists, on the other hand, not only had no intention of teaching the people, but asserted that it is we who ought to learn from the people. In their opinion, the people were socialistic by their very conditions, and quite ready for the social revolution; they hated the existing order, and properly speaking never ceased protesting against it: resisting actively or passively they have ever been in a state of mutiny. The task of the intelligentsia consisted of uniting and blending into one mighty torrent all these individual protests and petty riots. Among the revolutionist's proper methods they accepted agitation, all sorts of disturbing rumours, banditry, impersonation of pretenders to the throne. No one knew the hour of the people's vengeance, but so much inflammatory material had accumulated among the people that a small spark would easily flare up into a flame, and the latter into a gigantic conflagration. The conditions of the peasants were such that only a spark was wanted; the intelligentsia was to serve as the spark. The movement of a people in rebellion promised to be disorderly and chaotic, but their native sense would lead them out of chaos and enable them to build a new and just order. Such a programme required not even a special organisation or discipline among the agitators, and since the people were everywhere ready for the uprising, there was no need in deciding as to where it should start: no matter where the first spark struck, the fire would in any event spread in all directions.

In contrast to the south, the question of organisation was seriously considered in the north, and its adequate solution proved of great service for the cause of the revolution, for it secured continuity, accumulation of experience, and the gradual development of a superior type of organisation. As a matter of fact, the southerners disappeared, without leaving a tradition; they were uprooted, and the few survivors could only join new groups and be absorbed by them. Whereas in the north the presence of organisations was responsible for the continuity: the Tchaikovsky circle (the last group to be associated with the name of an individual) laid the foundation, in 1876, for the society Land and Freedom, from which was formed, in 1879, the party of The Will of the People.

Be it as it may, both the Propagandists and the Insurrectionists met with defeat, as far as their practical activity among the people was concerned. In the people themselves and in the political conditions of the country, they met with unexpected and insurmountable obstacles for the realisation of the programme as they understood it at that time. Yet there were quite a number of people willing to continue the revolutionary work and to follow a definite plan of action. Despite the numerous arrests, the more experienced among the survivors made a joint analysis of the past, and worked out new principles for revolutionary work. As a result of these efforts came the programme which became later known as that of the

Narodniki.[12] It was entirely incorporated in the programme of Land and Freedom, and later, in parts, in that of The Will of the People.

The basic idea of that programme was that as in the case of every other nation at a certain stage of its historical development, the Russian people have an outlook of their own, corresponding to the level of their moral and mental conceptions that have been formed under given environmental conditions. As part of this outlook one must regard popular attitudes toward political and economic questions. Under ordinary conditions it is extremely difficult to transform these established views, before changing the dominating institutions. Hence it is necessary to make an attempt in the revolutionary activity to use as a starting point the attitudes, aspirations, and desires prevalent among the people at the given moment, and inscribing on the revolutionary banner the ideals already ripe in the consciousness of the people. Such an ideal in the economic field was the possession of land by those who till it and only for as long as they till it. Communal ownership, and the confiscation of all land by the commune, was another such popular ideal, which coincided with the teaching of Socialism. As to the political issues, in order to disperse the peasant's faith in the Tsar, it was necessary to prove to him systematically that the Tsar was not the champion of the common people. For this purpose one had to encourage the people in sending petitioners to the Tsar; their sure failure would serve to destroy the illusion. Again, the revolutionists were to raise the people's spirit and intelligence by living among them in such capacities as village clerks, bookkeepers, assistant physicians, small traders, and the like.

LAND AND FREEDOM

In the fall of 1876, the society Land and Freedom was formed. I was among the initiators, but the leading spirit was Mark Natanson, a former member of the Tchaikovsky

[12] *Narod* means people. *Narodnik*—Populist. *Zemlya i Volya*—Land and Freedom. *Narodnaya Volya*—The Will of the People; *Naradovolets, Narodovoltsy*—adherent and adherents of *Narodnaya Volya*—*Translator.*

Circle who had recently returned from administrative exile. The name was chosen in memory of the Land and Freedom society which had existed during the early sixties. Our programme included work among all layers of society, extending our influence to the army, bureaucracy, rural officials, men of liberal professions, and endeavouring to organise public opinion against the government. One of these efforts was the celebrated demonstration at the Kazan Cathedral, in Petrograd, in which young Plekhanov [13] was one of the leaders. On that occasion many were beaten and arrested by the police, and were later tried and sentenced to prison.

After the Kazan demonstration, some of our members stayed in St. Petersburg, some set out for the provinces of Saratov and Astrakhan, while our circle, known as that of the "Separatists," chose the province of Samara for the region of its activity. In the spring of 1877, my friends went there first, made connections, obtained positions as county clerks, and enabled me to come in August, and take the place of an assistant physician.

FIRST STEPS

In Samara I was recommended to a young county physician, Nikolai Semenovich Popov, who proved to be in perfect accord with my plans and ideas, and managed to have me appointed to the large village of Studentsy, in his district. There were twelve villages under my management, and I had to visit them all every month. For the first time in my life I found myself face to face with the village life, alone with the people, far away from my relatives, acquaintances and friends, far from cultivated people. I confess, I felt lonely, weak, helpless in this peasant sea. Moreover, I had no idea how to approach a common person.

Heretofore I had not seen the wretched peasant environment at close range ; I knew of the people's poverty and misery rather theoretically, from books, magazine articles, statistical material. Now, at the age of twenty-five, I faced the people as a

[13] 1857–1918. Eventually one of the founders of the Marxian Socialist movement in Russia. —*Translator.*

baby into whose hands they thrust some strange, extraordinary object.

First of all, I began to attend to my official duties. Eighteen days out of thirty I had to be away from home, travelling through villages and hamlets. During these days I was enabled to plunge into the abyss of poverty and grief. I would usually stop at a hut, known as the "stopping hut," which would immediately be filled with thirty or forty patients apprised of my arrival by the elder of the village or his assistants. There were old and young, a large number of women and still more of children of all ages, whose screams and squeaks reverberated in the air. One could not look with equanimity at the filthy and emaciated patients. Most of their ailments were of a long standing; rheumatism and headaches ten to fifteen years old; nearly all of them suffered from skin diseases, yet only few villages had baths: instead most of them washed themselves in the Russian oven. There were numerous cases of incurable catarrhs of the stomach and intestines, wheezing chests heard from a distance, syphilis which spared no age, endless sores and wounds, and all this under conditions of such unimaginable filth of dwelling and clothes, of such unhealthful and insufficient food, that one asked oneself in stupor: was that the life of animals or of human beings! Tears often flowed in a stream from my eyes as I prepared medicine for these unfortunates.

Till evening I patiently distributed powders and salves, explaining three or four times how to use the medicine, and at the end of the work I would drop on the heap of straw prepared on the ground for my bed. Despair would seize me. Was there an end to this truly terrifying poverty? Were not all these prescriptions a hypocrisy amidst the surrounding squalour? Could there be any thought of protest under such conditions? Would it not be irony to speak of resistance, of struggle, to people completely crushed by their physical privations?

For three months, day after day, I saw the same picture. Only such close observation could give one a true conception of the condition of our people. These three months were a terrible experience for me, confined to the material side of the people's life. I had hardly a chance to look into their souls; my mouth could not open for propaganda.

At that time a certain Chepurnova was arrested in Samara, and among her papers were found compromising letters to me and other comrades from our Petersburg friends. We had been warned of this from Petersburg; besides, Alexander Kvyatkovsky was sent from Petersburg to transfer me from the village. One week after my departure, the gendarmes appeared at Studentsy.

VI

IN THE VILLAGE

KVYATKOVSKY, Solovyev, who had some time before given
up his position in a village blacksmith shop, and I decided to
settle next in the province of Voronezh, and thither we all
three betook ourselves. Shortly after this, the verdict of the
Trial of the 193 [14] was announced, which restored to us an
unexpected and incredible number of comrades. We could
not let slip this happy opportunity of enlisting from among
them people who might wish to join us immediately in our work
in the country. Accordingly, Bogdanovich and I left Voronezh
for St. Petersburg. Here we found great hilarity; the youth
of the nation rejoiced; old friends and new welcomed the released as though they were returned from the dead, while they,
exhausted and shattered physically, forgetting the sufferings
that they had just endured, dreamed with the ardour of youth,
and of long-restrained energy, of fresh labours for the cause.
They laid new plans for the realisation of their ideas. People
thronged their apartments from morning to night. It was an
uninterrupted session of a revolutionary club, where ninety to a
hundred visitors attended in a day; friends brought with them
strangers who wished to shake hands with those whom they
had looked upon as buried alive. At this time I made the
acquaintance of many of those associated with the movement
during the first half of the seventies, among them, Sofia Perovskaya, whom I met then for the first time. I had heard most
enthusiastic praise of her, and for my part was charmed by
her democratic tastes and ways, her simplicity, and the gentleness of her demeanour. Our friendly relations continued from
that time until her death, when, from behind the prison walls

[14] In 1878. Accused of revolutionary propaganda, the 193 prisoners had
spent a considerable time in jail before the trial. For many of them the
court adjudged the preliminary confinement as sufficient punishment.—
Translator.

she charged her companions to "guard Sukhanov and Verochka."

The members of the old Tchaikovsky Circle, both those who had been left at liberty, and those who had been freed by the court, decided to re-establish their organisation. They had in view some of their fellow-prisoners whom they considered especially desirable members for their party. And so a group of about forty was formed. At a general assembly of members, the Populist programme was read and adopted, and a committee was chosen to remain in St. Petersburg and manage the affairs of the group. After having made these decisions, the majority of the members dispersed: we, in order to establish ourselves in villages; others, to make final arrangements with their families and to settle their financial affairs; still others, to recover their lost health. Unfortunately, the existence of the group terminated at this point. As a result of the Tsar's failure to approve the sentence of the court, many members were rearrested and exiled by administrative order, a few fled abroad, our committee was broken up, and individual members, who had arranged their affairs or escaped from exile, returned to St. Petersburg one after another, and entered the organisation Land and Freedom. All this time they were urging me also to stay in St. Petersburg, for they considered me most adapted for work among the intelligentsia; but inasmuch as I was firm in my convictions, and relinquished my purposes only when experience itself proved them to be fallacious or inexpedient, I clung to my wish to go on living among the people. At that time some work had already been accomplished in Saratov. About a dozen workers were living in the villages, among them teachers, village clerks, cobblers, farm labourers, and pedlars. Besides this, active propaganda was being carried on among the city workmen in Saratov itself. Alexander Mikhaylov was living in the village Sinenkiye as an unofficial instructor among the Schismatics,[15] whom he greatly admired. He dreamed of founding a new rationalistic sect, the basic principle of which should be active struggle. He described to us with ardour the characters of the "Fugitives" and "Pil-

15 A sect of religious dissenters.—*Translator.*

grims," and typical examples of the Schismatic teachers who were far above the usual order of peasant in their intellectual development and general outlook.

While our men comrades managed to procure various county positions that would enable them to come in contact with the people, I also received a position in the Petrovsk district. My sister Evgenia, who had just passed the examination for assistant surgeon before the Saratov medical board, came to live with me. Our appearance in the district evoked a sensation, both in society and among the people themselves. Petrovsk society stood dumbfounded at the question: why were we, with our education and position in life, "burying" ourselves in the village, for what purpose, and *why?* [16] Fortunately for us, our manners and appearance made it impossible for them to imagine us to be Nihilists. Thanks to this, and still more to the quickly observed friendship between us and the President of the County Board and his wife, there was a turn in the liberal direction, and all doors opened before us. To be sure, certain officials regarded us with suspicion and decided to "watch out."

Under such auspices we began our work. For the peasants, the appearance of an assistant surgeon, "a she-healer," as they called me, was a great marvel. The muzhiks went to the priests for an explanation: had I been appointed to attend them all, or only the women? After they had been enlightened, I was besieged with patients. The poor country folk flocked to me by the tens and hundreds as though I were a wonder-working ikon; a whole train of wagons surrounded the county doctor's little cottage from morning till night; my fame spread swiftly beyond the boundaries of the three counties which I served, and later, beyond the district itself. I was unrestrained by the supervision of a doctor (for there never was one in my district during my stay), and received directly from the Medical Board as much medicine as I needed. Perhaps this explained the fact that I was able to help them, for

[16] In contrast to this viewpoint, the peasants, who knew well that man has needs other than material ones, found a higher explanation for our conduct, saying that it was "for the good of our souls."

I could dispense the remedies in their required quantities. One unfortunate peasant woman who was suffering from a hemorrhage, came to me on foot a distance of forty or fifty miles. On her return home, she declared that as soon as I touched her the hemorrhage ceased. Others brought water and oil, begging me to "speak a charm" over it, for they had heard that I "charmed away" sickness with marvellous success. They brought hoary old men to me, who had lost their sight fifteen and twenty years before, and who thought once more to see the light before their death, through my help. Attention, detailed questioning, and intelligent instruction in the use of medicine, were veritable marvels to the people. The first month I received eight hundred patients, and in the course of ten months five thousand, as many as a district physician receives in a city hospital in the course of a year, with several junior surgeons to aid him. If I helped one-tenth of these five thousand people, their prayers would win me forgiveness for my transgressions from the most cruel Jehovah. This immense task, of course, would have been beyond my strength if my sister Evgenia had not shared it with me.

We soon succeeded in opening a school. Evgenia informed the peasants that she would teach the children for nothing, if they would send them to her. We had all the school-books; the fathers would not have to buy primers or paper or pens. Immediately twenty-five pupils, boys and girls, assembled at our house. I must mention at this point that in all the three counties in my district, there was not one school. Some of the pupils were brought to Evgenia from other hamlets and villages, sometimes fifteen miles distant. There were adult pupils also, aside from little ones. A few muzhiks asked her to teach them arithmetic, a thing indispensable to them in keeping all kinds of village and county accounts. Soon my sister acquired the flattering title, "our golden-hearted little teacher."

When we had finished our work in the prescription room and the school, which were both located in the same doctor's cottage, we would take our work, or a book, and go to the village, to the house of some one of the peasants. And that evening would be a holiday in that house. The peasant would hasten

out to tell his neighbours and relatives to come and listen.
The reading would begin; at ten and eleven o'clock our hosts
would still be asking us to go on reading. We used to read
Nekrasov, sometimes Lermontov, or Shchedrin, or articles
from a magazine, the stories of Naumov, Levitov, Galitsinsky,
a few historical selections, and so on. We always had occasion
to talk about the conditions of peasant life, about the land,
their own relations to the landowner, to the authorities. We
had to touch on the needs of the peasants, listen to their complaints, their hopes, sympathise with their sorrows, share their
sympathies and antipathies. Sometimes they would ask me to
leave the book with them, so that they might read again a
passage that had pleased them, or even learn it by heart. They
invited us to come to the village assembly to detect the clerk's
trickery, his corruption and greed, the roguery of the elder,
and thereby defend the *Mir*.[17] They wanted to make Evgenia
village clerk, which office Chegodayev, whom the peasants hated,
was occupying at that time. They begged us to visit the
county court, and in general to call often at the County Board,
so that the clerk could not abuse them, insult, or maltreat
them. "He would be ashamed before you," said the peasants.
When at last it was time to go home, we always had to give
our solemn promise to make their children just as "learned"
as we were ourselves.

This life of ours, and the relations between us and these
simple folk, who felt that light was near at hand, possessed
such a bewitching charm, that even now it is pleasant for me
to recall it; every moment we felt that we were needed, that
we were not superfluous. It was this consciousness of one's
usefulness that was the magnetic force which drew our Russian
youth into the village. Only there could one have a clean soul
and a quiet conscience, and if they tore us away from that
life, from that activity, we were not to blame for it.

---

[17] *Mir* means world, peace, village commune. Here the word is used in
the latter sense. The *Mir* took charge of the communal ownership and distribution of land, of local taxation and other communal affairs in the
village.—*Translator.*

THEY FREEZE US OUT

The warfare against us was so typical, so characteristic, that I must touch upon it. And apropos of this I may mention that, in contrast to our other comrades, we were living under our own passports. No one in the district knew that one of our sisters was already in Siberia. We had not had time to make ourselves at home in the village before the peasants informed us that the priest of our district was spreading the rumour that we had no passports, that we had never studied anywhere, that we had no papers, and that he was as much of a healer as we were. When the peasants called on us to stand godmother, the priest refused to officiate, saying that he did not know who we were, where we came from, whether we were married or unmarried, or anything else about us. A little while later, this same servant of the Church made a declaration in the County Board, that from the time of our arrival in Vyazmino the religious spirit of his flock had changed; the temple of the Lord had been poorly attended, religious zeal had slackened, and the people had become insolent and wilful. At the Board they told the priest that all this had nothing to do with the manner in which I fulfilled my official duties, and therefore did not concern them. Then there began spying after the school: first the landowner's manager, then the clerk, then the priest, would call the little urchins in for an inquisition. "They're always asking us whether you teach us prayers," the children told my sister. Evgenia did teach them prayers. Nevertheless complaints reached Saratov that Evgenia was instilling into the children the principle that "there was no God, and we did not need a Tsar," while the rumour spread through the village from the county administration, that we were giving refuge to fugitives from the law. From that time on when any one came to our house, no matter who, a rural policeman would make his appearance also, on one pretext or another, to keep watch. When we made a trip to the town, our friends told us that Prince Chegodayev assured each and every one that we were going from one peasant hut to another, reading revolutionary proclamations, and that we did not let one sick man escape without expounding to him the theory that injustice reigned everywhere, and that every official was dishonest.

The grief of the peasants when they heard this news was beyond description.

THE TURNING POINT

Before our position had become strained to the breaking-point, Alexander Solovyev paid us a visit in order to consult with us on his project of going to St. Petersburg to assassinate Alexander II. He expounded to us his views on revolutionary work among the people, and on the general state of affairs in Russia. The first was, in his opinion, mere self-gratification when one considered the existing order of things, under which the struggle for the interests of the masses on a legal foundation appeared iniquitous and illegal in the eyes of the law, of all property-holders, and members of the administration. Working on this legal foundation, we had no chances for success, even though armed with the principle of justice and popular weal; for all the weight of material wealth, tradition, and authority, was on our opponents' side.

In view of this, we had already come to the conclusion at our last meeting in Saratov that terrorism against landlords and the police must be introduced into the village; that justice must be protected by physical force. This terroristic programme seemed all the more indispensable in that the people were crushed by their poverty, abased by the constant and arbitrary demands made upon them, and did not have the strength themselves to employ such means. But new revolutionary forces were necessary for such work, and the influx of these forces to the village had almost ceased, inasmuch as reaction and persecution had destroyed the energy of the intelligentsia and their faith in seeing fruitful results from their work in the country. Moreover, the revolutionary youth had not witnessed any hopeful change due to the labour of those who had previously been active among the people. The best impulses perished, finding no outlet for themselves in the face of the familiar force of reaction. This period in Russia marked the complete disappearance of public initiative; re-action might increase, but not decrease.

"The death of the Emperor," said Solovyev, "may bring about a turn in social life; the atmosphere will become purified; the intelligentsia will no longer be diffident, but enter upon a broad and fruitful activity among the people. A great stream of honest young vitality and strength will flow into the country places. And it is precisely this great stream of vitality, not the zeal of individual personalities like ourselves, that is neces-sary in order effectively to influence the life of all the Russian peasantry."

Solovyev was expressing the general conviction. We already saw clearly that our work among the people was of no avail. In our persons the revolutionary party had suffered a second defeat, but not by any means through the inexperience of its members, not through the theoretical nature of its programme, not through a desire to propagate among the people aims foreign to it and ideals inaccessible to it, not through ex-aggerated hopes in the forces and the preparation of the popular masses; by no means. We had to leave the stage while fully aware that our programme was applicable to life, that its demands had a real foundation in national conditions, and that the trouble was merely in the lack of political free-dom.

This absence of political freedom might be disguised, might not be keenly felt, were the despotic power to serve some way the needs of the people and the aspirations of society. But if instead, it goes its own way, ignoring both these factors; if it is deaf to the lamentations of the people, and to the demands of the zemstvo worker, and to the voice of the publicist; if it is indifferent to the serious investigations of the scholar, and to the figures of the statistician; if not one single group of its subjects has any means of influencing the course of social life; if all expedients are useless, all paths forbidden, and the younger, more ardent part of society, finds no sphere for its activity, no work in the name of the popular welfare to which it may devote its enthusiasm—then the situation becomes un-endurable, all the indignation of society centres itself on the man who expresses and represents that imperial authority which has diverged from the course of society, on the monarch who has declared himself to be responsible for the life, well-being, and happiness of the nation, but who has valued *his* wisdom, *his* strength, more highly than the wisdom and strength of millions of men. And if all means of convincing him have been tried and alike found fruitless, then there remains for the revolutionist only physical violence: the dagger, the revolver, and dynamite. And Solovyev took up the revolver.

Meanwhile the members of the city branches of the party had arrived at the same conclusion. Vera Zassulich, who had been acquitted by a trial by jury, had just escaped being arrested again. At the time that all Russia was applauding the verdict of the court, the members of the Tsar's family made a visit to Trepov.[18] When, in the Trial of the 193, the Senate recommended to lighten the sentence, the Tsar made it more severe. To every attempt at opposing his servants' arbitrary sway, he replied with augmented reaction and repressions; a state of siege resulted from a few political murders. It began to seem ridiculous to punish the servant who had done the will of him who had sent him, and to leave the master untouched. The political assassinations naturally led to the assassination of the Tsar, and this thought occurred to Goldenberg and Kobylyansky almost at the same time as it took possession of Solovyev. This thought did indeed possess him completely. I think that had we all rebelled against it, he would nevertheless have made the attempt. Moreover, he believed absolutely in its success. When I expressed to him the opinion that the failure of the attempt might bring about still more serious reaction, he began to assure me with such faith and enthusiasm that failure was unthinkable, that he would not survive it, and that he would enter the undertaking with every chance for success, that I could only wish that his hopes might be justified. And so we parted from this man, who united the courage of a hero with the self-renunciation of an ascetic, and the kindness of a child. From that time on we

[18] Vera Zassulich tried to assassinate Trepov, the St. Petersburg Chief of Police, for abusing the political prisoners.—*Translator.*

waited long and anxiously for news from St. Petersburg. Meanwhile, affairs in the village grew worse, and to remain there longer was useless and unendurable.

When, on the second of April, Solovyev's unsuccessful shot rang out,[19] my first thought was that we must go on with our work. Instead of destroying the power of reaction, we had given it occasion to vaunt itself yet more strongly, and we had to see the affair through to the finish. By this time, our comrades in the Volsk district had already been obliged to leave. Moreover, our friends wrote to us from St. Petersburg that Solovyev's sojourn in the province of Saratov had been discovered, and that a special commission had been appointed to investigate his activity. Soon came the news from Saratov that this commission had already arrived in the city, and was leaving for the Volsk District. Our friends urged us to leave for fear that our relations with Solovyev would be discovered. At last a messenger came from the Volsk District, to tell us that they had already discovered the cabmen who had driven Solovyev to the Petrovsk District. After that it was necessary to hasten our departure. Indeed, one day after my sister and I had left, the police appeared at Vyazmino.

So ended our stay in Saratov, begun in hope, and ending in failure. But although, in the light of those exterior conditions which pervaded the village, we had returned a negative answer to the question whether it was possible to work among the people, and had concluded that before all else it was necessary to destroy these very conditions, yet, at the same time, we bore away the consciousness that the people understood us, that it saw in us its friends. When the gendarmes and police appeared in Vyazmino, the peasants said: "That is because they are on our side." When the clerk later spread the rumour that we had been arrested, and Evgenia had been hanged, the peasants went at night to our friends to find out whether this was true. They returned home appeased and happy. When, a few months later, I met a young girl who had lived near us,

19 He fired at the Tsar from a revolver, near the Summer Garden in St. Petersburg. A peasant, Komissarov, pushed Solovyev's elbow, and the bullet went astray. Solovyev was hanged in May.—*Translator.*

she threw herself on my neck, with the warm greeting: "You did not live there in vain!"

When our little circle gathered for the last time in Saratov, I announced that I was going to withdraw from it in order to join the party, Land and Freedom, since I saw no good reason for the independent existence of a small group; and that in that party I would support those who stood for further attempts at assassinating the Tsar. Moreover, warfare with the government had become the watchword for all the other societies. After this we dispersed. In the meanwhile, the party Land and Freedom, anticipating my own wish, invited me through Popov who was then in Tambov to become one of its members. When I had given my consent, Popov told me that the organisation was calling a council meeting at Voronezh, where we afterwards went with a few other members of the party.

THE GENERAL SITUATION

From the end of 1876 up to the time of the meeting at Voronezh in the summer of 1879, the general situation in the revolutionary party was characterised by the fact that as yet it had shown no desire to unite into one all-Russian organisation which should include all adherents to the cause; with the result that, notwithstanding their solidarity of programmes, of aims and methods, they had scattered into several entirely independent groups which were united with each other only through the personal acquaintance of their individual members. At the time that the Society Land and Freedom was organised in the north into a firmly united group, bound by a general code, which regulated the mutual relations of the members, and outlined their rights and duties, the southerners were continuing to display the bold Russian spirit. Recognising no discipline, and only faintly distinguished from the mass of revolutionary youth, they wandered like nomads between Odessa, Kharkov, and Kiev. The series of government persecutions from 1877 to 1879 suppressed the movement in these cities. Prosecutions deprived them of their best forces. Such ordeals did not have these fatal results in the north, for the organised party had provided for an influx of new forces from the provinces whenever a loss in the central membership occurred. Thus it was that in the summer of 1879 the society Land and Freedom was the only example of an organised, revolutionary group which possessed a periodical (*Land and Freedom*, published since the autumn of 1878); and with a large contingent of members at its disposal. At the head of the society was a central group, with headquarters at St. Petersburg. This central group managed the printing press, the publishing of the periodical, and all the finances of the society; it also conducted relations with the provinces, directed all projects under way which did not relate directly to the work in the provinces, and in addition carried on the work of increasing the scope and strength of the organisation, and of sending new workers into the villages. The provincial members were scattered throughout the provinces of Saratov, Tambov, Voronezh, and the Don District, forming so-called "communes," which were autonomous and independent in their local administration of affairs. As the attention of the members of the party in St. Petersburg concentrated itself more and more on that portion of the programme which spoke of suppressing the despotism of the government agents, they took less and less thought of their comrades in the provinces. All their resources and personnel were devoted to the work of liberating political prisoners and to terroristic acts.

Moreover, disagreements over revolutionary principles began to arise. The members of the party in St. Petersburg, intoxicated with success, or chafing at failure, in the heat of battle which demanded the constant exertion of all their forces, but which at the same time gave an excellent means for agitation, began to look with amazement and contempt at the quiet villages of Tambov and Saratov. The absence there of any signs of active conflict, the evident lack of results in the country despite the fact that dozens of workers were living there, aroused them to the very depths of their souls. If dozens of revolutionists who had consecrated themselves to village activity for more than two years, proved unable not only to rouse the people, but even to produce any substantial

evidence that preparations might be made in the near future
for a popular uprising, then what was the use of their remaining any longer in the country? Every member who remained
among the peasants seemed to them to have been torn away
from that heated strife to which they devoted themselves with
enthusiasm. On the other hand, the Populists, in the strict
sense of the word, thought that the city members of the party
were playing with fireworks, whose brilliancy lured the youth
away from real business, from the midst of the people who
stood so much in need of their young strength. The murder
of generals and gendarme chiefs were in their eyes a less fruitful and necessary work than agrarian terror in the villages.
Terroristic acts went almost unnoticed in the village: there
was no one on whom to observe the effect they produced; un-
heralded and unmourned, they did not stir even the revolutionists themselves, who, dwelling in the country, had not lived
through the anxieties, dangers, and joys of the conflict. Amid
the monotony of the boundless steppes, and the sea of peasants,
they did not lament the loss of their comrades who had gone
to their death.

VII

DISSENSION

NOT only were the attitudes of the revolutionary groups in the city and in the country more or less estranged; factions began to arise within the Centre itself, in St. Petersburg, and sharp differences of opinion began to assert themselves.

The long series of dramatic attempts against the lives of those officials whose despotism had been most shameless, the armed protest of the party, had created such enthusiasm among the youth and seemed to offer such a practical means of dealing a direct blow at oppression, that a group arose within the central unit of the organisation, which favoured a programme of active conflict with the government. The "Blow at the Centre" was to them the only important consideration. But Popov and Plekhanov and their adherents in the central group, opposed their plan vigorously. They claimed that terroristic activity had only resulted in losses for the party and additional repressions on the part of the government; that it lured the youth from its constructive, legitimate work among the people, whose support was so indispensable to the party. So sharp was the cleavage that I was shocked by the exasperation expressed in meetings of the group when I returned to St. Petersburg.

AN ORGANISATION WITHIN AN ORGANISATION

After Solovyev's attempt, a general conference was urged by Plekhanov and Popov to determine the future policy of the party with regard to this question of political terror. They believed that the revolutionists in the provinces would favour their side, and throw their influence against terrorism. Fearing this event, the members of the more radical group (which later formed the nucleus for the Executive Committee of The Will of the People), secretly organised themselves into a separate group within the Land and Freedom and began to recruit members. At irregular intervals they published a leaflet in which a programme of violence was advocated and which was supplementary to the main party organ. They signed their communications with the name of the "Executive Committee," which term had been used in signing Osinsky's revolutionary proclamations in Kiev.

This group began to make preparations for its separate existence in case a break should become necessary with the main organisation, made preparations for establishing its own printing press and chemical laboratory. In Kibalchich it found a man, who, since the time of his release from prison early in the year 1878, had considered the problem of making dynamite at home, and who for that purpose not only studied its properties and preparation theoretically, but also made laboratory tests along that line.

LIPETSK AND VORONEZH

As soon as a general conference of Land and Freedom had been decided upon to take place at Voronezh, the members of the secret Executive Committee resolved to anticipate it by a congress of their own at Lipetsk, and invited the prominent southern revolutionists, Kolodkevich, Zhelyabov, and Frolenko. This group discussed and accepted a definite code of regulations, and named as its aim the overthrow of the autocratic order, and the establishment of political freedom through an armed struggle with the government. They then proceeded to Voronezh to join the conference of Land and Freedom.

The mutual distrust of the provincial and the St. Petersburg factions created a strained atmosphere, and it was with misgivings that the members assembled. They all feared a session of quarrels and dissension, but as soon as the conference opened it became evident that the cleavage was not as sharp as they had feared. A peace-loving and patient spirit, an earnest desire to preserve unity, prevailed. After mutual explanations and debates, the programme of Land and Freedom, and its by-laws, were left unchanged. It was decided to continue the work among the people, but also to include in it agrarian terror, and to continue terroristic warfare in the city, including therein attempts against the life of the Tsar. Plekhanov, however, was disappointed and exasperated at the turn of events, and withdrew from the party.

Generally speaking, the conference was rather weak and indeterminate, and not a decisive battle as the St. Petersburg members had expected. The radical group which had met at Lipetsk used it as a means to observe the various members in the party with a view to enrolling them later in their own organisation, in case a decisive break should become necessary in the future. Morozov approached me with this purpose, urging me to join in the formation of a secret group, but I refused, regarding it absolutely unpermissible to found a secret circle within a secret society. I did not know that this secret circle already existed.

VIII

LAND AND FREEDOM SPLITS

It was after the conference at Voronezh that my life under a false passport began. I left for St. Petersburg with Kvyatkovsky who escorted me to the Lesnoy suburb, where he and Ivanova kept a lodging for revolutionary meetings. These lodgings were the headquarters for the militant section of Land and Freedom. It was summer, and the location in the suburb offered many advantages for such headquarters. We all had false passports, and many other people in the same status used to come to us on business without attracting attention; yet it was easy to arrange meetings near the exit of the little pine grove in the park, under the guise of innocent outings. We would assemble at some remote spot where other people never ventured, and distribute ourselves here and there among the pines on the dry needles where every stranger could be observed from afar, should any chance to wander that way. These meetings began soon after our arrival, but they were no longer meetings of Land and Freedom, but only of those who had attended the assembly at Lipetsk, or who were constant visitors at our cottage in Lesnoy. It was at the first meeting there that Kvyatkovsky, Morozov, and Mikhaylov began to complain of the work of their adherents in the village, saying that they were hindering terroristic activity. They said that the decision of the conference at Voronezh, relative to the assassination of the Tsar, must be acted upon without delay, otherwise the preparations for the fall, when Alexander II was to return to St. Petersburg from the Crimea, could not be realised. Meanwhile, there was an ample supply of dynamite for attempts to be made in several places along the route of his party; and also an adequate staff of workers to accomplish the undertaking. But, they said, as before—so now—the opponents of the terroristic programme were delaying its fulfilment in every way possible. The strength of the organisation was being spent in quarrels and internal friction; the future offered only a series of concessions, waverings, and compromises, instead of decisive and unanimous action. The conference at Voronezh had not removed, but only stifled the dissension, and in order that the factions might not paralyse each other, it was better to divide forces, and permit each side to go its own way.

Again and again they discussed the subject, and there were now no objections. The chief opponents, Plekhanov, Popov, and Stefanovich, were absent. Sofia Perovskaya and I, who had not taken a definite stand at Voronezh in our efforts to preserve the unity of the organisation, no longer objected when the time had come for action, and our comrades from St. Petersburg showed us that all the means by which the attempt was to be made were in readiness; and that it only remained for us to carry out our plan, instead of standing at a dead centre. The general inclination was evidently towards division. The fate of Land and Freedom, and the question of its division, were brought to a head, and a definite break was resolved upon.

In order to determine the means by which the separation was to be effected, representatives were chosen from both sides. They proposed that the printing press on which the party periodical had been printed, should remain in the hands of the supporters of the old programme. Both sides agreed to this; and Mikhaylov's group, thanks to the supply of type secured by Zundelevich, was able to organise its composing room immediately. They also decided to divide the funds equally between them, but were unable to do so at the time. The comfortable fortune of Dmitri Lizogub, a former follower of Tchaikovsky, was tied up in landed estates, and he had given full control of them to Drigo, whom he trusted absolutely, to dispose of them in an honest and proper fashion. He authorised him to sell everything and turn the money over to Land and Freedom. But Lizogub had already been imprisoned for several months in Odessa. In the fall he was executed for his part in the Chubarov affair. As to Drigo, he betrayed his honour and sold himself to the government, hoping to profit from the wealth of his magnanimous and trusting friend. Alexander Mikhaylov, through whom the members of Land and Freedom carried on financial relations with Drigo, not only failed ever to receive any money from him, but barely escaped falling into the ambush laid for him by the traitor.

And so, as far as I can remember, our former comrades in Land and Freedom received nothing, but there were left for us resources amounting to twenty-three thousand rubles, which had been promised and were duly turned over to us by the Yakimovs (i.e. V.M. and N.S. Yakimov, members of the "Freedom or Death" group, who sympathised with a programme of political terror.

By mutual agreement, neither one of the two factions into which Land and Freedom had divided, was to use its former name, which had already won renown and sympathy in revolutionary circles. Both sides disputed this right, and neither one wished to yield to the other all the privileges of the continuer and heir of the previously active organisation. The supporters of the old tendency, who had concentrated their attention on the agrarian question and the economic interests of the peasantry, took as their name, the Black Partition, while we, who had aspired first of all to the overthrow of autocracy, and the substitution of the will of the people for the will of one man, took as our name, The Will of the People.

THE WILL OF THE PEOPLE

Whereas the Black Partition preserved in its general outlines the programme of Land and Freedom, only emphasising in it the point of direct activity among the people and the necessity of organising them for economic warfare against the bourgeoisie, the Narodovoltsy, *i. e.*, the members of The Will of the People, advanced an entirely new principle for their programme. This principle was based on the significance and influence of the centralised state authority on every phase of the life of the people. This element, in their opinion, had played an immense rôle throughout our entire history. In old times this state authority had crushed the federative principles of the political order in ancient Russia. The people, converted into a tax-paying class, were first bound to the soil, and then delivered into personal slavery. The state created the nobility, at first as a serving class, but later as an order of landowners free from the burdens of official duties. When this class became impoverished, and the houses of the most illustrious boyars became utterly destitute and perished towards the beginning of the eighteenth century, then by a series of "most gracious" colossal grants of imperial lands and crown serfs, it laid the foundation for those large, aristocratic and rich landed estates which existed at the time of the emancipation of the serfs. In our own times, the same state authority which had freed the serfs from personal slavery in 1861, took upon itself the rôle of the chief exploiter of free labour of the entire nation. It assigned the peasants allotments which were far below their working strength; it burdened this insufficient allotment with such incommensurate payments and taxes that they swallowed up all the returns which the peasant received from it, and in many places surpassed the producing capacity of the land by two hundred per cent. and more. Having created in this grievous fashion an immense national budget, eighty to ninety per cent. of which was furnished by the lower classes, the centralised state authority employed it almost entirely for the maintenance of the army, the navy, and the payment of state debts which had been incurred for the same purpose, assigning only pitiful crumbs to productive expenditures which satisfied such essential needs of the people as popular education.

It demonstrated perfectly the principle that the people existed for the government, and not the government for the people. Every individual exploitation paled before the exploitation that the government practised on the people. But, unsatisfied with its own achievements in this direction, the government used every means to encourage private exploitation. Just as in previous generations it had created a nobility of landowners, so now it strove to create a bourgeoisie. Instead of siding with the interests of the common people, it encouraged individual promoters, great manufacturers, and railroad magnates. Every economist testified that during all the twenty years that had elapsed since the liberation of the serfs, not one measure had been taken to secure an improvement in the economic life of the people; on the contrary, the entire financial policy of the government had been directed towards the creation and support of private capital, by means of subsidies, guaranteed profts, and discriminating tariffs. All economic measures during this period had been directed to this end; and while in the western European countries the central authority was serving as the instrument and representative of the wealthy classes which had already attained the sovereign power, in our country it appeared as an independent force, and to a considerable degree the source, the creator of these classes.

Thus in the economic sphere, the government of our time appeared to The Will of the People as the greatest of all proprietors, and the chief among the independent despoilers of the nation's labour, which used its power to uphold other more petty exploiters. The government left all classes without political rights, while oppressing the people economically; there was no religious freedom in Russia, as illustrated by the persecution of more than ten million sectarians and schismatics; fiscal and police measures deprived the people of the right of movement from one section to another; the absence of free instruction kept them in enforced ignorance; they were deprived of every means of acquainting the government with their requirements and necessities, for they had no right of petition; and, last of all, the entire life of the nation was at every point subjected to the arbitrary and unrestrained caprice of the administration. The only means through which society might influence the government, and through it, life, namely, literature and the press, were in a condition of complete suppression. In a country where there was no freedom of scientific investigation, or of speech, what could the press amount to? Its best representatives either had been, or were still in exile; those who had been imprisoned at various times lived under the constant surveillance of the police (Chernyshevsky, Mikhaylov, Herzen, Saltykov, Florovsky, Shelgunov, Pisarev, Lavrov, Dostoyevsky, Prugavin, Mikhaylovsky, Uspensky, and a host of others). The younger part of society, the students, were subjected to petty restraints, deprived of their rights of association, and were closely watched by the police. Every attempt

to secure a change in the existing order through one means or
another, either beat vainly against inertia, or met with furious
persecution. When the youth turned to the people with peaceful propaganda, the government met them with wholesale
arrests, exile, penal servitude, and central prisons. When, outraged by violence, these young Russians punished a few servants of the government, the central power replied with military rule and with executions. From the middle of 1878 to
1879, Russia beheld eighteen executions of political offenders.
Under such conditions the government machine was a veritable
Moloch, to whom both the economic well-being of the people,
and all the rights of citizenship and humanity were offered as
a sacrifice.

And it was against this lord of Russian life, this state power,
which rested secure in its vast army and all-powerful administration, that the revolutionary group, The Will of the People,
declared war, regarding the existing government as the greatest enemy of the people in every sphere of its life. This thesis
and its corollaries, political warfare, the transfer of the revolutionary center of gravity from the country to the city; preparation, not for a popular uprising, but for a conspiracy
against the higher authority, with the aim of seizing it and
turning it over to the people, together with the most rigid
centralisation of revolutionary forces as being the only condition to insure success in the warfare with a centralised enemy,
all these considerations brought about a veritable subversion in
the revolutionary world of that time. These ideas undermined
former revolutionary views, caused the socialistic and federal-
istic traditions of the organisation to totter, and destroyed utterly that revolutionary routine which had already become
established during the preceding decade. Therefore it is not
strange that a year and more of tireless propaganda, and a
whole series of illuminating facts, were necessary in order to
break up opposition and win a place of conclusive supremacy
for the new views in the revolutionary world. A general murmur of displeasure arose at the appearance of the issue of the
party's organ which pointed at the monarchy and proclaimed
its "Delendo est Carthago!" and a unanimous burst of applause

greeted the First of March, 1881 [the date of the assassination of Alexander II.—*Tr.*]

From the very first we decided in our program on the definition: "We are Populists-Socialists." It emphasised our revolutionary past, the fact that we were a party not exclusively political; that political freedom was for us not an *end*, but the *means* of breaking our way through to the people, of opening up a broad path for their development. On the other hand, by combining the words "socialist" and "populist," we indicated that, as socialists we pursued not the abstract, ultimate aims of the socialist teaching, but the attainment of those conscious needs and wants of the people, which in their essence included principles of socialism and freedom. Considering the incorporation of socialist ideals in life as a task of the more or less remote future, the new party placed as its nearest goal in the economic field the transfer of the chief instrument of production, the land, into the hands of the peasant commune; and in the political field, the substitution of the sovereignty of the entire people for the autocracy of one man. In other words, the establishment of such an order as would make the freely expressed popular will the highest and only arbiter of all social life. The most suitable means which presented itself for the attainment of these aims was the removal of the existing organization of state power through a revolution.

THE EXECUTIVE COMMITTEE OF THE WILL OF THE PEOPLE

In conformity with the demands of intensive warfare against our mighty antagonist, the plan of organisation of The Will of the People was designed along lines of strict centralisation, and on an all-Russian scale. A net of secret societies, groups of party members, some of whom might busy themselves with tasks of a general revolutionary nature in a limited region, while others might pursue special aims, having chosen for themselves one branch or another of revolutionary work, was to have one common centre, the Executive Committee, through which a general solidarity and bond was established. The local groups were obliged to obey this centre, to surrender to it their members and resources upon demand. All general party functions

and business of an all-Russian nature, came under the direction
of this centre. At a time of uprising, it was to direct all the
available forces of the party, and might call upon them for
revolutionary purposes. But until such a time, its main attention was to be directed towards the planning of a conspiracy,
that work of organisation which alone provided for the possibility of a revolution, through which the authority was to be
transferred to the hands of the people. The forces of the
party were generally applied in this direction. All the stranger
was the title of terrorist organisation which it later acquired.
The public gave it that name because of the external aspect of
its activity, the one characteristic which caught their attention. Terror for its own sake was never the aim of the party.
It was a weapon of protection, of self-defence, regarded as a
powerful instrument for agitation, and employed only for the
purpose of attaining the ends for which the organisation was
working. The assassination of the Tsar came under this head
as one detail. In the fall of 1879, it was a necessity, a question
of the day, which caused some to accept this assassination and
terroristic activity in general as the most essential point of our
entire programme. The desire to check the further development of reaction which hampered our organising activity, and
the wish to assume our work as soon as possible, were the only
reasons which induced the Executive Committee immediately
upon its formation as the centre of The Will of the People, to
plan for an attempt on the life of Alexander II to be made
simultaneously in four different places. And yet the members
of the Committee at the same time carried on active propaganda
both among the intelligentsia and the workingmen. Zhelyabov
directed it in Kharkov, Kolodkevich and I in Odessa, Alexander
Mikhaylov in Moscow, and Kvyatkovsky, Korba and others in
St. Petersburg. The work of propaganda and organisation
always went hand in hand with that of destruction; it was less
evident, but was nevertheless destined to bear its fruits.

Uniting the dissatisfied elements into a general conspiracy
against the government, the new party fully understood the
meaning of the support which a peasant uprising would give
them at the moment of the government's overthrow. Accord-

ingly it assigned a requisite place for activity among the people, and always regarded the ones who wished to devote themselves to it, as its natural allies.

The by-laws of the Executive Committee, by which we bound ourselves, were also written by those who had called the congress at Lipetsk. These requirements of the constitution consisted: first, in the promise to devote all one's mental and spiritual strength to the revolutionary work, to forget for its sake all ties of kinship, and all personal sympathies, love and friendships; second, to give one's life also, if necessary, taking no thought of anything else, and sparing no one and nothing; third, to have no personal property, nothing of one's own, which was not shared in common by the organisation of which one was a member; fourth, to devote oneself entirely to the secret society, to renounce one's individual desires, subordinating them to the will of the majority as expressed in the ordinances of that society; fifth, to preserve complete secrecy with respect to all the affairs, personnel, plans and proposals of the organisation; sixth, never in dealings of private or social nature, or in official acts and declarations, to call ourselves members of the Executive Committee, but only its agents; and seventh, in case of withdrawal from the society, to preserve an unbroken silence as to the nature of its activity, and the business transacted before the eyes and with the participation of the one withdrawing.

These demands were great, but they were easily fulfilled by one fired with the revolutionary spirit, with that intense emotion which knows neither obstacles nor impediments, but goes forward, looking neither backward nor to the right nor the left. If these demands had been less exigent, if they had not stirred one's spirit so profoundly, they would not have satisfied us; but now, by their severe and lofty nature they exalted us and freed us from every petty or personal consideration. One felt more vividly that in him there lived, there must live, an ideal.

IX

REVOLUTIONARY ATTEMPTS

WHEN the entire task of working out the principles and organisation of the society had been completed, the Committee passed on to practical matters, and decided, upon the return of Alexander II from the Crimea, to organise an attempt on his life at three different points. Several agents were appointed to go immediately to Moscow, Kharkov, and Odessa. Dynamite was the destructive element to be used in each case. At the same time, the Committee in St. Petersburg was making preparations for an explosion in the Winter Palace, but this was kept in strictest secrecy, and was under the management of a Directing Commission composed of three people chosen by the members of the Committee from their midst for affairs of the greatest importance.

Since I did not chance to be one of the people assigned to the organisation of the attempts to which I had given my approval, and since the thought was unendurable to me that I should bear only a moral responsibility, and not take a material part in an act for which the law threatened my comrades with the most heavy penalties, I made every effort to persuade the organisation to grant me some active part in the execution of its projects. After reprimanding me for seeking my own satisfaction instead of leaving it to the organisation to dispose of my services as it should itself think best, they made a concession and sent me to Odessa with dynamite. In order to maintain the lodgings necessary for the society's purposes, I asked my sister Evgenia to take my place in St. Petersburg, with the permission of the organisation. She had arrived shortly before this from the province of Ryazan, where she had spent the summer, and was living in St. Petersburg under the name of Poberezhskaya. Not suspecting that my sister in her inexperience had introduced herself to various people by the name

under which she was living, I suggested sending her to live with
Kvyatkovsky, under the same passport, and was thus the in-
direct cause of the terrible fate of Alexander Vasilyevich. The
college girl Bogoslavskaya, who was accused by her fiancé, declared that the copies of the periodical *The Will of the People*,
which were found in her possession by the police, had been given
to her by Poberezhskaya, and after a search in the city direc-
tory, Evgenia, and with her Kvyatkovsky, were arrested on the
24th of November, 1879. In 1880 he was executed, while she
was sent into exile under surveillance. In the apartment they
found dynamite, fulminates and a bit of paper which Kvyatkovsky, caught unawares, did not have time to burn. Crump-
ling it up he threw it into the corner. The gendarmes picked
it up, but could not understand its meaning; on the paper there
was sketched a plan, and on one spot a cross was marked. The
piece of paper cost Kvyatkovsky his life. After the explosion
on the 5th of February, 1880, in the Winter Palace, the police
made out that the plan was that of the Winter Palace, and
that the cross was placed over the dining room which had been
selected for the explosion because the entire royal family was
accustomed to assemble there.

Having received the necessary store of dynamite, I went to
Odessa with it, probably in the beginning of September. There
I succeeded in finding only Nikolai Ivanovich Kibalchich, who
told me that we must quickly arrange for an apartment which
the society needed for various purposes, for meetings, experiments with fulminates, and the storing of the materials necessary for the explosion. After a few days we found a suitable
apartment where we settled together under the name of Ivan-
itsky. Soon Kolodkevich and Frolenko joined us, and later,
Lebedeva. Our apartment was a place for general meetings
and assemblies; there all the conferences took place, there the
dynamite was stored, the guncotton dried, the fulminates prepared. Experiments were made with various types of induction
apparatus—in a word, all kinds of work went on there under
the direction of Kibalchich, but often with the very substantial
aid of others, including even myself. First of all, it was necessary to devise a plan for constructing a mine under the road-

bed of the railway track. It was proposed that we lay the dynamite at night, beneath the rails, in the immediate region of Odessa, during the intervals between trains, so that we might afterwards lay a wire into the field, but this plan presented many inconveniences and difficulties, both in the work of preparation and of execution. We decided that the best plan of all was for some one of us to get a position as railroad guard, and to lay the mine under the ground from his guard station. As for the timing of the action, one could imagine no surer or more convenient means. I offered to take it upon myself to find such a position. In case of my success, we decided that Frolenko should take the position, and that Lebedeva would play the part of his wife should he have to appear as a married man. After investigation, I applied to Baron Ungern-Shternberg, the future son-in-law of the governor-general, Count Totleben. When I had laid my request before the Baron to give a position as railroad guard to the janitor of the building where I lived, whose wife was suffering from tuberculosis, and needed healthy surroundings outside of the city, he said that the position of guard was not under his jurisdiction, but under that of the section master, and that he could do nothing since he did not know whether there were any vacancies. Then I asked for a note to the section master, saying that this would guarantee the future of my client, and the Baron wrote a few lines for me to give to Shchigelsky. Having observed that the reception given me by Ungern-Shternberg was not the one normally given by high society people to an "upperclass doll," I hastened to correct the mistake I had made in my costume, and accordingly appeared before the section master, clad in velvet, and adorned as befitted a lady-petitioner. I was greeted most kindly, and asked to send "my man" on the morrow. Returning home, and casting aside my peacock plumes, I wrote out a burgher's passport for Frolenko as Semen Alexandrov, the name I had devised for the benefit of his future superiors. On the next day he went to the section master and was assigned for service to a point seven or eight miles from Odessa, near Gnilyakov, to which he removed as soon as he had received a separate guardsman's cottage, taking Tatyana Ivanovna Lebedeva with him as his wife. Shortly afterwards, when the dynamite which was to be laid beneath the rails had already been taken to them, Goldenberg arrived unexpectedly with an order to give part of the dynamite to the Moscow group, since they did not think that they had a sufficient supply there, while the Emperor was more likely to pass over the Moscow-Kursk road. We had to submit. Goldenberg had not been in Odessa more than two days before the dynamite was brought from Gnilyakov. He left in good time, but was arrested in Elizavetgrad. A little later we learned that the sovereign would not pass through Odessa, so Frolenko and Lebedeva left first Gnilyakov, and later Odessa as well. Afterwards we heard that the imperial train had successfully passed through Kharkov on the Lozovo-Sebastopol railroad. The attempt which was to have been made on this route near Alexandrovsk, and which had been organised by the Executive Committee, acting through Zhelyabov, Yakimova, and the workingman, Okladsky, did not take place. The mine had been laid under the railroad bed, the conduits led far out into an adjoining field, and when the imperial train passed by, all the actors were at their posts, but the explosion did not follow because the electrodes were incorrectly joined and produced no spark.[20]

At the third point, on the Moscow-Kursk railroad, where preparations had been made near Moscow from a house near the station, two brightly lighted trains passed, one after another, on the 19th of November at the set hour. Stepan Shiryaev failed to join the electrodes at the first signal from Sofia Perovskaya, and the train passed unharmed. At the second signal, the second train was wrecked, but the Tsar was travelling in the first, while the second proved to be bearing only the court servants. This was a mishap, but the act in itself produced an immense impression in Russia, and found an echo throughout all Europe.

It was in St. Petersburg during the fall that our losses began. Kvyatkovsky perished, then Shiryaev, and others.

[20] It was later discovered that Okladsky was an agent provocateur, and was responsible for the failure of this attempt. He was recently identified and brought to trial before a revoultionary tribunal, at which veteran revolutionists testified against him.

Later the printing press of *The Will of the People* was destroyed after an heroic armed defence. In the middle of December Kibalchich left Odessa; in January, Kolodkevich, and at the same time others of the more influential members left, and all affairs were turned over to me and a few local workers who were little known in the revolutionary world.

My work was propaganda. After three months of life spent in my lodging, a life which demanded caution and did not permit personal relations with the outside world, with casual acquaintances, I longed for friends, for society and vital activity. My long-restrained energy welled up in me like a spring, but the assistants whom I had received from my predecessors were indolent and cowardly, and not particularly inspired with hope or enthusiasm. I had to abandon all these people afterwards as incompetents. Nevertheless, after the departure of Kibalchich I quickly formed a large circle of acquaintances in which representatives from all classes of society figured, from professor and general, landowner and student, doctor and government official, down to workman and seamstress. And wherever I could, I introduced revolutionary ideas and defended the activity of The Will of the People. My favourite sphere, however, was the younger generation, whose emotions were so strong, whose enthusiasm so sincere. Unfortunately, I had few acquaintances among the students, while those whom I did know regarded their fellows pessimistically and had no faith in the existence of revolutionary elements among them.

THE EXPLOSION IN THE WINTER PALACE

In the meantime, events were taking place in St. Petersburg. As I mentioned before, the Committee had in view one more undertaking staged for St. Petersburg itself, for which they were planning together with the preparations for the explosions near Moscow, Alexandrovsky, and Odessa. This was the undertaking at which Alexander Kvyatkovsky had hinted in his conversation with me.

At that time, Stepan Halturin, a member of the party and a very well-educated workman, a cabinet-maker by profession, with the encouragement of the Committee, got access to the

Winter Palace, ostensibly for work in his own line, but with the real aim of assassinating Alexander II. Having acquainted himself with the arrangement of the rooms and the surroundings of the Palace, and with the dispositions and habits of the servants, Halturin became friendly with them, and as a sober, skilful workman won the special favour of the police guard who lived with him in the palace basement, and who began to look upon him as a desirable suitor for his daughter. After such preparatory measures, Stepan slowly began to fill his trunk in the basement with dynamite which he received from the Committee. When a reasonable quantity had been collected and any additional amount might attract attention and cause investigation, it was decided to act.

On the day of the arrival in the capital of Prince Alexander of Battenberg, on the 5th of February, 1880, Halturin was to set off the explosion which would demolish the dining room and bury under its ruins the imperial family and their guest, when they would all be assembled at dinner. And so he did. At the appointed hour he joined a Rumford fuse of requisite length to the fulminate in the dynamite, lighted it, and left the Palace for the last time. A terrible explosion occurred at the moment when the imperial family entered the dining room. On the floor directly over the basement, where the bodyguard of the Finland regiment was quartered, fifty soldiers were mutilated and killed. The amount of dynamite proved insufficient, however, to destroy the dining room on the upper floor. It remained unharmed. The floor shook and heaved from the vibration, the dishes on the table fell to the floor with a crash. But the royal family remained unhurt.

Directly after this the dictatorship of Loris-Melikov was declared. He was greeted by the shot of Molodetsky, who died on the scaffold three or four days later with the smile of a hero.

Society, at any rate its more intelligent element, greeted our activity with great enthusiasm, and offered us sympathetic aid and ardent approval. From this point of view we had a right to speak in the name of society. We constituted to a marked degree the front rank of a part of that society. Knowing that this group sympathised with us, we did not feel ourselves a sect,

St. Petersburg, 1880

isolated from all the other elements of the empire, and this contributed not a little to that "implacable quality" which we showed in our actions, and of which the public prosecutors used to speak at our trials. In order to annihilate that quality, they would have had to annihilate the atmosphere of dissatisfaction which surrounded us; and the only way to do that, was to make the dissatisfied, satisfied. But in such a case, even we should have proved to be in large measure satisfied.

In March or April, 1880, Sablin and later Perovskaya, arrived in Odessa. They came to my lodgings and told me that they had been sent by the Committee to make preparations in Odessa for a mine, in case the Emperor should pass through the city on his way to the Crimea for the summer. I was then busy with preparations for a terrorist act, the assassination of Panyutin, head of the chancelry of Count Totleben, the governor-general. He was the right-hand man of the governor-general, who apparently granted him complete authority in directing the interior policy of the region under his charge. At least, during my entire stay in Odessa people spoke more of Panyutin than of Totleben, and Panyutin was the terror of the citizens of Odessa. At the time of the Trial of the Twenty-eight, which ended in five executions, he took measures for a thorough purging of the city. Comparing the city duma with the Paris Commune of 1871, he seized upon a few of its members; arrests of teachers, writers, students, officials and workingmen followed; vast numbers of people were exiled in a most arbitrary and revolting fashion. He was rough and coarse in his treatment of people, and the relatives of the exiles had to undergo humiliating scenes in his chancelry. When the pregnant wife of one of those who had been arrested could not restrain her sobs in his presence, he shouted, "Be off with you! I suppose you'll take it into your head to give birth to your brat here!"

It was against this Panyutin that I planned to turn the weapon of the party. A certain young man not only pointed him out to me, but described the usual course of his daily walks, so that at the appointed hour I was able almost daily to meet his stout figure, accompanied by two spies, one of whom walked beside him, while the other followed at a distance of four or five paces. A man was found to carry out our purpose: he was to stab Panyutin with a dagger during one of his walks. The place and time had already been decided upon, and I had planned to have a horse ready in order to give the assassin a chance to escape.

But the arrival of Sofia Perovskaya with an order from the Committee forced us to give up this project. Sablin and Perovskaya came with ready plans for the attempt. They were to select the street over which the Emperor was most likely to pass in going from the station to the steamboat wharf; on this street, they were to open a shop as husband and wife, and carry on trade, and from this shop it was planned to tunnel out under the street pavement and lay a mine. In a word, this was the project which was afterwards realised in St. Petersburg. Grigory Isayev, who arrived shortly afterwards with Yakimova, was to direct the technical details.

We rented a shop on Italyanskaya Street, and immediately set to work. We had to make haste, for the Emperor was expected in May, while our preparations were being made in April. Moreover, it was possible to work only at night, for the tunnelling had been begun not from the living apartments, but from the shop itself, where customers were likely to come. We had planned to lay the mine not by digging an excavation, but with a drill, and it proved to be very difficult to operate. The ground consisted of clay, and clogged up the drill, which moved only after tremendous physical exertions on our part, and with exasperating slowness. But finally we reached the stones of the pavement, and the drill went up and out into the light of day. Soon afterwards Grigory Isayev had three fingers blown off in an ill-guarded experiment with a fulminate. He bore it like a stoic, but we were deeply distressed. He had to go to a hospital. After this, all the things that had been stored in his room (the dynamite, mercury fulminate, wires, and so forth) were brought to me, for we were afraid that the sound of the explosion in his room might have turned the attention of the entire household upon him. We had one worker the less. We decided to give up the drill and to dig a tunnel a few yards long from the end of which we were to work with the drill; the

earth was to be piled up in one of the living rooms. We decided
to carry it all away without fail at the conclusion of our work,
fearing that there might be a general investigation of the houses
along the Tsar's route. Therefore we had already begun to
carry it away, whichever one of us was free at that time, and to
empty it out. I found a place in my apartment where a large
pile of this earth could be stored. They brought it to me on
foot and in carriages, in baskets, packages and bundles which I
emptied during the absence of the other lodgers, after sending
the servant out on an errand. In the meantime the rumours
of the Tsar's trip to Livadia ceased. Later we received word
from the Committee to stop operations. We then suggested
to the Committee that we make use of our work for blowing up
Count Totleben, but our offer was rejected, for this form of
assassination was being reserved especially for the Emperor.
We were permitted, however, to undertake the assassination of
Totleben through some other means.

After this, Sablin, I, and a few others whom I had enlisted,
began to observe the habits of the governor-general. We
planned to use bombs, and if the later invention of Isayev and
Kibalchich had existed then, the Count would not have escaped,
but we had only dynamite to work with, and the unperfected
fulminates. The bomb was therefore of inconvenient size, and
might not be sure of operation. Nevertheless, we should have
accomplished our design if Totleben had not been transferred
from Odessa. We longed to wash away the blood of our numerous comrades executed by him. The names of Totleben and
Chertkov were generally hated because of their blood-thirsti-
ness, and we planned by a systematic extermination of gover-
nor-generals, in order to obtain the annihilation of the very
institution which they represented.

After Totleben's departure, all preparations had to be
brought to an end. The shop on Italyanskaya Street was
closed; the excavation there had already been filled up with the
earth which had previously been taken from it. In this easy
task I, too, helped, dragging sacks of earth from the living
room and emptying them into the excavation where the men
trod down the earth. When everything had been restored to

its accustomed order, Sablin and Perovskaya departed, and Isayev and Yakimova followed them. I gave them a statement to hand to the Committee, asking them to recall me from Odessa, and to appoint some one to whom I might hand over the local business and party connections. I motivated my desire by the fact that I had already spent almost a year in the provinces, remote from the centre of the organisation, and felt myself somewhat estranged from the general activities; and that I must spend some time in St. Petersburg in order to report on my work up to that time, and to consult with them as to the future management of affairs. It must have been in July that I left Odessa for St. Petersburg without waiting for my appointed successor, Trigoni.

At that time new preparations for an attempt on the life of Alexander II were in progress in Petersburg, on Gorokhovaya Street, near the Stone Bridge. The details were then unknown to me. Like the explosion in the Winter Palace, this affair was kept in strict secrecy and was under the management of our directing commission. I knew only that an explosion was to take place along the route of one of the Tsar's drives, and this time from beneath the water.

I knew that at certain hours the Tsar was accustomed to drive to the Tsarskoye Selo station, and so I once walked along that course and actually did meet the open carriage which bore the Emperor. I wanted to see, if only once in my life, the man whose existence was of such fatal significance to our party. Neither before, nor ever afterwards did I see him. I think that that was his last trip along this route, for directly afterwards he set forth for the Crimea and did not return to St. Petersburg until late autumn. The attempt mentioned did not take place.

X

THE MILITARY ORGANISATION

THE fall of 1880 and the early part of 1881 were a time of increased ardour in the work of propaganda and organisation, carried on by our party. It was during this period that extensive connections with the provinces were formed, local groups organised, and a detailed plan of action in separate localities worked out. The agents of the Committee were covering in their travels certain selected regions, or were commandeered for permanent residence at points of special importance throughout the Empire. The increased distribution of our periodical, *The Will of the People*, propaganda by word of the Committee's programme, and, more than all, the outstanding episodes in the conflict, which spoke for themselves, won general sympathy for the party. Delegates came to the Committee from all over the country, to arrange connections, to offer their services for the fulfilment of new projects, and to request that agents be sent out to organise the local forces. The Committee, of course, lost no time in availing itself of this friendly and sympathetic attitude. It reaped the fruits of its toil and sacrifices. The profound mental stir which resulted from the activity of the Executive Committee was expressed in the outspoken desire of various circles and individuals to consolidate; in their efforts to join the party, and in their constant expressions of readiness to take part in active warfare with the government. Boldness is as infectious as panic; the energy and audacity of the organisation attracted to it vital elements, and death itself lost its terror.

In St. Petersburg itself, the work of propaganda, agitation, and organisation was carried on on the broadest of scales. The cessation of police attacks and battles with gendarmes during the period of Loris-Melikov's dictatorship was most favorable for work among the university youth and workingmen. It was a season of animation and hopes. All traces of the oppressive apathy that had grown up after the failures of the first half of the seventies disappeared as though those ten years had not been a continuous draining of the life-blood of Russia's protesting elements. A loud demand arose for the assassination of the Tsar, for Count Loris-Melikov's policy deceived no one. It created absolutely no change in the government's relations towards society, the common people, and the party itself. The Count merely replaced harsh and drastic forms with milder ones, but took away with one hand what he gave with the other.

Public opinion in the revolutionary world demanded that the programme of terror and assassination be continued, and that the Tsar's pseudo-liberal intimate meet the same fate as the Tsar himself. And while the majority of the Committee's agents were busy with propaganda and organisation, its technicians were working to perfect bombs which were to aid the exploding mines, the effectiveness of which had not been great up to this time.

It was during this brilliant period of its activity that the Executive Committee founded the Military Organisation of The Will of the People. At the same time it negotiated relations with the naval officers at Kronstadt, through Lieutenant Sukhanov; and with the artillery division in St. Petersburg, chiefly through Sergey Degayev. This man had served previously with the artillery at the Kronstadt Fortress, and had attended the Academy of Artillery for some time, though later he was excluded because of his political views.

Life itself could not have failed to influence the military order to some extent. There existed the literature which made its appeal on behalf of the people; the youth movement "to the people," had left a vivid trail; the political trials of the seventies were taking place, and also the arrests throughout the cities of Russia; then, too, even before the formation of The Will of the People, beginning with the shot fired by Vera Zassulich in the year 1878, a whole series of terroristic acts had deeply stirred public opinion in Russia. It would have been unnatural had all the men in the army and navy remained deaf to the things that were taking place outside of the military sphere. Indeed, we see that in 1878, an independently organised circle of naval officers and midshipmen was carrying on propaganda among the lower ranks at Kronstadt. The Russo-Turkish War, the liberation of Bulgaria and the inauguration of a constitution in that country, also had their effect. The war revealed in all its nakedness the shame of our officialdom; the conscienceless robbery and misappropriation of funds; the absence of any consideration whatever for the soldier, ragged and hungry, deprived of any medical help, suffering in numberless instances. The officers could not help but ponder over the causes of these abuses, and seek some means to eradicate them. Bulgaria had been freed from the Turkish yoke and a constitution granted her; but Russia had been left in political slavery under its former autocratic sway. "We thought," said Pokhitonov (who had participated in the siege of Plevna), at his trial in 1884, "that instead of freeing a foreign country, one should rather think of freeing Russia."

The military schools and academies of higher rank, which offered broader instruction, could not help in their turn but produce officers of a certain class, inspired with a longing to better society, a keen desire for freedom; and indeed, they did furnish them in the persons of such men as Rogachev, Pokhitonov, Butsevich, and others.

These were the main principles along which the organisation was effected: the Military Organisation was to be built from above, the nature of its structure being the same as that of The Will of the People, that is, along lines of strict centralisation; and to be entirely independent of the parent party in matters of organisation. At the head of the organisation, a central committee of officers, picked by the Executive Committee, was to stand. The local military groups which had been formed by the military centre of the party, were subordinate to this centre, while the centre itself *was subordinate to the Executive Committee.*

The aim of the Military Organisation was to lead an armed insurrection at the moment determined by the Executive Committee, which was in charge of all the forces accumulated during the period of preparation, not only in the army, but also among the workingmen, government officials, the intelligentsia, and the peasantry. Thus the rôle of the Military Organisation was not self-sufficient, but made subject to the Executive Committee, which had complete information on the general situation, and the moods of social groups and classes. The party thus consisted of two parallel organisations: the civil and the military, which were connected only through their centres. Such separation was by way of a precaution against exposing the military to avoidable danger; otherwise they would have been subjected to all the devastating hazards which wrought havoc among the local branches of the party. To rebuild these latter was much easier than to replace a compromised military circle.

At the same time that the naval officers at Kronstadt organised their group, a branch of the party among the artillerymen of St. Petersburg was formed, which included, beside Rogachev, Pokhitonov, and Degayev, of whom I have already spoken, also Papin, Nikolayev, and three or four others.

On such a basis the Military Organisation seemed to have every chance to grow and flourish. The sympathy with which the programme of The Will of the People met among the officers at Kronstadt and in St. Petersburg, the excellent personnel of the centre which was made up of people with the ability to enlarge the group as well as to direct it, all inspired great hopes. A census of members gave us close to two hundred, and later, a much larger number of references to members of various ranks of the army scattered throughout the cities, and sympathising more or less with the ideas of political freedom. These all had to be visited in turn by members of the organisation, in order to determine the degree of their revolutionary ardour, and in case they should prove useful, to organise them and later make them members of the central group.

The Will of the People also decided to organise abroad the propaganda of its actual aims and aspirations, and to enlist the sympathies of European society by acquainting it with the domestic policy of our government. Thus, while shaking the throne by the explosions of our bombs within the Empire, we might discredit it from without, and contribute to pressure from without and possibly to the diplomatic interference of a few countries which had been enlightened as to the internal affairs of our dark tsardom. For this purpose we had at our disposal those revolutionary forces which had been lost to the movement in Russia, that is, the emigrants.

Out of this number Hartman and Lavrov were selected by the Committee to undertake agitation as duly authorised agents of the party, in the spirit of The Will of the People programme. Lectures and gatherings might be employed as means for accomplishing this, but especial emphasis was laid upon the use of brochures, leaflets, and magazine articles portraying the economic and political state of affairs in Russia. Hartman was to visit the most important cities of the United States for this purpose. All the eminent figures in the socialistic world of Western Europe promised him their co-operation in one form or another. With some of them, as for instance, Karl Marx and Rochefort, the Committee communicated by letter, asking them to help their agent, Hartman, in the work of organising propaganda against Russian despotism. In answer to this request the author of "Capital" sent the Committee his autographed portrait, together with his expressed agreement to serve. Hartman declared that Marx showed the letter of the Committee with pride to his friends and acquaintances. But, according to the reports of all our friends abroad, it was not only Karl Marx who expressed his admiration for the Russian revolutionary movement. It had attracted general attention; the journalistic world seized eagerly upon news concerning Russia, and the events listed in the Russian revolutionary chronicle formed the most absorbing news. In order to check the stream of false rumours and canards of every kind, furnished to the European public through the daily press, it was necessary systematically to supply the foreign agents with correspondence from Russia covering all the current happenings in the Russian revolutionary world. The Committee chose me in the fall of 1880 as foreign correspondence secretary. I managed its business correspondence with Hartman, sent him copies of letters, biographies of those who had been executed, supplied him with current numbers of revolutionary publications, secured pictures of arrested and condemned revolutionists for him, sent him Russian magazines and newspapers, and, generally speaking, satisfied his demands to the best of my ability. After the assassination of Alexander II, I sent him a report of this event—the last one—including therein the letter of the Executive Committee to Alexander III, and a plan of the interior of the Kobozev cheese shop, drawn by Kobozev himself.

THE CHEESE SHOP

The Committee had been considering a plan to rent a store or shop on one of the streets of St. Petersburg along which the Emperor passed most frequently on his drives; from the shop they planned to make excavations for the purpose of laying a mine. With this end in view, a few agents of the party were entrusted with the task of examining all the available places for the execution of the plan, and since the Tsar was obliged to ride to the Mikhaylovsky Manège, they accordingly looked for a shop on one of the streets that led to it. Two such shops were found while Mikhaylov was still alive and apparently by him, and the Committee chose one of them. This was a shop in Mengden's house, on Malaya Sadovaya Street. It was decided to open a cheese shop there.

When the Committee began to choose the people necessary for this establishment, I suggested my friend, Yuri Nikolayevich Bogdanovich, as the shopkeeper. The exact location of the shop, and the name by which its master was to be known, were unknown to me until some time in February, when, as the date of the passport under which Bogdanovich was registered had expired, he asked me to write out a new one in the name of Kobozev. About the beginning of the year, Bogdanovich and Yakimova, as his wife, established themselves, and began to make excavations under the street.

XI

FEBRUARY DAYS

On Sunday, the fourteenth of February, the Emperor, who visited the Mikhaylovsky Manège on Sundays, and always chose a different route, passed along the Malaya Sadovaya. The underground excavation had by this time been completed, but the mine had not yet been laid. When we learned of this, we were indignant at the slowness of the technicians. We might have to wait for a whole month before the Tsar would pass that way again.

Exasperated, the Committee decreed in assembly that all preparations must be completed by the first of March, and the mine and its explosive charges prepared for action. Our plan consisted of three parts, which all had the same aim, namely, that this attempt, the seventh in number, should be decisive and final. The most important part was the explosion, which was to be directed from the cheese shop; only the members of the Committee knew about this. In case this explosion should take place shortly before or after the passing of the Tsar's carriage, then, the four bomb-throwers, Rysakov, Grinevitsky, Timofey Mikhaylov, and Emelyanov, were to hurl their bombs from opposite sides at the two ends of the Malaya Sadovaya. And if even these should fail of their purpose, Zhelyabov, armed with a dagger, was to spring upon the Emperor and finish the deed.

From this time on we lived a feverish and anxious life. The third month of the existence of the little cheese shop in Mengden's house had begun. The shopkeepers, Bogdanovich and Yakimova, satisfied all the external requirements of their position; Bogdanovich with his spade-shaped beard, his broad face, the colour of a burnished samovar as Bogdanovich used to say of himself laughingly, and his speech, quick-witted and to the point, and flavoured with jokes, all made him appear a genuine,

average tradesman. And Yakimova, with her "democratic" exterior, the bangs on her forehead, and her round "o" accent of
the Vyatka province, could not have made a better match for
him. But from a commercial point of view they were both incompetent, and the neighbouring tradesmen at once decided
that the newcomers would not be dangerous rivals. In addition to this, our supply of money was low during January and
February, and we could buy very few cheeses. So slight were
our funds for this most important purpose, that when, at the
critical moment, I secured three hundred rubles with which to
purchase stock, it was regarded as a piece of great good
fortune. And yet, at the first glance one did not notice how
small their stock was, as I convinced myself when in the guise
of a purchaser of Roquefort I once came to the shop on an
errand of the Committee, and surprised "Baska" in her rôle
as saleswoman behind the counter, which was covered with
cheeses of different kinds. The shop was located in a semi-
basement; I had come to warn them that the place was going
to be searched, and that a spy had approached Sukhanov, who
had been standing nearby, but that he had escaped in a cab.

Although the counter had a decent appearance, as became
a counter laden with cheeses, the cheese barrels on the ground
contained no cheese; they were filled with earth from the excavation under the street. Perhaps the inexperience of the shopkeepers aroused suspicion, or some one of those who worked at
night in the underground tunnel, was being followed (probably Trigoni, who, as we afterwards learned, was living in the
same house with a spy, on the Nevsky), but at all events, the
police had at last turned their attention to the shop.

On the evening of February 27th, the police appeared at
Trigoni's room in the house of Madame Missura, on the Nevsky, and arrested both him and Andrey Zhelyabov, who was
calling on him. The news of this misfortune, which struck us
dumb, was brought by Sukhanov, on the morning of February
28th, to our apartment near Voznesensky Bridge. At the
same time the rumour spread through the city that the police
were about to make an important discovery, and mentioned the
very precinct in which Kobozev's shop was located. Some

young people reported a conversation which they had over-heard between the porter of Mengden's house and a police officer, in which a search of the house was mentioned; "Kobo-zev" himself paid us a visit, and told of a call that some sup-posed sanitary commission had made on the shop, the veiled purpose of which was apparent. The whole matter hung by a thread.

"What is the cause of that dampness?" asked the constable, pointing to traces of moisture near one of the barrels that had been filled with damp earth.

"During the Carnival weeks we spilled some sour cream there," answered Bogdanovich. If the constable had looked into the barrel, he would have seen the kind of sour cream it contained!

In the corners of the back room, there lay on the floor a large heap of earth that had been removed from the excavation. It was covered with coal and straw, and a long strip of matting had been thrown on top. They had only to lift these up, in order to make their discovery. But nothing was noticed, and this inspection, the details of which were, in Bogdanovich's words, a lucky game of "to be or not to be," even gave the shop legal approval, since nothing of a suspicious nature had been found there. But when we heard the tale, we were struck with consternation. It was plain that this work which we had so long been planning, and which, with labour and peril, we had completed, this work, which was to end the two-years' warfare that had bound our hands, might perish on the eve of its con-summation. We could endure anything but that.

It was not the personal safety of our individual workers that aroused our anxiety. All our past, and all our revolu-tionary future were at stake on that Saturday, the day before the first of March; the past, in which there had been six at-tempts against the life of the Tsar, and twenty-one executions, and which we wished to end, to shake off, to forget; and the future, broad and bright, which we had dreamed of conquering for our generation. No nervous system could long endure such an intense strain.

And in the meantime, the entire tread of events had been

against us. We had lost Kletochnikov,[21] our guardian; the shop was in the greatest danger of discovery; Zhelyabov, that fearless comrade, who was to direct the bomb-throwers, and who was one of the most responsible people involved in the proposed attempt, had dropped out of the undertaking. We had immediately to dismantle and abandon his lodgings, after removing the supply of nitroglycerine that had been stored there. The lodgings on Telezhnaya Street, where all the technical preparations for the explosion were to take place, and where the signallers and bomb-throwers used to assemble, were unsafe, according to the declaration made the day before by Sablin and Gesya Helfman, its tenants; the police were evidently investigating it, and to complete the desperate situation, we learned with horror, *that the mine had not yet been laid, and that not one of its four charges was prepared.* And tomorrow was Sunday, the first of March, and the Tsar might pass along the Sadovaya.

It was in the face of these difficulties that we members of the Executive Committee hurriedly assembled at the apartment near Voznesensky Bridge, on February 28th. Not all of us were there, for there had not been time to notify every one. Besides myself and Isayev, the tenants of the apartment, there were Sofia Perovskaya, Anna Korba, Sukhanov, Grachevsky, Frolenko, Lebedeva, and possibly Tikhomirov and Langans. I do not remember for certain. In our agitation we were inspired by one feeling, one mood. Therefore, when Perovskaya asked the fundamental question of how to act if the Emperor should not pass along Malaya Sadovaya on the morrow, the first of March, and whether we should carry out the attempt with only the aid of loaded bombs, all who were present answered with one voice: "Act! Whatever happens, act to-morrow! The mine *must* be laid. The bombs *must* be loaded by morning and put into action, either when the mine explodes or independently." Only Sukhanov declared that he could say neither yes or no, since this type of bomb had never been used before.

[21] A clerk in the service of the secret police, who kept the revolutionists informed of his department's plans and movements.—*Translator.*

This all took place about three o'clock on Saturday afternoon. Isayev was dispatched at once to the shop, to lay the mine; the apartment of Zhelyabov and Perovskaya was dismantled, with the help of Sukhanov and his military comrades, and Perovskaya moved into our apartment. We did not have time to notify all our members, or even the signallers on Sadovaya; but their rôles, as well as those of the bomb-throwers, had been arranged in advance, and an appointment made with all of them for Sunday.

At five o'clock in the evening, three people were to come to our apartment and work all night on the bombs. These people were Sukhanov, Kibalchich, and Grachevsky. Up to eight o'clock, members of the Committee were constantly coming to the apartment, now with news, now on current business, but since this interfered with the work, they all left about eight o'clock, and there were only five of us left in the apartment, including myself and Perovskaya. Having persuaded Perovskaya, who was exhausted, to lie down in order to conserve her strength for the morrow, I began to help the workers wherever they needed a hand, even though it was an inexperienced one. Now I helped Kibalchich cast the weights, now I helped Sukhanov trim the kerosene cans which I had bought, and which served as cases for the explosives. All night long our lamps burned and our fire flared in the grate. At two o'clock I left my comrades, for they no longer needed my services. When Perovskaya and I arose at seven o'clock, the men were still working, but two explosive charges had been completed; Perovskaya took these to Sablin's apartment on Telezhnaya Street, and Sukhanov left directly afterwards. I then helped Grachevsky and Kibalchich fill the remaining two cans with nitroglycerine, and Kibalchich took them away. And so, at eight o'clock on the morning of the first of March the four bombs were ready, after three men had worked on them for fifteen hours. At ten o'clock, Rysakov, Grinevitsky, Emelyanov and Timofey Mikhaylov came to the apartment on Telezhnaya Street. Perovskaya, who with Zhelyabov had constantly been directing them, gave them definite instructions as to what posi-

tions they were to take for action, and where, after the Tsar's
carriage had passed, they were later to meet.

THE FIRST OF MARCH

By the order of the Committee I was to remain at home
until two o'clock on that first day of March, to receive the
Kobozevs, for Bogdanovich was to leave the shop an hour
before the Tsar's party should pass that way, and Yakimova
was to leave directly after the signal that the Tsar had made
his appearance on the Nevsky. A third person (Frolenko)
was to switch on the electric current, and then leave the shop
as a casual customer, in case he should escape perishing in the
ruins from the explosion wrought by his own hand.

At ten o'clock Frolenko came to see me. With astonishment
I saw him take from a package that he had brought with him,
a bottle of red wine and a sausage, which he put on the table,
preparing to have a little lunch. In my state of intense excitement, after our decision and the sleepless night spent in preparations, it seemed to me that to eat and drink was impossible.

"What are you doing?" I asked, almost with horror, as I
beheld this matter-of-fact procedure on the part of a man who
was destined to an almost certain death under the ruin caused
by the explosion.

"I must be in full possession of my strength," calmly replied
my comrade, and he imperturbably began to eat.

I could only bow in silent admiration before this disregard
of the thought of possible death, this all-absorbing realisation
that, in order to fulfil the mission which he had taken upon
himself, he must be in full possession of his strength.

Neither Bogdanovich nor Yakimova came to the apartment.
Isayev returned, and with him a few members of the party,
with the news that the Tsar had not passed the shop, but had
gone home from the Manège. Forgetting entirely that they
had not followed the return route of the Tsar, and also had not
been informed of the last decision of the Committee, to act,
whatever might occur, though it be only with bombs, I left the
house thinking that for some unforeseen reasons the attempt
had not taken place.

And indeed, the Tsar did not pass through the Sadovaya; but it was at this point that Sofia Perovskaya displayed all her self-possession. Quickly concluding that the Tsar would return by way of the quay along the Ekaterininskaya Canal, she changed the entire plan of action, deciding to employ only the bombs. She made the rounds of the bomb-throwers and instructed them to take new positions, after they had agreed that she was to give the signal by waving her handkerchief.

Shortly after two o'clock, two detonations that sounded like shots from a cannon, thundered out, one after another. Rysakov's bomb wrecked the Tsar's carriage, while Grinyevitsky's struck the Tsar. Both the Tsar and Grinyevitsky were mortally wounded, and died within a few hours.

When I left the house after Isayev's return, everything was quiet, but half an hour after I had made my appearance at Glyeb Uspensky's, Ivanchin-Pisarev came to him with the news that there had been some explosions and that a rumour was circulating to the effect that the Tsar had been killed, and that in the churches the people were already swearing allegiance to the heir.

I rushed home. The streets hummed with talk, and there was evident excitement. People were speaking of the Tsar, of his wounds, of blood and death. When I entered my own dwelling and saw my friends who as yet suspected nothing, I was so agitated that I could hardly utter the words announcing the death of the Tsar. I wept, and many of us wept; that heavy nightmare, which for ten years had strangled young Russia before our very eyes, had been brought to an end; the horrors of prison and exile, the violence, executions, and atrocities inflicted on hundreds and thousands of our adherents, the blood of our martyrs, all were atoned for by this blood of the Tsar, shed by our hands. A heavy burden was lifted from our shoulders; reaction must come to an end and give place to a new Russia. In this solemn moment, all our thoughts centred in the hope for a better future for our country.

Shortly afterwards Sukhanov joined us, joyful and excited, and embraced and congratulated us all in the name of that future. The letter to Alexander III [see *Appendix*], drawn up a few days later, is characteristic of the general state of mind of the members of the party in St. Petersburg, during the period that followed the first of March. The letter was composed with a moderation and tact that won the sympathetic approval of all Russian society. Upon its publication in the West, it produced a sensation throughout all the European press. The most moderate and conservative periodicals expressed their approval of the demands of the Russian Nihilists, finding them reasonable, just, and such as had in large measure been long ago realised in the daily life of Western Europe.

On the third of March, Kibalchich came to us with the news that Gesya Helfman's apartment on Telezhnaya Street had been discovered by the police, that Helfman had been arrested, while Sablin, who had always seemed a careless merry-maker, quick-witted and playful, had shot himself. He also told us about the armed resistance of a man who had appeared in the house after Helfman's arrest, and who proved to be the workman, Timofey Mikhaylov. The first thought of those who knew what members were accustomed to visit Helfman's apartment (which had a special significance and therefore was unknown to the majority of our agents), was, that it had been betrayed by Rysakov. In view of this supposition, the Committee changed its decision that the Kobozevs should leave their shop only after the dynamite had been removed from the mine; they were not only to give up their shop that very day, but to leave St. Petersburg that evening.

Not more than a week passed, and we lost Sofia Perovskaya, who was treacherously seized on the street. And directly after her arrest, Kibalchich met his ruin, betrayed by his landlady; while Frolenko, who was calling on Kibalchich, fell into the ambush and was also arrested. Ivanchin-Pisarev was the next to be seized. The White Terror had begun its activities.

At that time we thought that the government had in its employ some one who knew many of our agents by sight, and who had pointed them out on the street. But now, since the publication of the police archives, it has been discovered that one of the betrayers was the workman Okladsky, who had been condemned to penal servitude at the trial of Kvyatkovsky in

1880. In view of the danger of remaining in St. Petersburg, a few of us, at the suggestion of the Committee, were to leave the city. I was among this number. But we were all inspired with the desire to make use of these propitious moments for the purpose of organising the party. We saw around us the keenest enthusiasm; humble sympathisers, people who had hitherto been passive or indifferent, became aroused, asked for information, for work; circles of every kind imaginable invited representatives of the party to their meetings in order to establish relations with our organisation and to offer their services. If ambition had been the guiding motive of the members of the party, then surely we might then have drunk our fill, for our success was intoxicating. No one who who did not live through with us the period that followed the first of March, could ever conceive of the significance of that event for us, as a revolutionary party. It is easy to understand that departure from St. Petersburg at such a time was tormenting for any person who believed in his own strength, and who was convinced that the interests of the work in hand required his presence, even in spite of the demands of cool reason. Supported by Sukhanov, I presented such arguments in defence of my desire to remain where I was, that the Committee altered its decision in my favour, but, to my regret, not for long. On April 1st, Grigory Isayev failed to come home. He had been seized on the street, as I afterwards learned, by some traitor, as were several others of our comrades who came to their end during the course of that month of March. In order to avoid anxiety and misunderstanding, we had held to the rule that those who maintained lodgings for the use of the organisation were not allowed to spend the night away from home without a previous agreement. Consequently, I no longer doubted that Isayev had been arrested when he did not return by midnight of April 1st, to our common home.

At that time, through the force of various circumstances, our apartment had gradually been transformed into a storehouse for articles of every description. After the workingmen's press had been liquidated, the type and all the rest of the machinery were brought there. When the chemical laboratory was closed, Isayev brought all the apparatus and a large store of dynamite to our apartment. Sofia Perovskaya turned over to us her dynamite as well, and also everything else that she thought should be removed from her own apartment; after Frolenko's arrest, we received half of the passport equipment; and to cap the climax, all the literature and publications were brought to us from the printing shop of *The Will of the People*, and these filled to overflowing a huge trunk, which was afterwards found by the police empty in our apartment. Such treasures should not be lost, and I resolved to save everything and to leave the apartment absolutely empty on my departure.

On the morning of April 2nd, instead of going out to look for any of my friends, I decided to wait for some one to call, and I began to arrange the property of the party in such shape that it could be easily moved. It was one o'clock in the afternoon when Grachevsky made his appearance. He informed me that my comrades already considered me lost, since from early morning, the porters of various lodging houses had been filing through police headquarters in order to identify a young man who had been arrested the evening before, and who had refused to give his name and address. From the description given by the porters who had already been at police headquarters, no one doubted that the young man was Isayev. Nevertheless, Grachevsky approved of my wish to save our possessions. I asked him to inform Sukhanov of my situation, for he was so energetic and strong-willed that the most impossible things seemed possible to him.

A few hours later, Sukhanov appeared, accompanied by two naval officers, and with his customary efficiency and speed, he had, in the course of two hours removed all the necessary things from the apartment. Only two packages were left and these contained articles of no especial value. By this time it was eight o'clock in the evening. He then demanded that I, too, should straightway leave the house, but I saw no necessity whatever for leaving until morning; for I was convinced that Isayev would not tell where he lived, and I explained the circumstance that the police had not yet appeared by the fact that our porters had not yet gone to answer the summons. I thought that at night they would leave Isayev in peace, and I saw no risk therefore in remaining in my own rooms. After these arguments, Sukhanov left me, having promised to send two women in the morning for the remaining articles. On the morning of April 3rd, when I went out to survey my surroundings, a "pea-green overcoat" [22] stood in the gateway, giving instructions to the porters. "By twelve o'clock without fail, without fail, I say!" It was plain that they were summoning the porters to police headquarters. Then I put up the signal we had agreed upon that the apartment was still safe. Almost immediately two of my acquaintances came in and carried away the last bundles, begging me not to delay my departure. I waited for the woman who used to come to clean our apartment, and upon her arrival, I sent her away on some pretext after which I locked up my vacant dwelling and left. They say that the police arrived at our apartment before the samovar from which I had drunk tea had grown cold; they were an hour or so too late.

That day, April 3rd, was the day of the execution of our regicides. The weather was marvellous, the sky clear, and a radiant spring sun was shining; the snow was melting on the streets. When I left the house the public spectacle was already over, but everywhere they were talking about the execution. At the time when my heart was aching over the thought of Perovskaya and Zhelyabov, I happened to take a horse-car in which there were people returning from the Semenovsky Square where the execution had taken place. Many faces were excited, but there was no sign of regret or sorrow. Just across from me there sat a good-looking burgher in a blue overcoat. He was black-haired and swarthy, with a bristling beard and glowing eyes. His handsome face was distorted with passion; a real *oprichnik* [23] he was, ready to hew off heads.

SOFIA PEROVSKAYA

Sofia Lvovna Perovskaya both because of her revolutionary

---

[22] The well-known epithet for a police spy, used by Shchedrin.—*Translator.*

[23] One of the special bodyguard of Ivan the Terrible.—*Translator.*

activity and because of her fate as the first woman in Russia
to be executed for a political crime is one of those few characters destined to become historical.

From the point of view of heredity and the influence of environment, it is curious that this ascetic revolutionary was
the great-granddaughter of Kyril Grigoryevich Razumovsky,
the last hetman of Little Russia; the granddaughter of the
governor of the Crimea during the reign of Alexander I, and
the daughter of the governor of St. Petersburg in the time
of Alexander II.

By a chance concurrence of circumstances, her prosecutor
at the special session of the Senate, before which the case of
the first of March was tried, proved to be a man who had been
one of her childhood playmates. In Pskov, where Perovskaya
had formerly lived, her father and the father of her future
accuser had been colleagues and next-door neighbours, so that
the children met constantly.[24] This prosecutor in his speech
overstepped the boundaries of his official duties, and in addition to the reproach of "bloodthirstiness," usually applied in
such cases, he cast in the slur of "immorality." I refer to N. V.
Muravyev, who later became Minister of Justice, that guardian
of the law, who trampled it underfoot; that enlightened jurist,
who said of the court statutes of the year 1864 that they were
founded on the highest legal principles up to that time enun-
ciated in the civilised world, and who, nevertheless continually
shook those foundations. It was this legalistic Muravyev,
whom the Russian Government sent to Paris to procure from
the free republic the violation of the right of asylum, which
had been guaranteed by the law of that republic: namely, the
extradition of Lev Hartman, a revolutionist, and the tenant
of the house from which was directed the explosion of the
Tsar's train, near Moscow, on November 19th, 1879. It was
this Muravyev, the servant of impartial justice, who as Minister of Justice, was widely reported to be one of the most corrupt grafters of his time.

The conditions of her childhood kindled in Sofia Perovskaya
a sense of honour, and a radiant love for humanity, which never

24 After my arrest, Muravyev told me this himself.

grew dim. The older generation of that period had profited
from the institution of serfdom, with its disregard for human
personality. But when this despotic order was introduced into
family relations, it frequently aroused a protest and aversion
to despotism on the part of the children. And so it was with
Perovskaya. Her father, Lev Nikolayevich Perovsky, was a
despot among despots, who not only insulted the mother of his
children, but forced his little son to insult and abuse his mother,
who was a woman typical of her period in her unassuming spiritual beauty and gentleness. In the oppressive atmosphere of
her family, Sofia Lvovna learned to love *mankind*, to love those
who suffer, as she loved her mother who had suffered so long,
and with whom she maintained tender relations up to the last
tragic days of her life. During my own trial, the matrons of
the House of Preliminary Detention told me that while Perovskaya's trial was being held, Sofia Lvovna talked very little
whenever her mother, who had been summoned from the Crimea,
came to see her. Like a sick, tired child, motionless and speech-
less she would recline with her head on her mother's knee. The
two gendarmes, who sat in her cell day and night, remained on
duty during these visits.

Scarcely having begun her life as a conscious, thinking individual, Perovskaya resolved to leave her family, for to remain with them was morally unendurable to her. But her
father refused to give her a separate passport, and threatened
to have her brought back to his house under a guard of police
in case she should leave without his permission. Perovskaya
did not yield; she left her parents, and took refuge with the
Kornilov sisters, schoolgirl friends of hers at the Alarchinsky
Institute.[25] With one of them, Alexandra Ivanovna Moroz
(nèe Kornilov), she figured in the Trial of 193.

Perhaps Perovskaya had inherited her mother's tender heart,
and this may explain her womanly gentleness and overflowing
goodness toward the toiling masses, during the period of her activity as a member of the Tchaikovsky's circle. Upon com-
pleting her studies for the position of assistant physician, she
came in contact with these people in the village, in her ca-

[25] One of the first women's colleges in St. Petersburg.

pacity of propagandist from the Populist group. Those who witnessed her life there have stated in their reminiscences that there was something maternally tender in her treatment of the sick, as indeed there was in her entire attitude towards the peasants with whom she came in contact. How morally satisfying to her was this contact with village life, and how difficult it was for her to tear herself away from that obscure and wretched village existence, was indicated by her attitude at the conference of Voronezh, and her hesitation in the face of the breaking up of the party, Land and Freedom, into The Will of the People and the Black Partition. At that time both she and I had just left the village behind us, and were still bound to it with all our hearts. We were asked to take part in the political struggle, we were called to the city, but we felt that the village needed us, that without us it would be still darker there. Reason told us that we must follow the course chosen by our comrades, the political terrorists, who were drunk with the spirit of strife and animated by success. But our hearts spoke otherwise, our mood was quite different. It drew us to the world of the dispossessed. This mood, which we did not at that time analyze, was afterwards defined as an aspiration towards a clean life, towards personal saintliness. But, as I have before mentioned, after some hesitation we overcame our feeling, our mood, and having renounced that moral satisfaction which life among the people gave to us, we stood firmly side by side with our comrades, whose political sagacity was greater than our own.

From that time on, Perovskaya was first in all the terroristic projects of the Executive Committee of The Will of the People. It was she who took the part of the simple, hospitable housewife in the poor hovel bought for seven or eight hundred roubles in the name of Sukhorukov, who as a petty railroad clerk figured as her husband. At the decisive moment, it was she who was left in that hovel with Stephan Shiryayev, to turn on the electric current at the approach of the Tsar's train. Always watchful, always ready, she gave the necessary signal at the right time, and she was not to blame for the fact that it was not the Tsar's train, but the train in which his servants were travelling that was wrecked.

Later, after the explosion in the Winter Palace on the fifth of February, 1880, she went to Odessa to superintend the laying of a mine on Italyanskaya Street.

And finally, when on the first of March, 1881, the seventh attempt of the Executive Committee was in preparation, Perovskaya, together with Zhelyabov, organised the group of persons who were to observe the Tsar's goings and comings in the capital, and who were to be the signalists at the climax of the drama. She also directed the bomb-throwers, not only during the preparatory period, but also on the first of March, when she gave orders for a new disposition of forces, thanks to which the Emperor perished from the explosion of two bombs, hurled by the terrorists.

Of course, as with any complicated project in which many take part, it is hard to say definitely what each one contributed to the work as a whole; nevertheless, it seems only just to state, that had it not been for Sofia Perovskaya with her coolheadedness and incomparable good judgment and wise management, the assassination of the Tsar might not have taken place at all on that day. It was she who saved the day, and paid for the victory with her life.

I became acquainted with Sofia Lvovna in 1877, in St. Petersburg, when she was out on bail, as one of those indicted in the Trial of 193. Alexandra Kornilova brought her to my room to spend the night. Her appearance attracted my attention. In her country smock, that served as a nightgown, she looked like a young peasant girl with her short flaxen braid, her light grey eyes, and her childishly rounded cheeks. Only the high forehead was at variance with the general peasant cast of her features. In all her fair, pleasant little face there was much that was youthful and simple, much that recalled the child. This childlike element in her face was preserved up to the very end, notwithstanding the tragic moments that she lived through during those March days.

Looking at the simplicity of her exterior, no one would have suspected the environment in which she was born and amid which she spent her childhood and early youth; while the general expression of her face with its soft contours, did not speak at all of her strong will and firm character, which she had perhaps inherited from her father. Generally speaking, there was in her nature both feminine gentleness and masculine severity. Tender, tender as a mother with the working people, she was exacting and severe towards her comrades and fellow-workers, while towards her political enemies, the government, she could be merciless, a trait that made Sukhanov almost shudder; his ideal of woman could not be reconciled with this trait. When the Trial of 193 was ended, her apartment in St. Petersburg was the centre where her acquitted comrades met, but only the "Protestant" comrades, those who had not recognised this trial as legal, and therefore had not attended its sessions. The forceful personality of Myshkin, and his celebrated speech at the trial, produced on her so strong an impression, that the thought of liberating him from the Chuguyev Central Prison in the province of Kharkov, became her *idée fixe*. She devoted much energy in attempts to realise it.

Perovskaya's two most beloved comrades were people remarkable for their spiritual qualities, but entirely different from each other—the one endowed with great brilliance, the other quite devoid of it: Andrey Zhelyabov and Frolenko, "Mikhaylo," as she and all his friends called him. It was at the conference at Voronezh that I first met these two men, and Perovskaya, who had known them previously, told me a great deal about their excellencies. One could see, though, that however much she esteemed "Mikhaylo," Zhelyabov awoke her warmest admiration and enthusiasm.

Perovskaya, in accordance with the ideals of our epoch, was a rigid ascetic. I need not mention the modest simplicity of all the domestic régime of her daily life, but here is a characteristic example of her attitude toward the funds of the organisation. On one of those March days, she came to me and said, "Get me a loan of about fifteen rubles! I have spent that amount for medicine, and it shouldn't come out of the general expense account. Mother has sent me a silk *sortie de bal;* the dressmaker will sell it for me, and I will pay the debt." I think none of us had yet become so rigidly conscientious.

During those same memorable days, I came to know all her fine sensitiveness and her disinterested solicitude for her comrades. After Zhelabov's arrest on February 27th, Perovskaya abandoned the apartment that Zhelyabov and she had occupied, and removed all illegal property. From that day until March 10th, when she was arrested near the Anichkov Palace, she spent the night, now with one friend, now with another. Circumstances at that time made such a homeless state particularly wearing, and it was by no means unavoidable, for we had several lodgings held in common for the organisation, where every comrade could feel that he had the same rights as his host, and be perfectly at home. But Perovskaya feared to endanger her comrades.

"Verochka, may I spend the night with you?" asked Perovskaya, a day or two before her arrest. I looked at her with astonishment and reproach. "How can you ask that? Indeed, is such a question possible?" "I am asking," said Perovskaya, "because if they come to search the house and find me here, they will hang you." Embracing her, and pointing to the revolver which lay at the head of my bed, I said, "I shall shoot if they come, whether you are here or not."

Such was the soul of Perovskaya, or a part of her soul, because only a small part of it was revealed to me. In those hurried times, we took only a superficial interest in the psychology of one another; we acted, but did not observe.

She was a woman; she could feel pain, physical pain. When they led her out, clad in her black prison dress, to the tumbril waiting in the court of the House of Preliminary Detention, they first seated her with her back to the horse, hung a placard on her bosom with the inscription, "The Regicide," and then bound her hands together so tightly that she said, "Loosen the cord a little, it hurts me."

"You'll feel worse than that later on," growled the rough gendarme who was supervising the train.

This man was the warden of the Alexey Ravelin in the Fortress of Sts. Peter and Paul, where, a little later, members of our party were dying a lingering death. It was this same man, Yakovlev, who became the last commandant of the Schlüsselburg Fortress.

In a similar manner they brought to Semenovsky Square our four other comrades, who were involved in the affair of the first of March: Zhelyabov, a peasant; Kibalchich, the son of a priest, and the inventor of the bombs; Timofey Mikhaylov, a workman, and Rysakov, a middle-class citizen, who, together with Perovskaya, the noblewoman, represented symbolically all the classes in the Russian Empire.

On the scaffold Perovskaya was firm, with all her steel-like firmness. She embraced Zhelyabov in farewell, she embraced Kibalchich and Mikhaylov; but she did not embrace Rysakov, who in an effort to save himself, had betrayed the apartment on Telezhnaya Street, and had brought to their ruin Sablin, who shot himself, Gesya Helfman, who died in the House of Preliminary Detention, and Timofey Mikhaylov, who died on the scaffold.

So died Perovskaya true to herself both in life and in death.

THE SIGNIFICANCE OF THE FIRST OF MARCH

Whatever people have said or thought concerning the first of March, its significance was immense. In order to appreciate this, one must recall the conditions under which it was consummated. It cut short the twenty-six year reign of an Emperor, who had opened a new era for Russia, by starting her on the road of development followed by the rest of humanity. After the stagnation of ages, he had given her a powerful forward impulse by the liberation of the serfs, by the new system of local government, and by the reform of the judiciary. Yet the first and greatest of these, the liberation of the serfs, had failed to satisfy, even at the outset, the demands of the best representatives of society; while later, when fifteen years had passed since its realisation, and the period of adulation had changed to a period of criticism, the press openly asserted that this reform had been promulgated under the pressure of the landholders, and that it was a compromise which did not in the least correspond with its avowed purpose—"the improvement of the economic existence of the peasantry, in order to enable them to discharge their obligations and taxes regularly." The works of Yanson, Prince Vasilchikov, and other investigators, revealed the utter economic disintegration of the peasants: insufficient land allotments, the development of a village proletariat, and such a discrepancy between the income yielded by the peasants' land, and the payments they made, that Prince Vasilchikov compared the position of our peasantry with the utter helplessness of the French peasantry before the Revolution of 1789, and stated that Russia was menaced by the same calamities that had broken out in France toward the end of the eighteenth century. Government commissions confirmed this view, and testified to the impoverishment of the masses.

The other reforms were curtailed and distorted by various supplements, exemptions and interpretations, under the increasing influence of the opponents of reform, and of the reaction which took place in the Emperor himself. Little by little social forces and governmental authority parted company; public opinion lost all influence over the course of the national life and of the administration.

The dissatisfaction of one section of society broke out during the sixties, at the very beginning of Alexander's reign, in the disturbances of the student body, and found expression in the trials of Chernyshevsky, Mikhaylov, and the groups of Karakozov and Nechayev. These expressions of dissatisfaction, together with the unrest aroused by the Polish Revolt (1863), served as a signal for increased reaction, and its supporters could not have made better use of them. By the beginning of the seventies, the break between the government and the nation was already complete. From this time on, the rebellion of a portion of the citizens against the policy supported by the Tsar became, one might say, chronic. But each manifestation of this rebellion resulted in a still heavier oppression of the people, which, in its turn, led to still sharper resistance. By the end of the seventies, all Russia's internal life, all her internal policy, was absorbed in the government's struggle against sedition. Governor-generalships, military courts, a special state police, and a series of pitiless executions, made their appearance; but at this same time there began a series of attempts against the life of the Emperor. And though the authorities had employed their most extreme measures in combating the evil, neither their hundreds of thousands of bayonets, nor the throng of guards and spies, nor the gold of the Tsar's treasury, could save the sovereign of eighty million people, and he fell by the hand of a revolutionist.

The instructive feature of the first of March is the fact that it proved to be the finale of a twenty-years' conflict between the government and society, twenty years of persecutions, cruelties and oppression, directed against a minority, but falling as a burden on every one—and as a result: Rysakov with his phrase, "We shall see yet whether all is well!" [26]

The assassination of the Emperor took place at a time when there was a general conviction that the attempt was going to be made. All society was divided into two camps on this question, one of which feared the event, while the other awaited it with impatience. Such a situation was unprecedented in the history of nations and was a worthy subject for the meditations of philosopher, moralist and statesman. The bomb of the Executive Committee made all Russia tremble and placed before her the questions: Where is the escape from this abnormal situation? What has caused it? And what will happen in the future if nothing new is introduced into our life? We thought that the government's failure to destroy the revolutionary movement through repressions, and the fruitlessness of its attempt to overcome dissatisfaction by removing the most energetic among the dissatisfied, had been clearly demonstrated by the experience of the past twenty years, which culminated in the event of the first of March. We thought that if Alexander III failed to draw the right conclusion, Russia itself did not; that public opinion, if freely expressed, would suggest as a means of suppressing internecine strife, not war-

[26] On the first of March, after the explosion of the bomb hurled by Grinevitsky, Alexander II came out of the carriage, and said to his entourage: "Thank God, all is well!" Whereupon Rysakov shouted his words, and threw the fatal bomb.—*Translator.*

fare with individual manifestations of discontent, but the annihilation of the cause of that discontent; we believed that it would point out that this cause was not to be found in the activities of individual agitators and outstanding personalities, by whose apprehension the government had vainly hoped to establish tranquillity, but in the general oppression, the complete elimination of the educated class from any activities which would affect the life of the people and the state, and the lack of any sphere of activity whatever for them except the pursuit of plunder and personal gain; in the continuous conflict between the policy of the government on the one hand, and the interests and needs of the people and the intelligentsia on the other. And in case the former régime should continue, this voice of the people would proclaim that the first of March would be repeated inevitably under circumstances perhaps still more tragic.

Thus the dilemma that had been brought to an issue, appeared to us to have been solved in the public consciousness, and to be awaiting only the moment of its embodiment in actual life. The unusual circumstances under which the event of the first of March took place, and the very immensity of its scale, helped in a large measure to elucidate this public consciousness, and it was impossible to deny its significance, in this respect, for society.

But the first of March also agitated all the peasantry. It drew them forth from the sphere of their daily cares and village interests, and concentrated their attention upon the question: "Who killed the Tsar, and why was he killed?" All who lived in the villages, at that time and long afterwards, unanimously testified that the murder of the Tsar, and the motives for that murder, deeply agitated the minds of the peasantry, and forced them to think intensely. This process of reasoning could lead to only one of two conclusions: the true one, that the Tsar had been killed by the Socialists, who were fighting for the interests of the people and wished to secure land for them and free them from the yoke of the officials; or the other interpretation, that the nobles, the landowners, were fighting against the Tsar for their rights, and that, in the hope of restoring serfdom, they had killed him for having freed the peasants. In the one case, the people would be united with the Socialist party by a community of interests, and the party would acquire among the masses a basic support which decades of propaganda by word would not have secured. In the other case, their rage against the wealthy class would increase; and in the terrible economic situation in which the people were living, this rage might break out in a massacre of the privileged class, which would be little different from the extirpation of the Roman patricians by the Lombards during their invasion of Italy, or from the horrors of the Pugachev uprising. In this case, the party's only task would be to make use of the outburst of popular indignation and passions. In either case, the first of March made certain or probable an alliance between the people and the revolutionary struggle.

In its relation to the party itself, and to the revolutionary world in general, this event was of immense importance. In the eyes of its supporters, it raised the Committee to an unheard-of height. "Come and rule over us," people cried to them with one voice; it created such an atmosphere as would have satisfied the demands of the most fiery revolutionist, and if there was anything to regret in the situation, it was that though the harvest was plentiful, the reapers were few.

But aside from the fact that The Will of the People had acquired for itself on the first of March a most advantageous position, and new opportunities for enlarging its organisation, this moment was a triumph for the general principles of the organisation. No efforts on the part of an individual or even of a separate group would have been sufficient to direct and bring to an end this two-years' warfare, with its remarkable episodes and conclusion—a warfare in which on one side there had been all the advantages of authority and material power, while on the other were only energy and organisation. The inevitable necessity of organisation, in a conflict with the government, organisation as the only condition that could make victory possible—that was what the first of March proclaimed. After this there was no longer any need of championing this idea—it had become the common property of the milieu from which the members of the party came.

On the other hand, this important moment in the history of the revolutionary movement did not evoke a popular uprising, was not accompanied by attempted insurrections in the cities, and did not force the government to make radical changes in the economic and political order of Russia, or to yield to the demands of the dissatisfied. With regard to the first point, I may say positively that the party at no time, and in no place, either in its periodical or in its programme, or in verbal declarations of its immediate aims and problems, indicated regicide as an infallible means of producing a popular uprising; this uprising may have been the hope of individuals, but it was not counted on by the party. People expected an insurrection because they were unacquainted with the state of affairs in the organisation, which was still too young for the accomplishment of such attempts; and even if among the revolutionists there were some who were dissatisfied because their suppositions had failed to materialise, they were people who had been accustomed to reap where they had not sown. The insurrection was still a matter of the future, which demanded much labour.

It is perfectly true that the first of March did not accomplish the political and economic reconstruction of Russia. But, although our party was not in a position to bring about this reconstruction through revolutionary means, it had never regarded the governmental authority in its present form of organisation, as a power capable of sincerely assuming the initiative in this matter. To be sure, it did expect concessions, a relaxation of the rigid régime, the cessation of reaction, partial liberty, which would have made existence endurable and peaceful activity possible. This expectation proved to be a mistake, a very sad and unfortunate mistake, not only for the revolutionary party, but for the people also, and for society, for the wealthy classes and the bureaucrats, for the whole empire, and for its head; unfortunate because it involved new catastrophes in the future, new social and political disturbances. It would have been difficult to find many people in Russia at that time who believed in the future peaceful progress of their native land, and in an undisturbed existence for their monarch; and without such faith, such certitude, the future could not but appear gloomy and alarming. In its own time this future was to have its say.

I must here say a few more words about the demoralisation brought about in society by the methods of the struggle between the government and the revolutionary party. This struggle was accompanied by violence, as is the case with any conflict waged by means of force rather than ideas. And violence, whether committed against a thought, an action, or a human life, never contributed to the refinement of morals. It arouses ferocity, develops brutal instincts, awakens evil impulses, and prompts acts of disloyalty. Humanity and magnanimity are incompatible with it. And from this point of view, the government and the revolutionary party, when they entered into what may be termed a hand-to-hand battle, vied with one another in corrupting everything and every one around them. On the one hand, the party declared that all methods were fair in the war with its antagonist, that here the end justified the means. At the same time, it created a cult of dynamite and the revolver, and crowned the terrorist with a halo; murder and the scaffold acquired a magnetic charm and attraction for the youth of the land, and the weaker their nervous system, and the more oppressive the life around them, the greater was their exaltation at the thought of revolutionary terror. Since the effects of ideas are hardly perceptible to a revolutionist during the brief span of his lifetime, he desires to see some concrete, palpable manifestation of his own will, his own strength, and at that time only a terroristic act with all its violence could be such a manifestation. Society saw no escape from the existing condition; one group sympathised with the violence practised by the party, while others regarded it only as a necessary evil—but even they applauded the valour and skill of the champion. And the repetition of such events made them a normal element of society's life.

But the gloomy side of revolutionary activity was brightened by the concord and brotherhood which existed among the revolutionists themselves; moreover, the party committed its deeds of violence under the banner of the people's welfare, in defence of the oppressed and insulted. Outsiders became reconciled to terrorism because of the disinterestedness of its motives; it redeemed itself through renunciation of material benefits, through the fact that the revolutionist was not satisfied with personal well-being, the possibility of which he rejected, once he had set out on his dangerous path; it redeemed itself by prison, exile, penal servitude and death. Thus, though society became somewhat callous by accustoming itself to the violence practised by the revolutionary party, yet it nevertheless beheld, if not in the party as a whole, at least in individual representatives of it, examples of self-sacrifice and heroism, persons of rare civic virtues.

Parallel with the violence practised by the revolutionary party, but on a larger scale, was the violence practised by the government. It enchained thought, forbade free speech, and despoiled the people of life and freedom. Administrative exile was an ordinary occurrence, the prisons were filled to overflowing, executions were numbered by the dozen. In addition to this, prisoners were violently abused in the Siberian mines, and humiliating treatment was common in the central prisons. Throughout all the prisons harshness and violence were the daily order; in the House of Preliminary Detention, Bogolyubov was flogged and the modesty of women was insulted.[27]

The officials who carried out the orders became callous, the sufferers and their relatives, friends and acquaintances became more and more incensed. Society became accustomed to this degradation of human dignity. The spectacle of public executions aroused mob bloodthirst; retaliation, an eye for an eye and a tooth for a tooth, became the watchword of all. Secret police were necessary in order to avert the government from impending danger; official gold created an army of spies. These were recruited from all ranks of society; among them were generals and baronesses, officers and advocates, journalists and doctors, college men and women; alas, there were even

27 Three women revolutionists, Malinovskaya, Kolenkina and Evgenia Figner, were forced to remove all of their garments in the presence of three men physicians.

high-school students, little girls fourteen years old, while in Simferopol the department of the gendarmerie induced an eleven year-old high-school boy to become a paid spy. We know well that there is no stronger passion, or one leading to baser crimes than the passion for gold. Persian gold forced the Greek chieftains to sell their native land; thirty pieces of silver seduced Judas Iscariot. Our government took every advantage of the greed and covetousness of the human race, and utilised in every possible way the power of gold. Young women used the charms of their beauty and youth to seduce and betray; spies played the parts of initiators, organisers, and moving spirits in revolutionary work; secret accusations, treachery of the most perfidious kind, a clever trick at an examination, as a means of extorting a confession, or the inauguration of a great trial, under the most artificial pretences, and at the price of the well-being of dozens of people—such were the exploits that won the prize of gold, or advancement in office. In addition to all this, the government enticed the weak members of the party to become renegades. Remission of penalties, an agreement to forget the past, freedom and money—all served as a means for seduction. This was the greatest moral blow dealt to us revolutionists, a blow which shook our faith in mankind. It was not so hard to lose one's freedom, as to see a former comrade for whose sake you had been ready to risk your life, whom you had trusted and protected, and for whom you had performed every possible brotherly service—to see him helping the gendarmes to arrest you, and to hear his cynical words, "So you didn't expect it, did you?"

Of course, all this was done in the name of "legal" justice, for the sake of saving the fatherland, or rather that state of society in which they wished to preserve the fatherland. But who, who will deny the base degradation of human character made manifest by these facts?

But a veritable moral pestilence was spread by another, still more pernicious means. The government strove to disorganise our ranks by arousing the mistrust of one another; by tricks of espionage and by police plots they tried to cast a shadow of suspicion on certain of our comrades who had worked side by side with us. Thoughtlessness and carelessness on the part of some, a chance train of circumstances directed by the hand of a detective against others, served as a means of introducing into the midst of our revolutionary brotherhood, the dark suspicion of the venality and treachery of its members. This was the policy: to create a situation in which brother would rise up against brother. And indeed, we might soon have reached a stage when our hands would have been crimsoned by blood, perhaps as innocent as the blood of Ivanov, which Nechayev had shed.[28]

I knew a youth who had been so ensnared by the machinations of spies that he appeared in the eyes of everybody to be a traitor. He was on the point of committing suicide, so great was his despair at the suspicion that had fallen upon him. The people who had known him personally believed in his innocence, but when he asked me the question whether it would be possible for him to continue his revolutionary work, I answered, as I had to answer, "No." And thus a situation was created in which one became positively "alarmed for man." And if we, people who had long been connected with the movement, who had been brought up on the pure principles of Socialism, had prepared ourselves for peaceful propaganda, and had passed through the school of asceticism and personal morality, were rightly called malefactors by the government, then those whom the government trained must surely have been demons!

[28] At the end of the sixties, Nechayev organised a shady group of revolutionists in Russia, advocating the principle that all means were justified by a revolutionary aim. When Ivanov, one of the leading members, recanted and decided to withdraw from the organisation, Nechayev had the other members kill Ivanov. The Nechayev affair did great harm to the reputation of the revolutionists. Dostoyevsky made use of the affair in his novel, "The Possessed."—*Translator.*

XII

AFTER THE FIRST OF MARCH

AFTER the alarming March days, during which Isayev was
arrested, and after the discovery of our lodgings by the
police, on the 3rd of April, the Committee decided that I
should leave St. Petersburg and go to Odessa to manage local
affairs. There I found many dependable and energetic workers. Through Svedentsev, who had formerly served in the
army, we had a connection with the officers in the Odessa region, and serveral of these I met. I found them upon closer
acquaintance admirable men and of high ideals, but lacking
confidence in their ability for the work of actively organising
and spreading revolutionary propaganda among their friends
in the army. These men had never in their lives worked actively along revolutionary lines and when I pointed out to them
the necessity of widening their acquaintanceship for the purpose of enlisting the services of sympathising persons, they
replied unanimously that no such persons were to be found
among the officers. However, it turned out that active agitation was being carried on by several of the naval officers, and
the two groups became very friendly.

It was proposed that a member of the central group of the
Military Organisation be sent to Odessa to invite the circle
officially to affiliate with the military centre. A. Butsevich
was chosen for this mission. He easily succeeded in organising
this group as a branch of the main party, and the officers assumed those serious obligations implied by the statutes which
Butsevich had proposed, and promised to join an armed uprising and sway their troops to the same cause at the first
call of the Military Centre. Thus Butsevich's mission was
accomplished, and a bond established between the officers of
revolutionary sympathies in the North and the South. The
entire Military Organisation at that time numbered fifty
members.

XIII

THE CENTRE OF THE PARTY MOVES TO MOSCOW

In the latter part of October, I received an invitation to go to Moscow. Six months had passed since I had left St. Petersburg, and up to this time I had had almost no news as to the direction events had taken in party affairs, or as to the activities of the central group which had been transferred to Moscow. One can imagine how impatiently I hastened to this meeting with my comrades who had escaped arrest in St. Petersburg during the preceding spring.

I must mention here that life in Odessa, which had not reverberated to the shock of those March days, had not prepared me for such changes as awaited me in Moscow. After my arrival I beheld with grief the destructive significance of the losses which the Executive Committee had experienced shortly before the first of March and still more after it.

The headquarters of the Committee had been transferred from St. Petersburg to Moscow, not through any lofty considerations, but merely through the stress of necessity. It was impossible for those of its members who had not yet fallen into the hands of the police to maintain themselves in St. Petersburg after the arrests in March and April. To remain there meant to court destruction, for it was plain that some one who knew the members of the organisation by sight, was pointing them out on the street to the police.

The transfer of the centre of the revolutionary party from the capital could not help but injure the affairs of the party. If we consider the revolutionary movement only from the period of the seventies, every one acquainted with it would say that St. Petersburg was its main centre. Being the centre of the Empire, and the cynosure of all the intellectual forces of the land, it was year after year the place in which the opposing elements gathered. It was here that the most important revolutionary organisations of a more serious and all-Russian character arose and succeeded one another: the Tchaikovsky Circle, Land and Freedom, The Will of the People, were successive stages in the movement. And here also it was that these organisations in large part recruited their adherents. Without mentioning the more remote periods, but beginning with the Tchaikovsky Circle, revolutionary activity centred here, and here the leaders of revolutionary organisations established their headquarters. To St. Petersburg the provinces stretched out their hands, and thence they received their inspiration; here the passwords were given out, and from this place proceeded moral support, and the network of the organisations. All the most important political trials, which had immense significance from the point of view of agitation, were held here, and here too, all revolutionary outbreaks found the warmest echo. In St. Petersburg were concentrated the main literary forces of Russia, and that portion of them which touched upon the revolutionary movement. The revolutionary periodicals were published only in St. Petersburg, and from there circulated throughout Russia.

The working population of St. Petersburg, more firmly rooted, and better educated, was better fitted to receive the ideas of socialism and revolution. Propaganda had been carried on here throughout the factories and mills, longer, more systematically, and on a larger scale, than in any of the other industrial centres.

The students of St. Petersburg were more numerous than in other cities, and led the Russian student body in its protests and revolts, being the first to give the signal for every movement, and then assuming the leadership. In other cities, revolutionary tradition might be interrupted, but this never occurred in St. Petersburg from the seventies on. It was never left without an organisation, while around it there always existed a circle of sympathisers and supporters. To leave St. Petersburg, to transfer the revolutionary centre to another city, meant to lose the ground on which up to that time revolutionary organizations had been founded, had grown up, and had their existence—to lose the ground which had been enriched by all the revolutionary past. Such a transfer was a species of emigration, an exile, a tearing asunder, and was fraught with most grevious consequences.

Moscow, whither the Executive Committee had moved its headquarters, was a city in which revolutionary tradition had not existed continuously. The organisations which appeared there had been active for only a short time, being broken up by arrests, and had not been succeeded by any group which could continue their activity.

THE CONDITION OF THE CENTRE

GREAT was the change I found in the Executive Committee, both in number and in character. There was no use deceiving oneself—the Committee of the year 1879 had been destroyed. Strangely enough, none of us mentioned the fact; we would assemble, discuss various questions, and adjourn as though we had not noticed the desperate position of our centre. Or perhaps we all beheld the misfortune, but never spoke of it. Only once, in a private talk with Grachevsky, did I express to him my fears for the future and my sorrow over the present. But he was of another opinion, or did not wish to admit that the situation was catastrophic. Out of twenty-three founders of The Will of the People, and members of the Executive Committee chosen up to the first of March, only eight were left at liberty: three women, Oshanina (who was a complete invalid), Korba, and I, and five men. The main pillars of our organisation, who had established its new policy and committed revolutionary acts that "had attracted the world's attention," were no longer among us. They had left the revolutionary arena, they had been condemned, or were awaiting stern judgment. We had lost many comrades from among the intelligentsia and the workingmen, who had been indispensable for the common cause, and who had, by the versatility of their talents and abilities, co-ordinated the various branches of activity in our organisation. But now there was only a desert where these had been. There were not minds or hands enough—initiators at the top and skilful workers to carry out their plans. In 1879 the Executive Committee had united in its personnel all the revolutionary forces which had accumulated during the preceding decade, and which had escaped the devastating violence of this period. It had launched them into political warfare, and after accomplishing a tremendous task, at the end of two years had lost all its capital. Now, at the end of the year 1881, only a small group was left, in addition to those whom the counsel for the defence at my trial (in 1884) termed "disciples."

So the Executive Committee had in reality come to an end, and at the time of which I speak, the centre of the party was unable to play its former rôle. There was left in the arena of the conflict with autocracy hardly a single name that was known throughout freedom-loving Russia. Together with its members had disappeared the ability of the Executive Committee to wage war. The work of propaganda and organisation remained; it was necessary, whatever the cost, to plan for a new levy of forces. But working conditions had become tremendously complicated. Espionage and detective work had been perfected; virtuosi in that line appeared, ambitious, capable people like Sudeykin. On the other hand, personal qualifications of the revolutionists had to be higher than they had been in the seventies. It was necessary to search for more mature elements in the intelligentsia and the working class, but there were few that satisfied the requirements. Ordinary workers were easily found among the young people; they were perfectly suitable for work in the local groups and the provinces, but we demanded different requirements from the candidates for positions in the central group, judging them by the standard we had set at the founding of The Will of the People, and only a few approached this standard.

With the ruin of the former organisation, and the loss of many of our comrades, the control that the party had exercised over the individual became weakened. I had already noticed this in April, when I passed through Moscow on my way south. Several devastating arrests took place because individual workers had risked their safety and utterly neglected precautions.

THE Executive Committee, that is, the Committee of 1879, had in reality come to an end, but in the meantime Russia, profoundly stirred by the assassination of the Tsar, was still reverberating from the shock of the first of March. Public opinion, which was uninformed as to the real strength of the party, was dazzled by the performance of the Committee, greatly exaggerated its power, and awaited still further blows, for the Committee had reiterated in its publications that assassinations of the tsars would continue to take place, and that arms would not be laid down until autocracy should surrender, and free institutions should take the place of the tsarist régime.

It is fitting here to relate an episode which has not yet been mentioned by any one; to tell of a possibility which remained unrealised. On the third of March, Kibalchich came unexpectedly and in great excitement to our apartment near the Voznesensky Bridge, where he was not supposed to come without giving special notice. He told us that the lodgings of Sablin and Gesya Helfman on the Telezhnaya had been seized by the police. Sablin had shot himself, while Timofey Mikhaylov had been arrested on the stairway that led to their apartment. This event involved the safety of the cheese shop on Malaya Sadovaya Street. It had not yet been vacated, and its shopkeepers, Bogdanovich and Yakimova, were still at their posts there. At any moment it might be discovered by the police. The question of dismantling the shop was debated, and it was decided that this should be done immediately, and that the shopkeepers should leave St. Petersburg that very evening. I alone held a different opinion. I proposed that they retain the shop two or three days longer. On considering the events that had taken place on the second and third of March, it became evident that the new Emperor had passed from the Anichkov Palace through Malaya Sadovaya Street, that is, past the shop that had prepared a death for his father. This indicated that there was as yet no direct information against the shop. Therefore, notwithstanding the danger of the situation, for the police held information against the street, and had made an investigation of the shop on the twenty-eighth of February, in the guise of a sanitary commission, and might, of course, repeat it, I proposed to remain in the shop a few days longer, and if the Emperor should pass by once more, to explode the mine which had been prepared for his father. I pointed out that in this case it would be worth risking the lives of those who should remain in the shop, and that the Executive Committee had the right to take such a risk. However, all the others were against me. Impulsively I exclaimed, "That's cowardly of you!" Tikhomirov and Langans, who were standing next to me, broke out angrily, "You've no right to say that!" The rest were silent, and the proposal was rejected.

The chance for a speedy assassination of another tsar passed with the closing of the shop. There was a lull. It was forced, as far as we were concerned, but popular opinion interpreted it as the calm before a storm. The government itself shared this view and awaited new tragedies. A strained expectation was the universal mood, the actions of the Committee during all this period were shrouded in secrecy; no one knew exactly when, or in what form the blow would fall. No one even knew what forces, either in personnel or technique were at the disposal of The Will of the People. Glyeb Ivanovich Uspensky [29] expressed jokingly and metaphorically this complete ignorance, and at the same time, the recognition of the Executive Committee as the decisive factor in Russia's destiny when he said to me shortly after the first of March, "And what's Vera Nikolayevna going to do with us now?" meaning by Vera Nikolayevna, the Executive Committee.

After a short period of indecision and wavering, which was reflected in the bureaucratic circles by the prediction that the most vicious reaction would hold sway for twenty-five years, it became clear that there was no use in expecting any progressive innovations from the new Tsar. The reactionary tendency of his internal policy was evident to every one. The manifesto of April declared that the principle of autocracy was unshakable; the removal of Loris-Melikov, Milutin, and

[29] A populist writer.

Abaza, showed that the attempt of the liberal party to give even slight satisfaction to the general demand for freedom, had ended, and that everything would remain unchanged.

But would the revolutionary party, the Executive Committee, remain silent after all its declarations? After the letter to Alexander III, in which were formulated demands which had not yet been complied with? All those who had been dissatisfied with the old order believed, longed to believe, that it would not. The conduct of the government supported this faith. The coronation of the new Emperor did not take place; no mention was even made of it, and fear of the terrorists served as the only explanation for this fact. Fabulous rumours as to their intentions and plans circulated among the people. In actual fact the Executive Committee had no such intentions. The first few days after the assassination, Perovskaya, greatly excited and agitated by the strain of the events she had lived through, as if engulfed by a mania and forgetting her good judgment, thought only of making preparations for a new attempt at assassinating the new Tsar. She made various inquiries, sought out laundresses and milliners who worked for the palace households, and collected on all sides information concerning people who might chance to meet the members of the Tsar's family. She herself kept watch of the Tsar's departures from the Anichkov Palace, until she was finally arrested nearby. After her arrest and the departure of the members of the Committee for Moscow, these convulsive attempts ceased. We knew that the Tsar had hidden in Gatchina and was living there like a prisoner, access to whom was forbidden. The Committee did not undertake to make any inquiries, to collect any information, nor to make any observations; and none of the projects to make use of the coronation festivities at Moscow materialised. The very question of assassination was not raised. Not once during the course of my stay in Moscow, was it even spoken of at our conferences, so evident was the utter impossibility of considering such an undertaking with the resources that we possessed at the time.

THE MOSCOW GROUP IS BROKEN UP

I ARRIVED in Moscow about the 15th of March, and stopped at the poor, cramped lodgings of Andreyeva, who, like her brother, was a member of the Moscow group. And this time I found my comrades in an evil pass. The rooms themselves, their very atmosphere, possessed an eerie foreboding. My comrades did not know which of them was under suspicion, who had been followed, or who might expect arrest at any moment. Uncertainty held sway and for the time being no attempts to communicate with each other were made. The rumour went that some one among the local members was giving the police full information. A general flight, a run for one's life, as we spoke of it later began. Only Savely Zlatopolsky came to see me, bringing the proclamation of the Executive Committee which had just been published, concerning the assassination of Procurator Strelnikov on March 18. He insisted that I leave Moscow immediately, without waiting to see the other members of the organisation, since we were all threatened with arrest. We decided that the best plan was for me to establish myself in Kharkov, where there was a local group but no agent of the Committee, since Marya Zhebuneva, who had been working there, had decided to follow her husband to Siberia after his arrest.

At the end of a fortnight, Zlatopolsky was also arrested. After this the printing shop of *The Will of the People* was closed, and its entire staff scattered, going their various ways. This was the end of the Moscow group.

XIV

IN KHARKOV

In Kharkov, I found a small local group of worthy and energetic people. The main, and one might say, the only activity of the group, was propaganda and socialist instruction among the workingmen. But Kharkov was still a very unimportant centre from the point of view of productive industry, and with respect to culture and education. The group, like other local groups of The Will of the People, had its own sphere of activity in a number of cities in its region. It had few connections in the student body and in intellectual circles, because of the absence of good leaders; the young people whom we had occasion to meet did not seem valuable material. The group had no financial resources whatever. It turned out once that among us all we had one ruble and twenty or forty copecks. Under such conditions it was unthinkable to make visits to even the very nearest towns, and it was very rarely that we did so.

Such was the state of affairs when in June the news began to arrive of the arrests of the remaining members of the Executive Committee, and of the further apprehension of party laboratories and centres. Since Oshanina and Tikhomirov had gone abroad, I was the only representative of the Committee left in Russia.

From that time on all my efforts were concentrated in the attempt to unite the strongest forces available, and to create from them a group which should compensate as far as possible for the absence of the central organisation, which had been utterly annihilated by the successful manœuvres of the police. The situation was catastrophic both in St. Petersburg and Moscow, as well as in Odessa; the local groups in Kiev and Kharkov were still not sufficiently experienced. Still a few of the old party members scattered about the country remained unharmed, and though they had not been members of the Executive Committee, we had long worked together in various branches of activity. It was necessary to assemble them in one place and talk over plans regarding the renewal of our labours. This work I accordingly undertook.

I was striving to create anew an organisation similar to the one which had been destroyed. Perhaps my choice of new members was faulty, but I worked with the material at hand, and, casting a retrospective glance over the ten years that followed, I am forced to say that they were all filled with similar vain attempts on the part of individuals and small groups to re-create that which, in its very essence, could no longer be created. The Will of the People as an organisation had lived its allotted span. In the Russia of those days there was no accumulation of revolutionary forces which, in spite of all arrests and all the skilled technique of police investigation, would permit the organisation to maintain that lofty position it had held at the time of the formation of the party. But The Will of the People had accomplished its mission. It had shaken passive and inert Russia to its foundations; it had created a revolutionary policy, the main elements of which never became extinct. Its experiment had not been in vain, the recognition of the necessity of political freedom, and of active warfare in order to attain it, remained in the minds of the following generations, and became a part of all ensuing revolutionary programmes. In its aspiration to secure a liberal form of government, it was the advance guard of the Russian intelligentsia which was composed both of the privileged and the working classes. This advance guard proved to be at least a quarter of a century in advance of its time, and it remained isolated. The Will of the People had hoped that the political attempt of the first of March would liberate the living forces of the masses dissatisfied with their economic position, that they would join the movement, while at the same time middle-class society would take advantage of the opportune moment and voice its political demands. But the people were silent after the first of March, and society in its turn remained dumb. Thus The Will of the People proved to have no support in society, no deep root in the popular mind, and all attempts to renew the organisation for the immediate continuance of active conflict against the existing orders, were vain. The profound backwardness of the peasantry owing to the low level of Russia's economic development; the absence during the eighties of an industrial proletariat in the western-European sense of the word; the impossibility, under the despotic police control, of addressing the masses either directly or through the written word—these circumstances were the causes of the isolation in which The Will of the People found itself after all its political demonstrations. It was necessary to create a new basis, and to build a new party upon the foundation of Russia's economic development; this was to be the work of the future. In anticipation of this future a new party must arise, and indeed, its embryo did arise, the Liberation of Labour Group,[30] later developing into the Social-Democratic Labour Party,[31] which began to lay this foundation by appealing chiefly to the working class.

Yet, as is usually the case, the old order could not at once disappear. The generation that had taken part in The Will of the People movement, educated during the brilliant period of the Committee's activity, and inspired by the example of its warfare, could not give up the hope in the immediate resumption of the conflict in the same spirit and form under which The Will of the People had waged it. The recent past blinded one's eyes by the glowing activity which had taken place in view of the whole country—of the whole world. It was difficult, psychologically, to descend to petty, grey, and obscure toil for the future, instead of offering spectacular resistance to the government which had cut off the foremost of our revolutionary workers. The future was not yet clearly defined, and did not lure one with hopes of quick results.

My own plan for renewing the central group was to invite five members of the military organisation, who were especially gifted, both in ability and character, to join us. They were to

[30] The first Marxian socialist group organised in 1883.—*Translator.*
[31] Formed in 1898, of which the present Communist Party is the outgrowth.—*Translator.*

assume with us the duties of the late Committee, which dealt
with matters of general importance to the party, and in order
to do so, they were to resign from the army and withdraw from
the military organisation, preserving only such relations with
this group as the Committee had formerly maintained. The
two new members, Spandoni and Degayev, approved of this
plan of mine, and it was resolved that Degayev should visit the
military organisations. At the same time we decided that after
his trip to St. Petersburg, to Odessa and Nikolayev, Degayev
was to settle with his wife in Odessa, where I was organising a
printing press which he and his wife were to manage.

MY MEETING WITH MIKHAYLOVSKY

On the fifteenth of October, during Degayev's absence,
Mikhaylovsky [32] unexpectedly came to Kharkov to see me.
Having sought me out, he said that the purpose of his visit was
a very important matter, to which he must receive an answer.
The matter was as follows: Nikoladze, a noted man of letters,
had come to him in St. Petersburg, and declared that a certain
man prominent in government circles (Count Vorontsov-Dash-
kov), had asked him to act as mediator between the government and The Will of the People party, and had commissioned
him to enter into negotiations with the Executive Committee
for the purpose of concluding a truce. Mikhaylovsky said
that the government, according to Nikoladze, was tired of
waging war against The Will of the People, and longed for
peace. It recognised that society should be given a larger
share in political activity, and was prepared to enter on a
policy of well-considered reforms. But it could not do so under
the threat of revolutionary terror. It was this terror alone
which prevented the realisation of these reforms. If The Will
of the People would cease its destructive activity, such reforms
would be introduced. If the party would refrain from terroristic acts up to the time of the coronation, a manifesto would be
published at that time which would grant: first, complete po-

---

[32] 1842–1904. Sociologist and literary critic of the Populist strain. He
kept in close contact with the Narodovoltsy and, later, with the Socialist-
Revolutionists.—*Translator.*

litical amnesty; second, freedom of the press; and third, the permission to carry on peaceful socialistic propaganda. In proof of its sincerity, the government would liberate some one of the condemned party members, Isayev, for example.

After listening to Nikoladze's proposal, Mikhaylovsky resolved to confer with some one of the members of the Executive Committee, and since I was its only representative left in Russia, he reported to me what he had heard from Nikoladze. Mikhaylovsky himself ascribed great significance to the mission which the high official had entrusted to Nikoladze. I, on the other hand, saw in it only a repetition of the ruse by which the procurator Dobrzhynsky seduced Goldenberg in 1879. Dobrzhynsky, too, assured Goldenberg of the benevolent intentions of the government, which had been prevented by the terroristic activity of the Executive Committee from introducing indispensable reforms. In the name of his country's welfare he exhorted Goldenberg to sacrifice his friends and comrades, and to clear a broad pathway that should lead to the liberty of the Russian people. The results are well known: Goldenberg told everything that he knew, and although he did not actually betray any one into the hands of the government, he described the appearance and the characteristics of all the people whom he had ever met during his life as a revolutionist; and when he saw that he had been deceived, he hanged himself in the Fortress of Sts. Peter and Paul.

To all my objections, pointing out the uselessness, and even the danger of negotiating over the matter, Mikhaylovsky asked the question: "But could the party actually commit any acts of a terroristic nature at the present time?" In reply I was forced to admit that the state of affairs in the revolutionary organisation offered no hope of this. "In that case," said Mikhaylovsky, "you will lose nothing, while you stand a chance of gaining some advantage."

We finally decided to refuse to carry on any negotiations whatever with Nikoladze in *Russia*. I, however, without his knowledge, was to dispatch some person abroad, who was to communicate to Tikhomirov and Oshanina both Nikoladze's mission and my attitude towards it, giving them the opportunity of acting on their own judgment in case he should visit them; while on the other hand, we in Russia would not consider ourselves bound, whatever the result of their conferences might be. And, if the circumstances should prove favourable, we would remain free to carry on our terroristic activity. Mikhaylovsky, moreover, promised to tell Nikoladze that he had not found any one belonging to the Committee, and that its members were living abroad. When Degayev returned from his circuit of conferences and investigation, I informed him and Spandoni, whom I had summoned from Kiev, of my interview with Mikhaylovsky. They approved entirely both of my attitude towards the matter and of my proposal to send my own envoy to Tikhomirov in Paris. Salova, whom I had known since 1880, was well suited for this. I summoned her from Odessa, gave her all the necessary information, and commissioned her to take out a foreign passport which would enable her to visit Tikhomirov and communicate to him the above-mentioned proposal, all of which she did without delay.

XV

DEGAYEV

In September Sergey Degayev and his wife came to Kharkov. I had made the acquaintance of Degayev and his family in St. Petersburg in the fall of 1880. My comrades on the Committee were already well acquainted with him, and vouched for him as a very capable, intelligent man, devoted to the party and serving its interests. Degayev was not an accredited visitor of our conspirative lodgings, and never knew their addresses, not because we distrusted him, but because in our organisation we observed the most strict secrecy in this matter. The members of the Committee themselves had knowledge of and visited only such lodgings as they were obliged to through business necessity. Such were the rules. Moreover, Degayev was under the suspicion of the police, and spies might be interested in investigating his daily walks and the persons with whom he came in contact. We used to see him at the home of some neutral person, or at his own home, for he lived with his family, who were all sympathetic to the movement, and received all the members of the party, myself among them, with the greatest cordiality. He was indeed a most energetic person. He successfully passed the examination of the Institute of Railroad Engineers, served in the administration department of a certain railroad company, devoting the hours from ten to four to his office duties, gave lessons in mathematics, and with all this, made friends in the revolutionary group, maintained his connections with his comrades in the Artillery Academy, from which he had been expelled for his "unsafe" views, and carried out to the letter all the requests and commissions entrusted to him by the members of the Committee. The Degayevs lived modestly, just managing to make both ends meet, as the saying goes. His mother, evidently, had a pension or some small savings laid by, which, however, were utterly insufficient for living necessities; and Sergey's financial assistance in meeting the household expenses was the main source of their means of support.

Volodya, his brother, a good-hearted, gentle lad, had also been expelled from the Naval Training School for "unsafe" views. With childish naïveté he used to ask me when the revolution would take place. He expected me to reply that it would come to pass within three or four months, or at the most six, and was bitterly disappointed on hearing that no one could set a stated time for its consummation. A year later I learned with astonishment that, with the approval of Sergey Degayev and Zlatopolsky, Volodya had become ostensibly one of Sudeykin's agents, his work being to deceive that clever, adroit, and experienced detective, and, without betraying the revolutionists, to keep the party informed of Sudeykin's activities.

Upon his arrival in Kharkov, Degayev briefly related to me the happenings of those eighteen months during which we had not seen each other; and, among other things, informed me that after the first of March he had been arrested as having taken part in the excavation on Malaya Sadovaya Street, but that he had fortunately escaped prosecution. I was greatly surprised at such a reprieve, because the natural witness against him could have been only the traitor Merkulov, and to survive the damaging testimony of such a man was difficult. But Degayev was utterly silent with regard to the suspicious circumstances surrounding him. In the spring of 1882, Sudeykin had decided that Volodya Degayev was useless to him as a detective, and refused to retain his services any longer. The St. Petersburg group of The Will of the People then thought of a new scheme by which to maintain their connection with Sudeykin, and, tracking him down, to kill him. In pursuance of this plan, Volodya was to tell his patron that his brother Sergey was in need of work, and would be glad to obtain some work as draughtsman. Sudeykin agreed to this proposal, and Sergey received the required commission. They met several times, and according to Degayev, conferred on purely business matters, the nature of which he reported to Grachevsky. Later Degayev left for the Caucasus, without securing for Grachevsky any of the information needed by the party.

THE NECESSITY FOR RE-ESTABLISHING THE CENTRE

When Sergey Degayev came to Kharkov, I greeted him as an old, tried comrade, and after the arrest in St. Petersburg of the remaining members of the Committee, it was absolutely necessary to take him into the central group, where he might help in regulating the affairs of the party. He had earned the right to this through his participation in revolutionary work during a period of from two to three years; he had possessed the confidence of our dead comrades; he had been the chief leader among the artillery corps of St. Petersburg and Kronstadt, with members of which he had been acquainted through his attendance at the Academy, and his former service at Kronstadt. He knew many members of the navy branch, Sukhanov's comrades, and, as a member of the group from the artillery, which had entered the military organisation, had been initiated into all the affairs of this organisation. Under the stress of this situation we were to bend all our energies to the reorganisation of the centre, and having mustered our forces together, assume upon ourselves all the responsibility which circumstances might impose upon us, however heavy that responsibility might be. Degayev listened to my recital in silence, and agreed to become a member of the central organisation which was to assume the direction of the party's affairs.

XVI

THE SEIZURE OF THE PRINTING PRESS IN ODESSA

In the latter part of December news came from Odessa that the secret printing press there had been discovered, and that the five people who had been associated with it, Degayev and his wife, Kalyuzhnaya, Surovtsev, and Spandoni, had been arrested. So it came about that the newly organised printing press existed for only five weeks, and the whole enterprise crumbled to the ground. This was a heavy blow. It shattered our last hope for a speedy re-establishment of the party organ, by the presence or absence of which the government and wide circles of society usually judged of the state of the revolutionary cause.

With a heavy heart do I recall that dark period into which I plunged after this news reached me. I saw that all my preparations had come to naught, that all my work had been fruitless. Whatever plans I devised were swept away to destruction, bearing with them the ruin of those whom I had engaged to take part in them. I had persevered, but all in vain. And yet, was it possible for me to retreat when young souls were watching me hopefully from afar, seeking moral support for their convictions? I remember one letter that I received at that time. A young girl of my acquaintance, a political outlaw, persecuted by the police and bewildered, wrote to me that there was one star on the dark horizon of her gloomy soul—myself. After my arrest she committed suicide, casting herself beneath the wheels of a train. Everything was perishing, going down to destruction around me, and I was left alone, like Eugene Sue's eternal wanderer, to travel my path of sorrows to which there seemed no end.

Now, even more than in previous months, I lived a dual life, an external existence for others, and an internal existence for myself. Outwardly I had to preserve a calm, courageous aspect, and this I did; but in the stillness of the night I would think with painful anxiety: Would the "end" come? "My end"? In the morning I would put on my mask and begin my Penelope toil. When Mikhaylovsky visited me in October on the business which I have already mentioned, he asked me, when taking his leave, what my plans were. I replied with the symbolic phrase, "I shall gather up the broken threads and tie them together." Mikhaylovsky took my head in both his hands and covered my face with kisses. It was only after I had read his verses about me, published after his death, that I understood why he, who had never before been demonstrative, had kissed me then. I think it was because he was deeply moved by the steadfastness with which I held to my purpose.

I do not think that my mental attitude was perceptible to others, during ordinary business meetings, but my close acquaintances used often to say to me, "Why are you thinking so deeply? Why do your eyes look beyond us, far in the distance?" That was because in my soul the words constantly echoed, "It is hard to live!" And my eyes unconsciously gazed beyond, for there, in that beyond, lay hidden "the end."

But more bitter times were yet to come. The seizure of the printing press in Odessa was the external side of the misfortune. There was another side which remained still hidden, and which had the most fatal consequences.

THE "FUGITIVE"

The printing press had been seized by the police on December 20th, and on January 23rd or 24th, I received a special summons to go to the house of my friends, the Tikhotskys. When I arrived at the Tikhotskys', I stopped short in astonishment. Before me stood Degayev, the director of the printing press, who had been arrested in Odessa. "What has happened? How did you get here?" I asked, excited and agitated by the joy and the unexpectedness of this meeting.

"I escaped," stammered Degayev, pale, unnerved, with the face of a man worn out by anxiety. And then he told me the following story. He did not know by what means the police had been guided in their discovery of the printing press and its workers. Perhaps the boxes and trunks containing the type, which had astonished the porters by their weight, had caused suspicion and a report to the police. After his arrest, he began to plan for an escape, and mentioned Kiev as his place of residence previous to Odessa, saying that he wished to give his testimony there. For a long time the gendarmes withheld their consent, but they later agreed to this demand. And when, one night, they sent him to the station in a cab accompanied by two gendarmes, and they were driving over the vacant space of ground which separated the station from the city, he threw a handful of tobacco into the eyes of the gendarmes, sprang from the cab, and disappeared in the darkness.

"In Odessa," he continued, "I found refuge with officers with whom I had become acquainted during my visits to the various branches of the military organisation. At the end of a few days one of them took me by carriage to Nikolayev to the group of officers with whom I had stayed during my visit there, and yesterday I arrived in Kharkov. Being unable to find your address, I applied to Gursky in whose care I was to write to you. After repeated refusals and much quizzing, he finally agreed to tell me how to find you."

"Where did you spend the night? Did you walk the streets all night long?" I asked sympathetically.

"In a place of ill repute," answered Degayev in confusion. I was also confused. But I was confused because I took "a place of ill repute" in its entirely specific sense; while Degayev's embarrassment arose from the fact that his refuge (as I afterwards learned) had been not a house of prostitution, but a quite different place.

"But how did it happen that you threw tobacco into the eyes of the gendarmes?" said I, continuing to question the successful fugitive. "You don't smoke, do you?"

This question was more than absurd, for in such cases people do not throw smoking tobacco, but snuff. Degayev did not lose his composure, but took up my foolish question.

"I don't smoke," he explained, "but I had bought the tobacco in advance."

Degayev's appearance aroused my sympathy. I understood

that he could not rejoice in his freedom, while his wife remained in prison. This circumstance was enough to deprive a man of his calmness and self-possession. I made every effort to encourage him.

Afterwards I recalled strange, random phrases which might have been taken for vague hints, perhaps warnings on his part, had we been at all on our guard. But we were far from such suspicions and could only share his grief over the misfortune which had descended upon him.

"Some one of those arrested in Odessa is giving information," Degayev said once.

"But who could it be?" I asked him.

"One of the 'illegal'," he replied.

"But there are no 'illegal' persons there, save your wife, Surovtsev, and Kalyuzhnaya, and they are trustworthy people; besides, they have nothing to betray."

"You are wrong," Degayev insisted, "some one of the 'illegal' is giving information."

I was perplexed.

Once, when Degayev and Chernyavskaya were at my apartment, he asked me, "Are you really safe here in Kharkov?"

"Yes, absolutely so," I replied confidently.

"Are you quite sure of that?" he persisted.

"Of course! Unless I meet Merkulov [33] on the street!" I said, regarding such an event quite improbable.

Later, in conversation, Degayev inquired casually at what hour I usually left the house. There was nothing out of place in such a question from a friend with whom I exchanged visits frequently, and I answered immediately, "Usually at eight o'clock, when the students of the assistant-surgeons' school go to their classes, for my passport is a duplicate of one of theirs."

Another time, when he was taking his departure, he asked me whether there was another exit besides the gate that opened on the street.

"Yes, through the notion shop kept by my landlord and his wife, but I never go that way," I replied.

And Degayev made use of all this information.

[33] The traitor, who knew Vera Figner personally.—*Translator.*

MY ARREST

A day or two had elapsed after this conversation, when on the morning of February 10, I glanced at my watch; it was eight o'clock, and I accordingly left the house. I had not gone ten paces when I met Merkulov face to face. One look—and we recognised each other. He did not seize me at once, and there were no gendarmes or police in sight. I walked on, rapidly considering the situation. There was no place to hide, no courtyards that opened on another street, no lodgings of any of my near acquaintances. What did I have in my pocket? I ransacked my memory. There was a notebook with two or three names of people who did not belong to the organisation; a postal receipt for money which had been sent to Rostov, to A. Kashintsev. I must destroy it without fail. I was still walking along Ekaterininskaya Street and approaching a little semicircular garden plot which had been laid out on one side of the street. Instead of the lofty buildings which now loom up beyond this little part, there stood at that time an old frame house. A good friend of mine lived there, N. A. Ivashev, a turner, who had a little shop of his own. Probably the gendarmes knew that friends of mine lived there, for the thought had barely flashed into my mind to go to them, when I was surrounded by gendarmes who sprang up from nowhere. A moment later I was seated in a sleigh with two gendarmes, on my way to police headquarters.

There, in a private room, my clothing was searched. I noticed immediately that the women who had been summoned for this task were inexperienced, and I took from my pocket the purse which contained the postal receipt. In a second the paper was in my mouth. The women raised a cry for help, a gendarme rushed in and seized me by the throat. I laughed affectedly, in order to show that he was too late, and the gendarme released me. In reality I could not possibly have swallowed the dry, smooth paper, and only later succeeded in doing so.

A police officer came in, and drew up a short report. When he asked for my name, I said, "If you have arrested me, you must know that yourself." Then Merkulov entered the room, and in his usual rapid speech said brazenly, "So you didn't expect it, did you?" "Blackguard!" I cried, and raised my hand threateningly. The coward fell back towards the doorway.

They took me to the prison, dressed me in convict garb, and brought me a jug of milk, demanding that I drink it. The authorities feared for my life. They imagined that I had swallowed not a piece of paper but poison. They mistook small particles of yellow potassium, which I kept in my purse to make invisible ink, for deadly cyanide of potassium.

In the morning I was taken to the railroad station, accompanied by two gendarmes, on my way to St. Petersburg.

XVII

IN THE POLICE DEPARTMENT

It was towards evening on Saturday when we arrived in St. Petersburg, and I was installed in one of the cells of the building occupied by the Police Department. The following day being a holiday, I was able to give myself over to my thoughts. Of whom, of what was I to think? Of my mother, whom I had not seen for several years, of a meeting with her, and the grief which awaited her?

They kept me there for three days. Later I learned that my arrest had caused great rejoicing in the imperial circles. Alexander III, on receiving the news, exclaimed, "Thank God, that terrible woman has been arrested!" It was evidently for him that the picture was destined which they took of me at the studio of Alexandrovsky and Taube on the Nevsky, where the pictures of all those who had been placed under arrest were usually taken. When Dobrzhynsky, the public prosecutor, in my presence examined the proofs which had been made in the studio, he turned to M. V. Muravyev, and looking at him significantly, said with especial emphasis, "We must select a good one, you know for whom." He selected the picture taken in the year 1883, which was afterwards most widely distributed among the public, and printed in the collection of my poems.

V. D. Nabokov, the son of the Minister of Justice, then a child, remembers the joy which his father expressed when they brought him the telegram communicating the news of my arrest. In the department itself, when they summoned me from my cell, I passed a veritable gauntlet of officials, idly crowding along my path. The political trials of former years, during which my name had been repeatedly mentioned, had evidently made me an object of curiosity. They also exhibited me to a few of the high dignitaries: to the Director of the Police Department, to the Associate Minister of the Interior, and to the

Minister himself. I remember the three figures, Plehve, Orzhevsky, and Count D. A. Tolstoy.[34]

The first was rude, purposely so. Carelessly nodding his head, partly in salutation, and partly to indicate a row of chairs ranged along the wall, he growled harshly, "Take a chair!" And after I had seated myself he began to scoff at me, saying that it was impossible for them to arrest any one of the students without hearing enthusiastic reports about me.

"Can such enthusiasm have satisfied you?" he asked me. He shrugged his shoulders with an expression of disdain on his face. "Perhaps," he continued ironically, "you would now be disposed to occupy that position in society which you might have occupied earlier." But a moment later, as though wishing to look into the soul of a person who had been utterly worn out by an "illegal" existence, he said, "Perhaps you have become so wearied that the end seems welcome?"

Orzhevsky was gallant and refined, and behaved like a cultured gentleman. Kind and considerate in his address, tactful in conversation, he wished to draw me into a discussion on political topics, but I evaded him, saying that I could express my views better at the trial.

Tolstoy was a good-natured, somewhat stolid old man.

"How unassuming you are!" he exclaimed, when I entered Orzhevsky's private office. "I had expected you to be quite different." And he immediately began to discuss classical education, and the fact that we revolutionists opposed this system, and had, as he knew, evil designs against his life. Then, changing the subject to political assassinations, and to attempts against the imperial family in particular, he continued, "But what can you gain by this? Supposing you do kill one tsar, another will take his place," and so on and so on. He spoke tritely, without force, and assumed the attitude of a grand-

[34] As Minister of Education, and later of the Interior, Tolstoy carried out a most reactionary policy. In his former capacity he reduced education to a farce, and particularly embittered the college youth. Von Plehve became Minister of the Interior under Nicolas II, and won the hatred of all groups by his brutal persecutions. In 1904 he was assassinated by Sazonov, by order of the Terrorist Organisation of the Socialists-Revolutionists.—*Translator.*

father reproving his grandchild, so that there was no use in replying to his arguments.

"I am sorry that I have not the time," he said at last, "or I would convince you of your error."

Not wishing to leave him the last word, I said, "I am sorry too. I hope I could convert you to The Will of the People programme."

The jest took wings, and on my first meeting with Dobrzynsky he amused me by asking: "Is it possible that you really believed you could win Count Tolstoy over to your creed?"

With a smile I replied, "And why not?"

From the Police Department they transferred me to the Fortress of Sts. Peter and Paul, and kept me there for twenty months before I was tried. At first they summoned me several times for examination to the Police Department. I said from the first that I saw no necessity, and had no intention, of concealing any of the details of my revolutionary activity previous to the first of March, 1881, since my testimony would refer to events which were already well known, and to persons who had already been condemned. As for events relating to a more recent period, I would remain silent.

My visits to the Police Department, accompanied by Captain Domashnev, and my meetings with the state's attorneys, Dobrzynsky and Muravyev, were oppressive, and I suggested that they cease summoning me personally from the Fortress, but instead to give me paper and ink in my cell, so that I might write down everything that I felt like revealing, consigning the pages to the Inspector as they were completed.

Perhaps a month or more had passed, when one day a tall, elderly general of gendarmes made his appearance in my cell. His features were attractive and well formed.

"My name is Sereda," he said, introducing himself. "I have been appointed by the imperial authority to investigate political propaganda throughout the troops of the Empire." He took my hand and kissed it, in spite of my resistance. "You are a good woman," he said. "Your misfortune is that, although you married, you had no children."

After this peculiar overture, we seated ourselves and I asked how he proposed to make use of his far-reaching authority. He replied that he had no intention of arranging a huge trial. Only the most active conspirators would be prosecuted. And he was true to his word. Fourteen people were arraigned in our trial, and among them only six army officers, while dozens of them might have been prosecuted.

Then the general began to confess his political ideas to me: he was not a reactionary, not a supporter of the existing system. Only his debts forced him to remain in office. "Were it not for that, I should not be here," he declared. "I love freedom, but I do not approve of political assassinations. I can understand a battle on the barricades, but not a stab in the back with a dagger."

After this visit I was left in peace, since my testimony, which presented an authoritative outline of the revolutionary movement, had already been completed and submitted, even before Sereda's visit, and he had come to me after having perused it.[35]

IN THE FORTRESS OF STS. PETER AND PAUL

A period of calm succeeded. The agitation aroused in me by my arrest and the new surroundings, and which had been sustained by the retrospection of all my past, from childhood to imprisonment, a retrospection which is probably common to all those who fall into prison, and who think that their life has come to an end, this agitation, so natural during the first period of one's imprisonment, subsided, and a grey, monotonous life began, filled only with reading. For whole days and weeks I was silent. I was allowed twenty-minute visits from my mother and sister once every two weeks. Such were the regulations. Two gratings, about a yard apart, separated us. Not once did they let me kiss my mother's hand. Once, when I was especially despondent, I begged the Inspector to let me do this.

---

[35] This testimony deeply impressed the gendarmes. "It passes from hand to hand, and we read it as a novel," said Captain Domashnev to me. N. V. Muravyev had a copy made for himself, and a few years later lent it to my ex-husband, A. V. Philipov, who was serving in the Ministry of Justice.

I so longed to caress, to touch with my lips her warm little hand. It was useless. The regulations did not permit this.

In the spring I pined for flowers. I longed to have just one little flower, one of those bulbs which are sold on the streets of St. Petersburg in little pots. My sister brought a hyacinth to the Fortress. She asked permission to give it to me, but they refused to give it to me even cut. All gifts were forbidden in the Fortress, and the Inspector remained inexorable.

When summer came the visits ceased. My mother departed for our old village in the province of Kazan, while my sister Olga went to the island of Osel for treatment.

Silence, eternal silence. Akhsharumov, a member of the Petrashevsky Circle,[36] as I read much later, tried to preserve the functions of his vocal cords during his imprisonment in the Fortress by reading aloud. I did not avail myself of this expedient, for it had not occurred to me. My vocal cords became weakened and atrophied from disuse; my voice became weak and broken. From a deep contralto it became thin, strident, quavering, like the voice of one convalescing from a serious illness; words came from my tongue with difficulty, and haltingly. And together with this physical breakdown of my organ of speech came a psychic change. The desire arose in me *to be silent*. In addition to the enforced necessity of being silent, I lost the inner impulse for speaking—I *wanted* to be silent, and when it was necessary to move my lips, to speak, I had to summon all my strength of will.

When my mother returned in the autumn, it was hard for me to go out to that first meeting with her. And as time passed it became harder for me to emerge from solitude, from silence. And what was the use of it? Why change the tempo of life, the natural order of the day and one's own mood? Why destroy one's spiritual balance for twenty minutes in which one did not know what to say, what questions to ask, and then, on returning to one's cell, to strive long and vainly to regain one's

[36] In 1849, a number of persons were arrested in St. Petersburg for meeting at the home of Petrashevsky and discussing various problems. The accused were severely punished. One of these victims was F. Dostoyevsky.—*Translator.*

composure and sink into apathy for another two weeks? Every time that the gendarmes threw open the door of my cell, and uttered the words, "A visit from your family!" I so longed to refuse to go, to say that I did not want to, that I *would* not. And only the thought that my mother and sister would be frightened and hurt made me rise and go to them.

A long time passed, when in the spring of 1884 they again summoned me to the office. There I found Dobrzynsky and General Sereda. They were sitting near the table, which was laden with large, bound notebooks. They were weary, preoccupied, and their faces were grave and serious.

"Do you recognise this handwriting?" asked Dobrzynsky, laying before me an unbound notebook. I did not recognise the handwriting, and answered, "No." Then he opened the notebook, and showed me the signature. There it stood, Sergey Degayev, the date and the month. My memory recalled it afterwards as *November* 20th, but this was of course a mistake; the printing press in Odessa was seized by the police on the eighteenth, or, according to other testimony, on *December* 20th.

Then, turning over the pages, one after another, Dobrzynsky pointed out to me separate passages in the notebook, covering others with his hand. There was no longer any doubt. Before me there lay a document of the greatest importance; the author had delivered into the hands of the government everything that he had learned during his association with the party. Not only were the important members of the organisation mentioned by name, but even the most insignificant helpers and active sympathisers were revealed and identified, from first to last, insofar as the author had knowledge of their existence. The army officers from the north and the south were to a man treacherously betrayed; not a member of the military organisation escaped betrayal. All the available forces of the party lay in the palm of the government's hand, and all the people who had belonged to it lived from now on under a glass cover.

I was stupefied. Degayev! Degayev had done this thing! I sprang from my chair and for a few minutes paced back and forth through the room, while Sereda and Dobrzynsky silently turned the pages of the folios which they had brought with them. When I returned to my place, Dobrzynsky began to show me the various testimonies of the officers from the south. Each one began with the shameful words, "Repenting of my errors, I make the following statement . . ." and so forth. They repented of their errors, these men thirty-five and forty years of age, whom I had trusted and had so wished to add to the party, as men of strong and reliable character, who would not fail us. All these conspirators, who had promised to join an armed revolt at the command of the party and give their lives for the cause of the people, now faintheartedly recanted the declaration of faith which they had made, and to which they had bound themselves by their word. They had "gone astray," they who for many years had discussed the themes of revolution, barricades, and so on. These statements produced a miserable impression on me; but what did they signify in the face of what Degayev had done, who had shaken the foundation of life itself, that faith in people without which a revolutionist cannot act? He had lied, dissimulated, and deceived; he had asked questions in order that he might betray, and at the same time he had flattered and praised. His escape had been fictitious; the gendarmes had released him in order to conceal his treachery, and, having begun his career of betrayal, he became a provocateur, so that by attracting dozens of new people to the revolutionary movement he might secretly surrender them into the hands of the government. To experience such a betrayal was a blow heavy beyond all words. It took away the moral beauty of mankind, the beauty of the revolution and of life itself. From the ideal heights I was hurled into the lowliest slough.

When I met my family for the first time after receiving this news, they knew that some shattering blow had fallen upon me. I longed to die. I longed to, but I had to live; I was obliged to live so that I might attend my trial, that final act in the work of an active revolutionist. As a member of the Executive Committee I had to tell my story, to fulfil my last duty, as all those who had gone before me had fulfilled theirs. And, as a comrade of those whom Degayev had betrayed, I had to share our common fate to the end. But the only way I could live was to fill my mind with something which had no bearing on the misfortunes of the revolution. I had to occupy myself constantly with work of some kind. I began to study the English language, and so zealously that at the end of two weeks I was reading Macaulay's *History of England* in the original. This would have been incredible, as I recalled many years afterwards, had I not taken a few lessons in this language from an Englishwoman while I was attending the Institute, at the insistence of the headmistress, in spite of my great reluctance and poor success. Evidently some traces of these lessons still remained in my memory, and now, after sixteen years, were revived.

Having gained a ready command of the English language, I did not leave my book for whole days, allowing myself not a moment for meditation. I had already applied myself zealously to reading during the first months of my imprisonment, and never in my life did I read with such enthusiasm, with such satisfying results as at that time, during my stay in the Fortress. My education had been, generally speaking, irregular and unsystematic. I need not mention the Institute, where every one was persecuted for reading, and where there was practically no library for the students. At the University of Zurich my medical studies occupied too much of my time for me to avail myself of all the possibilities offered by the excellent library which the Russian emigrants and students supported. I had to hasten my medical education, for I did not have sufficient funds to support me during a long sojourn abroad. And after I had left the University and returned to Russia, the active revolutionary environment in which I lived was not conducive to serious intellectual pursuits. In the revolutionary circle in which I moved, science and learning were never disdained, but obstacles accumulated to such an extent that it was impossible for one to devote himself to them. The revolutionary cause demanded all one's attention; thought was to be directed only to what was for the good of the party, and to what the organisation was undertaking and performing.

Only in prison, where there was no other occupation, no

external impressions and events, was I able to surrender myself fully to the subjects which had especially interested me, to history, political economy, sociology, and read everything of Spencer on biology and psychology. My letters to mother and sister Olga, which she kept, reflect this omnivorous reading. Fifty in number, these letters which I wrote in the Peter and Paul Fortress are filled almost entirely with short accounts of the works of various authors, which I recommended to my sister for one reason or another. These letters could not have contained anything else, for they had to pass through several censors, beginning with the Fortress and ending with the Police Department. Only here and there, in a few words, a trace of the psychology of a prisoner slipped through.

The books helped me to live. From the very beginning of my imprisonment they deadened the pain which misfortunes of a general nature brought into the prison. They also helped me to endure even the moral catastrophe wrought by Degayev. My painful mental and spiritual state was diverted in yet another way. My finger began to pain me; an infection appeared on my little finger and caused me great pain. When I showed the finger to Doctor Wilms, he shook his head and said, "We must lance that." And when he had done so, he added, "I was afraid that it might develop into tetanus." This severe, elderly man, whose soul had turned to stone from the gloomy secrets of the Fortress and the Alexey Ravelin, now for the first time looked about the large, but dark, damp and dirty cell where I had lived for more than a year, and which was covered with mould and dust, and said, "They must transfer you to a lighter cell."

The following day, they did in fact transfer me to a cell opening off another corridor. It was a small, but far more comfortable room, which, I think, must have had a southwestern exposure. In spite of the rampart which rose up outside the window, a few oblique rays of light from the invisible sun penetrated the cell towards noon. The wall was farther from the window that it was in cell No. 43, where I had lived up to that time. I clambered up on the iron table, which was screwed to the wall of my new quarters and next to the cot, so that I might survey my surroundings, and saw in a little hollow on the sloping side of the wall, a weak little seedling tree. A capricious elder had grown up there on the rock, from a tiny seed carried by the wind. It demanded little; a ruined section of wall, tumbling down in rubbish, was enough to nourish it. At the approach of spring, I would climb up on the table every day about noontime to look at the green, budding foliage of the little tree, which I called *mine*, because there was no one besides myself who could see it, or who watched it grow.

On September 16 or 18, 1884, my indictment was handed to me. Together with thirteen other prisoners, I was delivered to the court martial. The counsel appointed to defend me appeared. I asked his pardon that I could not accept his services. He was left alone with me, and lowering his voice he whispered, "Sudeykin has been killed. Degayev killed him and disappeared."

For a moment the darkness lifted from my soul, was rent. . . . Convulsively, in a sharp zigzag, there bust forth a flood of deep and hidden emotion, complex and contradictory; it flashed like lightning, and all became dark once more.

XVIII

"THE COURT IS IN SESSION"

It was Saturday, September 21, 1884, when, at ten o'clock in the evening, a gendarme unexpectedly brought me a coat and hat; they transferred me from the Peter and Paul Fortress to the House of Preliminary Detention. Just why it was necessary to surround this act with mystery, and to alarm me at a late hour, when I was already preparing to retire, I do not know. But the entire prison régime, insofar as I myself experienced it prior to my trial and thereafter, was so organised, either designedly or otherwise, as to lead to a complete breakdown of one's nervous system, which it kept in a state of tension, now by means of silence and solitude, now by various unexpected happenings.

Of course, I did not close my eyes that night. They put me in a cell directly opposite the place where the woman supervisor was stationed. Through some incomprehensible idea of precaution, the peep-hole in the door had been left open, and remained so all night long. The two guards on duty spent the whole night chatting outside my door between their tours of inspection, and gave me no opportunity to sleep for a moment. The next day I could hardly stand it when they took me out to meet my mother and my sister Olga. This time there was no pair of gratings set at a yard's distance from each other, and for the first time after twenty months of imprisonment, I could kiss my mother's hand. We could sit down and talk as much as we pleased, but having grown accustomed to silence and twenty-minute visits once in two weeks, I soon became so tired that I myself asked my mother to go. The next day my court martial was to begin.

The following morning, Monday, at ten o'clock, they led me through a maze of passages, stairways and corridors to the room where my thirteen co-defendants had already been ranged.

Between every couple there stood a gendarme with drawn sword. It was impossible to embrace one another, or to press the hand of a friend. This was for the best, for the change in their appearance was in itself enough to make one weep. How could one look calmly at the pale, sallow faces, which had formerly been so courageous and full of joy and life; on the figures bent with exhaustion, some of which bore plain signs of physical breakdown? [37] Think of the bitterness and sorrow, that we were all of us united in this trial not only through our revolutionary activity, but through the fact that we had been brought to the bar by the treachery of a friend who had broken faith with us! And during the entire course of the trial, through all its manifold incidents, one could feel, consciously or unconsciously, the hand of Degayev, which had left its shameful imprint on us all, and had crushed our spirits with its heavy weight.

The state witnesses arrived; experts were summoned—at the insistence of the state—and endless evidence against the accused was read.

There were almost no retorts. Only Chemodanova, who had once been a political exile, attempted, with easy loquacity, to convince the court of her innocence. She told her story so coherently and in such detail, that even I, who had myself summoned her to Kharkov, was ready to doubt. Well, perhaps she really had come to Kharkov on personal business, and by mere accident had chanced to become associated with the secret printing press of The Will of the People!

My other comrades were reserved and silent, thinking their own serious thoughts. Only Ludmila Volkenstein was perfectly unconcerned, and subjected herself to the loud, disagreeable reprimands of the president of the court: "Defendant Volkenstein! do not talk to your neighbours." "Defendant Volkenstein! I am speaking to you—stop whispering. Move to the end of the bench!" and so on.

As for me, I succumbed to exhaustion. After the silence and

[37] Shortly after their transfer to Schlüsselburg, the officer Tikhonovich either died or committed suicide, while Nemolovsky died from consumption.

solitude of the Peter and Paul Fortress, the nervous tension which came from the change of surroundings was unendurable. Dizzy from the sight of my comrades, agitated by the proximity of people, by the sound of their voices, as well as by the brilliant evening lights, I was unable to endure to the end one single session, and would go to my cell to rest my worn-out nerves.

During intermissions my mother and sister would come to me, and this laid a fresh burden upon my nerves, until I had to say with sorrow, "Go away! I have not the strength. . . ."

During the preparatory investigations, I had set forth in writing everything which related to my own part in the revolutionary movement, not wishing to diminish by one iota my responsibility before the existing laws, and so, during the trial, my conduct was guided by the same motive. Therefore I needed no defence whatsoever. Nevertheless I requested the services of Attorney Leontyev, explaining to him that the only reason for my request was that it gave me an opportunity to speak with him in private. I had to make some last arrangements, but this was impossible during the meetings with my mother, for an inspectress always attended our visits.

During the period of my preliminary confinement, my sister, knowing that I loved flowers, had more than once asked for permission to give me some, but no exchange of any gifts was permitted in the Peter and Paul Fortress. Now, on the very last day of the trial, she brought me a beautiful bouquet of roses. These marvellous roses gave me one of the most tender recollections that I bore away with me to Schlüsselburg.

Another touching episode during these sad days, was an unexpected greeting from a French woman, Madame Matrosov, née Valdon, who had taught in the Rodionovsky Institute at Kazan, and had known me as a little twelve year old girl in a schoolroom. Now, in the hall of the Criminal Court, she remembered her little pupil, and greeted me warmly.

There came at last the most memorable day of my life, the most profoundly moving moment in any trial, when the president turning to the accused, says in a peculiarly solemn voice, "Defendant, the last word is yours!"

The last word! How great, and how deep a significance is in that brief phrase! The accused is given an opportunity, unique in its tragic setting, and perhaps the last, the very last opportunity in his life, to express his spiritual individuality, to explain the moral justification of his acts and conduct, and to speak aloud, for all to hear, those things which he wishes to say, which he must say, and may say. A few minutes more, and this opportunity, this last possibility, drops into the past, retreats irrevocably and forever. If this moment is allowed to escape, the man whom they are trying, and whom they are ready to condemn, will never more lift his voice in speech: they will not listen to him, and his voice will either grow dumb in prison, or die with him on the scaffold.

How many torturing fears did I experience, in awaiting that day and hour in the loneliness of my cell!

Under the circumstances created by the investigation, I was the central figure of the trial, the person of most importance in the case under consideration. The previous trials (dating from 1879 to 1884), of Alexander Soloviev, Alexander Kvyatkovsky, of the conspirators of the first of March, and the trials of the twenty, and of the seventeen members of The Will of the People, during which my name had been frequently mentioned, had created for me, the last of them all to be arrested, an exceptional position. This position demanded that, as the last member of the Executive Committee, and as a representative of The Will of the People, I should speak at the trial.

But I was in no mood for making speeches. I was crushed by the general situation in our native land. There was no doubt that the conflict and the protest were ended; a long, dark period of reaction had come upon us, all the more difficult to endure morally, because we had not expected it, but had hoped for an entirely new form of social life and government. The warfare had been waged by methods of unheard-of cruelty, but we had paid for such methods with our lives, and had believed and hoped. But the common people had remained silent, and had not understood. The advanced elements had remained silent, though they had understood. The wheel of history had been against us; we had anticipated by twenty-five years the course of events, the general political development of the city people and the peasantry—and we were left alone. The carefully selected and organised forces, small in number, but audacious in spirit, had been swept from life's arena, suppressed and annihilated. My comrades on the Executive Committee had been arrested and condemned before me. Some of them had died on the scaffold, others had died slowly from exhaustion and ill-treatment behind the walls of the Alexey Ravelin. The entire organisation of The Will of the People party, insofar as it had not been destroyed, had been reduced to fragments, over the ruins of which played the demoralising activity of Sergey Degayev, who, after the founders of The Will of the People had met their fate, began his career of betrayal in prison, and, emerging therefrom by means of a pretended escape, continued his career of treachery and espionage outside.

So it came about that at the time of the trial in 1884, in which, betrayed by Degayev, I was the central figure, the secret society which had striven to destroy autocracy, and which through its activities had not only shaken to the foundations our native land, but had aroused the whole civilised world, now lay prostrate. It lay prostrate, with no hope of soon arising from its ruin.

And at the very time when my body was shaken and weakened by the conditions of my preliminary imprisonment in the Fortress, when my spirit was broken and devastated by all that I had lived through, the moment arrived in which I was inexorably bound to fulfil my duty to my dead comrades and to our shattered party, to confess my faith, to declare before the court the spiritual impulses which had governed our activities, and to point out the social and political ideal to which we had aspired.

The presiding judge had spoken; my name was called. There was an unnatural silence, and the eyes of those present, strangers and comrades alike, turned to me, and they were all listening, though as yet I had not uttered a word.

I was nervous and timid: what if in the midst of my carefully thought-out speech that mental darkness should suddenly descend upon me, which in those decisive days frequently overwhelmed me, without causing me to lose consciousness?

And in the midst of the stillness, vibrant with the general attention, I spoke my last words in a voice wherein sounded my repressed emotion.

"The court has been examining my revolutionary activities since the year 1879. The public prosecutor has expressed astonishment in his speech of indictment, both with respect to the character and to the extent of those activities. But these crimes, like all others, have their own history. They are logically and closely bound up with my whole previous life. During the period of my preliminary imprisonment, I have often debated whether my life could have followed a different course, or could have ended in any other spot than this Criminal Court. And every time I have replied to myself, No!

"I began my life under very happy surroundings. I had no lack of guides in the formation of my character; it was not necessary to keep me in leading strings. My family was intelligent and affectionate, so that I never experienced the disharmony which often exists between the older and younger generations. I had no knowledge of material want, and no anxiety concerning daily necessities or self-support. When, at the age of seventeen, I left the Institute, the thought was borne in upon me for the first time that not every one lived under such happy conditions as I. The vague idea that I belonged to the cultured minority, aroused in me the thought of the obligations which my position imposed upon me with respect to the remaining uneducated masses, who lived from day to day, submerged in manual toil, and deprived of all those things which are usually called the blessings of civilisation. This visualisation of the contrast between my position and the position of those who surrounded me, aroused in me the first thought of the necessity of creating for myself a purpose in life which should tend to benefit those others.

"Russian journalism of that period, and the feminist movement which was in full swing at the beginning of the seventies, gave a ready answer to the questions which arose in my mind, and indicated the medical profession as being a form of activity which would satisfy my philanthropic aspirations.

"The Women's Academy in St. Petersburg had already been opened, but from its very beginning it was characterised by the weakness for which it has been distinguished up to the present time, in its constant struggle between life and death; and since I had firmly made up my mind, and did not wish to be forced to abandon the course which I had undertaken, I decided to go abroad.

"And so, having considerably recast my life, I departed for Zurich, and entered the University. Life abroad presented a sharp contrast to Russian life. I saw there things which were entirely new to me. I had not been prepared for them by what I had previously seen and known; I had not been prepared to make a correct evaluation of everything which came into my life. I accepted the idea of socialism at first almost instinctively. It seemed to me that it was nothing more than a broader conception of that altruistic thought which had earlier awakened in my mind. The teaching which promised equality, fraternity, and universal happiness, could not help but dazzle me. My horizon became broader; in place of my native village and its inhabitants, there appeared before me a picture of the common people, of humanity. Moreover, I had gone abroad at the time when the events which had taken place in Paris, and the revolution which was progressing in Spain, were evoking a mighty echo from the entire labouring world of the west. At the same time I became acquainted with the doctrines and the organisation of the International. Not till later did I begin to realise that much of what I saw there was only the brighter side of the picture. Moreover, I did not regard the working-class movement with which I had become acquainted, as a product of western-European life, but I thought that the same doctrine applied to all times, and to every locality.

"Attracted by socialist ideas while abroad, I joined the first revolutionary circle in the work of which my sister Lydia was engaged. Its plan of organisation was very weak; each member might take up revolutionary work in any form he chose, and at any time suited to his convenience. This work consisted of spreading the ideas of socialism, in the optimistic hope that the common people of Russia, already socialists because of their poverty and their social position, could be converted to socialism by a mere word. What we termed at that time the social revolution was rather in the nature of a peaceful social reorganisation; that is, we thought that the minority who opposed socialism, on seeing the impossibility of carrying on the strife, would be forced to yield to the majority who had become conscious of their own interests; and so there was no mention of bloodshed.

"I remained abroad for almost four years. I had always been more or less conservative, in the sense that I did not make speedy decisions, but having once made them, I withdrew from them only with great difficulty. Even when in the spring of 1874, almost the entire circle left for Russia, I remained abroad to continue my medical studies.

"My sister and the other members of the circle ended their careers most miserably. Two or three months' work as labourers in factories, secured for them two- and three-year terms of preliminary detention, after which a trial condemned some of them to penal servitude, others, to lifelong exile in Siberia. While they were in prison, the summons came to me: they asked me to return to Russia to support the cause of the circle. Inasmuch as I had already received a sufficiently thorough medical education, so that the conferring of the title of doctor of medicine and surgery upon me would satisfy only my vanity, I cut short my course and returned to Russia.

"There, from the very first, I found a critical and difficult situation. The movement 'To the People' had already suffered defeat. Nevertheless, I found a fairly large group of persons who seemed congenial, whom I trusted, and with whom I became intimate. Together with them I participated in the working out of that programme which is known as the Programme of the Populists [*Narodniki*].

"I went to live in the country. The programme of the Populists, as the court knows, had aims which the law could not sanction, for its problem was to effect the transfer of all the land into the hands of the peasant communes. But before this could be accomplished, the rôle which the revolutionists living among the people must play, consisted in what is called in all countries, cultural activity. So it was that I too went to live in the country with designs of a purely revolutionary nature, and yet I do not think that my manner towards the peasants, or my actions in general, would have aroused persecution in any other country save Russia; elsewhere I might even have been considered a useful member of society.

"I became an assistant surgeon in the Zemstvo.[38]

"A whole league was formed against me in a very short time, at the head of which stood the marshal of the nobility, and the district police captain, while in the rear were the village constable, the county clerk and others. Rumours of every kind were spread about me: that I had no passport, while I really had one, and was living under my own name; that my diploma was forged, and so forth. When the peasants did not wish to enter into an unprofitable agreement with the proprietor, it was said that I was to blame; when the county assembly reduced the clerk's salary, it was said that I was again to blame.

"Public and secret inquiries were made: the police captain came; several of the peasants were arrested; my name figured in the cross-questioning; two complaints were made to the governor, and it was only through the efforts made by the president of the executive board of the County Zemstvo that I was left in peace. Police espionage rose up around me; people began to be afraid of me. The peasants came to my house by stealthy and circuitous routes.

"These obstacles naturally led me to the question: what could I accomplish under such conditions?

"I shall speak frankly. When I settled in the village, I was at an age when I could no longer make gross mistakes through any lack of tact, at an age when people become more tolerant, more attentive to the opinions of others. I wanted to study

38 The Zemstvo (Rural Boards) was established in 1864, as a self-governing institution for the management of the material and cultural needs of the village. Eventually this important reform shared the fate of the other liberal reforms of Alexander II: it was curtailed and mutilated.— *Translator.*

the ground, to learn what the peasant himself thought, what he wished. I saw that there were no acts of mine which could incriminate me, that I was being persecuted only for my spirit, for my private views. They did not think that it was possible for a person of some culture to settle in the village without some horrible purpose.

"And so I was deprived of the possibility of even physical contact with the people, and was unable not only to accomplish anything, but even to hold the most simple, everyday relations with them.

"Then I began to ponder: had I not made some mistake from which I could escape by moving to another locality and repeating my attempt? It was hard for me to give up my plans. I had studied medicine for four years and had grown accustomed to the thought that I was going to work among the peasants.

"On considering this question, and hearing the stories that others had to tell, I became convinced that it was not a question of my own personality, or the conditions of a given locality, but of conditions in general, namely, the absence of political freedom in Russia.

"I had already received more than one invitation from the organisation Land and Freedom, to become one of its members, and to work among the intelligentsia. But as I always clung fast to a decision once made, I did not accept these invitations, and stayed in the village as long as there was any possibility of my doing so. Thus, not vacillation but bitter necessity forced me to give up my original views and to set out on another course.

"At that time individual opinions had begun to arise to the effect that the political element was to play an important rôle in the problems of the revolutionary party. Two opposing divisions grew up in the society Land and Freedom, and pulled in opposite directions. When I had come to the end of my attempts in the country, I notified the organisation that I now considered myself free.

"At that time two courses were open to me: I could either take a step backwards, go abroad and become a physician—

no longer for the peasants, to be sure, but for wealthy people—which I did not wish to do, or I could choose the other course, which I preferred: employ my energy and strength in breaking down that obstacle which had thwarted my desires. After entering Land and Freedom, I was invited to attend the conference at Voronezh, where there took place no immediate split in the party, but where the position of each member was more or less clearly defined. Some said that we must carry on our work on the old basis, that is, live in the village and organise a popular insurrection in some definite locality; others believed that it was necessary to live in the city and direct our efforts against the imperial authority.

"From Voronezh I went to St. Petersburg, where shortly afterwards Land and Freedom broke up, and I received and accepted an invitation to become a member of the Executive Committee of The Will of the People. My previous experience had led me to the conviction that the only course by which the existing order of things might be changed was a course of violence. Peaceful methods had been forbidden me; we had of course no free press, so that it was impossible to think of propagating ideas by means of the printed word. If any organ of society had pointed out to me another course than violence, I might have chosen it, at least, I would have tried it. But I had seen no protest either from the Zemstvo, or from the courts, or from any institutions whatsoever; neither had literature exerted any influence to change the life which we were leading, and so I concluded that the only escape from the position in which we found ourselves, lay in militant resistance.

"Having once taken this position, I maintained my course to the end. I had always required logical and harmonious agreement of word and action from others, and so, of course, from myself; and it seemed to me that if I admitted theoretically that only through violence could we accomplish anything, I was in duty bound to take active part in whatever programme of violence might be undertaken by the organisation which I had joined. Many things forced me to take this attitude. I could not with a quiet conscience urge others to take part in acts of violence if I myself did not do so; only personal participation could give me the right to approach other people with various proposals. The organisation really preferred to use me for other purposes, for propaganda among the intelligentsia, but I desired and demanded a different rôle. I knew that the court would always take cognisanse of whether or not I had an immediate part in our work, and that the only public opinion which is permitted to express itself freely, always descends with especial rancour upon those who take immediate part in acts of violence. And so I considered it nothing short of baseness to thrust others into a course which I myself did not enter.

"This is the explanation of that 'bloodthirst,' which must seem so terrible and incomprehensible, and which is expressed in those acts, the very enumeration of which would seem cynical to the court, had they not proceeded from motives which at all events do not seem to be dishonourable.

"The most essential part of the programme in accordance with which I worked, and which had the greatest significance for me, was the annihilation of the autocratic form of government. I really ascribe no practical importance to the question whether our programme advocates a republic or a constitutional monarchy. We may dream of a republic, but only that form of government will be realised for which society proves itself ready—and so this question has no special meaning for me. I consider it most important, most essential, that such conditions should be established as will allow the individual to develop his abilities to the fullest extent, and to devote them wholeheartedly to the good of society. And it seems to me that under our present order, such conditions do not exist."

When I had finished, the president asked gently, "Have you said all that you wish to say?"

"Yes," I replied.

And no earthly power could have urged me to speak further, so great was my agitation and weariness.

The sympathetic glances, handshakes and congratulations of my comrades and defenders at the end of my speech, and in the following intermission, convinced me that my address had produced an impression.

The Minister of Justice, Nabokov, who had attended this session and had noticed that Attorney Leontyev had made a stenographic report of the speech, approached him after the session and asked him to give him a copy of it.

My last duty had been fulfilled, and a great peace descended on my spirit. They say that a similar blissful state of serenity precedes death. The past, with its burning experience in the construction and destruction of social ideals and aims, with its agitating impressions of people of opposite types, some astonishing one with their courage, some driving one to despair by their shameful cowardice, everything which I had lived through in life's kaleidoscope of the base and the noble, everything withdrew to some remote distance. The curtain fell for the last time on the tragedy which I had lived through to the last act. Yes, the past withdrew, but the future, the threatening future, which tore one away from life and humanity, had not yet come. There was a breathing space, when the alarming, eventful period of life had been completed, while the dead years of the future had not yet revealed themselves even in anticipation. And I breathed freely. The cycle of my service to an idea, with all the recollections which poisoned it, was completed, as the cycle of life seems to be completed to the person who is dying. And was I not in fact dying? Is not civil and political death, to a person who has devoted himself to social activity, the same as physical death to a person living a private life? And as one may experience a feeling of blissful serenity at one's physical death, I had a similar feeling on looking back over my life, knowing that I had made every effort, had done all that was possible, and that if I had received anything from society and from life, I had also given to society and to life all that I could give.

I had outlived my spiritual and physical forces—there was nothing left—even my will to live had vanished. And at the time when I was overwhelmed by a feeling of liberation from my duty to my native land, to society and my party, I became only a human being, the daughter of my mother, the sister of my sister, who were the only persons that remained to me in the midst of the social ruin.

I felt like one who has been grievously wounded. The knife of the surgeon has long hung threateningly over him. But now the operation has been performed, it is finished; he is taken from the operating table, the anesthetic has worn off, and he rests in the clean, cool, white bed. They have cut off an arm, they have cut off a leg, but all the fear and the danger are behind, there is no pain now, and he is happy, unconscious of the boundless misfortune which awaits him, and which will at any moment knock at his door.

The sentence ran: capital punishment by hanging for me and seven of my comrades, six of whom were army officers.

When the trial was over and I had returned to my cell, the superintendent of the jail, a retired naval officer, came to me and said:

"The army officers who have been condemned to death, have decided to appeal for a commutation of the sentence. But Baron Stromberg is undecided, and he wants to know what you think he ought to do: shall he, in view of his comrades' desire, also make an appeal, or shall he refuse to join them in their action?"

"Tell Stromberg," I replied, "that I would never advise another person to do a thing which I myself would not do under similar circumstances."

The superintendent looked at me reproachfully.

"How cruel you are!" he said.

TEN DAYS

My mother and sister came to see me on the Sunday after the trial. I did not suspect that I was seeing them for the last time.

"My mother hoped to see my face once more,
  And so she turned, and so she went away;
  My sister lingered at the open door
  To speak with eyes the words she could not say." [39]

It was painful to sustain that long, sorrowful gaze. Did she know, or did she only have a premonition, that this was our

[39] From a poem by Vera Figner.—*Translator.*

last meeting? A moment more and I could not have endured it, but the door closed heavily, and forever.

On Monday, about one o'clock, I was finishing my lunch— they had brought me a small partridge, a duchesse pear, and a box of sweets—when the inspectress hurried in with the words, "They have come for you!" Ten minutes later I had gathered together my belongings, and the cab was taking me back to the Fortress of Peter and Paul.

There I once more found myself in number 43. I was very thirsty. "Please make some tea," I said to the guard, "and bring me the box of sweets from my things."

It grew quiet in the corridor; the gendarmes did not come back. Expectantly I lay down on the cot and fell into a sound, sweet, sleep. I think that I had never yet slept so soundly, so sweetly during the term of my imprisonment.

Perhaps I dreamt that I was again with my mother, and that, seeking a caress from her, I said, as I had said so often before, "How charming, how interesting you are, mother dear. One could fall in love with you!" Or did I dream that my sister had brought me a bunch of tea roses, still more tender and fragrant than those others?

The lock grated, and before I had time to spring up, the stout, rude officer Yakovlev stood in my cell, accompanied by a gendarme and a soldier from the Fortress. Without giving me a moment to collect myself, he began to read the document which he held in his hands.

I did not understand a word, I could not. The sweet slumber had enchained my body and my consciousness. What was it? What were those words, that strange, disjointed enumeration: "Shoes, a linen kerchief thirty inches square, a tin cup, five thousand blows of the rod. . . ." I did not understand a word!

"Wait a moment," I said with difficulty, covering my eyes with my hand, "I was asleep, and cannot seem to wake up; come back a little later."

A quarter of an hour later the officer returned; again he read the paper. I understood.

"Go into the other cell," said the gendarme.

There was a vacant cell next to mine; it was there that I was usually searched by a woman who came for this special purpose. And she was there now.

I had been wearing an exquisite gown of thin blue material. My mother had brought it to me during the time of the trial. I took it off, and all my other garments; I even took off the holy image with which my mother had blessed me. On the bench there lay a heap of nondescript rags. The woman slipped over me a peasant shirt of harsh grey hemp that had not been washed yet, and a kerchief of the same material, thirty inches square; she wound my legs with coarse linen strips, pushed towards me a pair of huge, clumsy peasant's shoes, and gave me a skirt of grey soldier's cloth. I looked with astonishment at this skirt: it had been eaten all over, not by a moth, but by some large, greedy caterpillar, who had gnawed dozens of long, oval runs. Then she gave me a grey cotton gown with a yellow diamond on the back. The lining was saturated with dirt and grease and sweat; some one had evidently worn it for a long time. The shoulders of the wrapper hung far down on my arms, while the sleeves covered my wrists.

Probably they would have changed these garments for new, had I made a protest. But I did not protest; I was at the mercy of others, and preferred to remain silent.

The ugly metamorphosis was completed, and I returned to number 43, transformed into Cinderella. The change was so sudden, the contrast so vivid, that I was ready to laugh wildly, unnaturally, to laugh at myself, at the blue dress, at the little partridge and the pear.

In my cell also a change had taken place: though this was no goldfish's castle which had been changed into a hut with a broken water trough, still everything was bound to make a strong impression upon me.

The two mattresses which had always lain on the cot, had disappeared; a sack of straw had taken their place. Of the two pillows, only one remained; instead of the blanket, there was an old piece of baize, while the white china cup that had stood on the table had been replaced by a tin one. It was battered, as though it had been purposely mutilated; it was covered with rust, and jagged on the edges; when, in the mornings, they gave me boiling water instead of tea, with black bread and salt, I had to search for a safe place on the rim, so that I might not cut my lips.

The bright serenity which had so comforted me during the last few days departed with the change in my surroundings. My thought gave a feverish start, and began to work rapidly, excitedly. I did not think now of myself and the present, nor of my family and the end that awaited me. My thought for some reason turned to the fate of revolutionary movements in general, in the west and at home; to the continuity of our ideas, and their dissemination from one country to another. Pictures of times long past, of people who had died long ago, awoke in my memory, and my imagination worked as never before. I had no books, but during those days I could not have concentrated my attention on anything outside of myself. They gave me the Gospels to read. At one time in my childhood they had entranced me; now they did not satisfy my mood. The first few days I did not even turn their pages; later, when I had thought all my thoughts, and my excitement had subsided, I read words, phrases, but without comprehending their meaning and significance; the reading was mechanical —I merely began to translate the text at first into French, and then into German.

On Saturdays, Doctor Wilms usually visited all the prisoners in the Peter and Paul Fortress. On this Saturday he also came. He walked along the corridor with Lesnik, the inspector, and carried on a jovial conversation. His deep-toned laugh called forth a muffled echo throughout the long, empty corridor, and it was still rumbling when the gendarme unlocked my cell. His laugh broke off sharply when he caught sight of me; his stern old face with its harsh lines grew long; for almost two years he had attended me, and now for the first time he beheld me after my transformation.

Slightly averting his face, he asked, "How is your health?"

A strange question to ask a person who has been condemned to death!

"All right," I replied.

On the evening of the eighth day I heard in the corridor the sound of doors being opened and shut. Evidently some one was making a tour of the cells. They unlocked mine also. An old general, the commandant of the Fortress, entered with the inspector and various attendants. Raising the document which he held in his hand, he read in a loud, distinct voice, "His Majesty the Emperor has most graciously ordered that your death sentence be commuted to penal servitude for life."

Had I believed, had I expected that they would execute me? Had I prepared myself for it? No, I had not. They had executed Perovskaya after the first of March, and it seems that this first execution of a woman had disturbed and oppressed every one. At that time, the execution of a woman had not yet become a common occurrence, and three years had passed since the execution of Sofia Perovskaya.

But had the sentence remained in force, I should have died with complete self-possession; my mind was prepared for death. I should hardly have been exalted and inspired thereby; I had outlived all my strength, and I should merely have preferred a speedy death on the scaffold to a slow process of dying, the inevitability of which I clearly recognised at that time.

Ten days passed before, on the twelfth of October, they took me away, I knew not whither.

BOOK TWO: WHEN THE CLOCK OF LIFE STOPPED

I

THE FIRST DAY

ON the morning of October 12, 1884, into my cell, which was dim, almost dark at that hour, rushed a "pledged" guard, as they called the retired soldiers, who together with the gendarmes had the supervision of the prisoners in the Fortress of Peter and Paul. He was a most malignant jailer, a white-haired rat, tired of his work, his duties, his responsibility, and of the very prisoners whom he had guarded for decades like a chained dog. Life evidently had not pampered him, and now, old, sick, and embittered, he vented on whomever he could, his grievances against fate.

He was impressed upon my memory from our first meeting. As soon as I was brought into the Fortress, he muttered angrily, just before shutting the door of the cell which I was entering as a novice, "Singing is forbidden here!" I was stunned; I had never thought of singing. "Singing?" I said. "But who would ever think of it?" Indeed, was not my soul full of serious feelings and grave thoughts as I passed within the walls of the Fortress? Would not singing, at such a moment, be a profanation of a place sanctified by the sufferings of many generations?

Now, on October 12, 1884, breaking into my cell while I was still in bed, he testily set down a pair of felt boots on the floor, threw an unlined sheepskin coat on my bed, and hissed angrily, "Get up! Hurry! And dress rather warmly!"

"What is the matter?" I thought. "What are they going to do to me?"

From the very moment of my arrest, I had felt that I no longer belonged to myself. I no longer asked myself, what I was going to do, but what they were going to do to me. Verily, to lose one's freedom means to lose the ownership of one's own body.

"What are they going to do to me? What?" I meditated, while quickly finishing my convict toilet. It was a simple one: rags for leg wrappers, peasant shoes, a filthy, old, moth-eaten skirt, made from soldier's cloth, a prison coat saturated with some one's sweat, and a white linen kerchief for my head. I had had no soap for ten days; nor was a convict allowed a comb, tooth powder or brush.

And all the time—the thought: "What are they going to do to me? Perhaps they will take me to execution?" But then, it was only three days ago that they had informed me of the pardon, and the old warden had solemnly declared: "Hard labour for life." My head had become confused. At the end of two years of absolute solitude, reality had become blurred; the possible and the impossible had strangely changed places, and the impossible now appeared rather possible.

"Well then, maybe they will execute me after all? Or will they execute not me, but my comrades, while I shall be placed alongside of them, that I may witness and live through their experience? Why not, indeed? Did this not happen to Dostoyevsky, and to others? Why should it not be repeated? But then, why did the 'pledged' guard say, 'Dress rather warmly'? Evidently they are going to take me somewhere, to some distant place where it will be cold. But where, then, where? To a large, public square overflowing with people, with a scaffold in the middle? Or to Siberia? Will they put me into a sleigh, between two gendarmes, and shall we gallop to the Kara mines, where I shall find other women, exiled earlier?"

Though it was autumn, and only yesterday there had been no snow on the ground, the felt boots and sheepskin coat insistently pictured in my mind a snow-covered plain, a sleigh, and a troika.

Accompanied by gendarmes I passed through the corridor, and went down the stairway to a room in front of the guardhouse. At the desk stood the warden in his uniform, and near the window, with his back to me, a short and stocky civilian.

"Your hand!" said the warden.

I held out my hand, perplexed. The dark-garbed civilian

at once turned towards me, and for a moment he held my wrist cautiously, as a physician feels one's pulse. "What does it mean?" I thought. "It is probably the assistant surgeon. What is he here for? Why my pulse? Is there something ahead of me that will cause me to faint?" A dark, improbable idea flashed through my head. I felt my heart beating more and more slowly in my breast. I summoned all my strength.

Meanwhile the supposed surgeon turned again to the window, with his back to me. And again the warden said, "Your hands!"

At the same moment the dark-garbed creature faced me squarely, a chain in his hands. My fear of the unknown gave way to fury at the actual. Uncontrollable rage gripped me. "What! Upon me, a free individual, they are putting a chain, the emblem of slavery! With this chain they wish to fetter my thought, my will!" All my blood stopped flowing, trembling with anger I stamped my foot, and while they chained my hands I addressed the warden with vehemence:

"Tell my mother! Tell her that no matter what they do to me, I shall remain the same!"

"All right, all right," muttered the warden, almost frightened.

"And tell her not to grieve. If there are books, and if only I get some news of her, that is all I want."

"All right, I will tell her everything," muttered the warden in confusion.

We passed between rows of soldiers standing at attention in the guardhouse, and came out into a little court. A carriage guarded by two armed gendarmes, wearing overcoats, stood on the other side of the iron gate which separated the Trubetzkoy Bastion from the Fortress square. While taking a few steps needed to reach the carriage, I noticed one of the guards, the most jovial and kindly fellow of them all. He was small of stature, with a coppery red face covered with a reddish growth, and a large scar on his left cheek, which ran past the eye up to the temple. He used always to gaze at me amiably, and to smile. He seemed to be saying, "Ah, little lady! I see you're growing thin, growing pale all the time. Do stop

it! Upon my word, there is some joy in life." I would feel
relieved in my solitude.

Now he had evidently planned to meet me; his face was
serious and sad. Our eyes met, and a lump came into my
throat. The kindly chap looked at me with such compassion.
"Oh, don't weep, don't think of weeping, Vera! To burst into
tears at such a moment would be sheer disgrace," I kept on
arguing to myself. But how moved I was, how moved. I carried his glance with me into my living grave, and there it served
to comfort me: a simple-hearted Russian, a little soldier who
conscientiously guarded me—his soul was with me, he sympathised with me, pitied me. He was the last and only person
to see me off—and with a caress—to my new life, dark as
the night.

"Where are they taking me?" I asked the warden, when we
were seated in the carriage.

"I do not know," he answered.

From the Fortress we turned to the right, along the quay of
the Neva. The minutes seemed like hours. When the carriage
finally stopped and we came out, I faced a small gangplank
and a steamer, on which not a soul was to be seen. The gendarmes caught hold of me and almost carried me to the deck.
Then I was taken down into a cabin with carefully curtained
windows. The steamer started, and moved on and on.

Two or three hours later an officer came and asked whether
I wanted something to eat.

"No!"

Again he came. This time he asked whether I wanted some
tea.

I answered sternly, "No."

Let him not come near. Let him not ask questions. I wanted
to be silent. I must be silent. During the twenty months of
complete solitude, when I could speak only once in two weeks,
at the twenty-minute meetings with my mother and sister, my
poor voice had changed so; it had become so thin, so pitiful
and ringing. It had a treacherous sound—it betrayed me.

The steamer moved on and on, carrying me off into the unknown. At first I thought that perhaps they were taking me

to some isolated harbour, thence to proceed by railway or in a horse cart. Perhaps to Keksholm? I had heard of this fortress in Finland. Or maybe to Schlüsselburg? At the Fortress of Peter and Paul I had read in some book or other, that a prison which would hold forty persons had been erected there for the members of The Will of the People. At the trial one of our comrades had shouted, "All of us are off for Schlüsselburg!"

In about five hours the steamer reached land. There was a stir among the gendarmes, and they commanded me to go up on deck. There they seized my arms, swiftly and firmly as though in iron vises, carried me down to the shore and led me forward. In front of me loomed white walls and white towers made of limestone. Way up on a tall spire shone a golden key. There remained no doubt—it was Schlüsselburg. And the key rising to the sky, like an emblem, seemed to say that there would be *no coming out*. The two-headed eagle spread its wings, brooding over the entrance into the Fortress, above which a weather-beaten sign bore the word: "Imperial." There was something vindictive, personal in this word, and it stung me painfully.

Accompanied by a whole crowd of people, whom I much later realised to have been officers, gendarmes, and soldiers, I passed through the gates. And then I saw something quite unexpected. The place was idyllic. A summer villa? An agricultural colony? Something of the sort—quiet and simple. To the left there was a white two-story building, that might have been a girls' boarding school, but really was a barrack. To the right stood several single houses, so white and nice, each one with a little garden, while in the space between spread a vast lawn with shrubs and clusters of trees. The leaves had already fallen, but how splendid it must be here in the summer with everything green all around! At the very end one could see a white church surmounted with a golden cross. It spoke of something peaceful, quiet; it called to mind one's native village.

On and on moved the crowd, and soon I saw a two-story red brick building, with dingy windows and two tall chimneys on the roof—a typical factory. Iron gates, painted red, stood wide open in a red brick wall in front of the building, and through them the crowd swept me along and brought me up on a porch which looked almost amiable. Through a corridor we entered a rather spacious vaulted room—the office. A bathtub stood in one corner.

"Your hands!" said the warden.

I held them out, and after fussing a bit, he unlocked the chain and had it removed. Everybody left, except myself, a young man in the uniform of a military doctor, and a middle-aged woman, who had suddenly made her appearance, and who had the physiognomy and manners of a housekeeper in charge of a "respectable" house.

Then the doctor sat down by the table, with his back to me, and the woman began to undress me.

In a few minutes I stood naked.

Did I suffer? No.

Was I ashamed? No.

I felt—indifferent. My soul flew off somewhere, or rather it retreated and shrunk into a tiny lump. There was left only my body, which knew neither shame nor moral pain.

The doctor rose, walked around me, and noted down something. Then he left.

They had brought me here, to stay forever. I was never to leave this place, and yet, it was necessary to strip me naked, it was necessary to write down in a book whether I had any special marks on my body or not.

Four years before they had treated my sister, Evgenia, in the same way after her trial. When Count D. Tolstoy, Minister of the Interior, had an interview with me following my arrest, I indignantly related this to him.

"That is malfeasance," he said. "That must not occur."

And now, in spite of that—perhaps for the very reason that I had been indignant—they had subjected me to the same treatment. And I did not protest, did not scream. I did not scratch or bite.

When in our childhood we read of ancient Rome, how, for the amusement of the mob, the Cæsars had young Christian maidens brought into the arena, and then let lions loose upon them—

St. Petersburg, 1884
(before entering Schlüsselburg)

Nizhmi-Novgorod, 1906
(after her release)

what did we learn from our reading? That those women did
not scream, did not resist.

But I, too, had my God, my religion: the religion of liberty,
equality, and fraternity. And for the glory of that doctrine
I was bound to endure everything.

After the bath, which I had to take, probably in order to
let them find out whether I had anything concealed, the woman
disappeared, and I was led upstairs.

The two stories of the prison were separated by nothing save
a netting, and a narrow walk which ran like a balcony along the
row of cells on the upper story. Owing to this arrangement,
one could see at once the whole interior of the prison, all the
forty iron doors of the cells.

The rope net was divided in the middle by a narrow bridge,
which led to Cell 26. "The bridge of sighs," I thought, as I
was being led across it. I recalled the palace of the Venetian
doges, where the bridge of that name was the only road over
which the rebels of Venice walked from their cells to the block.
The Schlüsselburg bridge of sighs I crossed every day for
many, many years. I was locked up in Number 26. The door
slammed, and I dropped, exhausted, on my cot.

A new life began. A life amidst deathly stillness, that stillness to which you always listen and which you hear; the stillness which little by little overpowers you, envelops you, pene-
trates into all the pores of your body, into your reason, your
very soul. How dreadful it is in its dumbness, how terrible it
is in its soundlessness and in its chance interruptions. Gradually there steals from it to you the sense that some mystery
is close at hand; everything becomes unusual, puzzling, as on
a moonlit night, in solitude, in the shadow of a still forest.
Everything is mysterious, incomprehensible. In this stillness
the real becomes vague and unreal, and the imaginary seems
real. Everything is tangled up, confused. The long grey day,
wearying in its idleness, resembles a sleep without dreams; and
at night you have such bright and glowing dreams that you
have continually to assure yourself that they are only the

fruit of your imagination. You live in such a way that dream seems life, and life, a dream.

And the sounds! Accursed sounds which suddenly and unexpectedly break in upon you, frighten you, and vanish. Somewhere begins a loud hissing, as though an enormous snake were creeping from under the floor, to enwrap you in its cold, slippery coils. But it is only water hissing somewhere below, in the pipes. You imagine people immured within stony sacks. You hear a very soft, suppressed groan, and it seems as though some one were suffocating beneath a heap of stones. But no! It is only the faint, very faint, dry cough of a tubercular prisoner. If a dish clatters somewhere, or the metal leg of a cot drops on the floor, your imagination pictures men rattling their chains and fetters.

What, then, is real here? What is actually here, and what is nonexisting? It is still and quiet as in a grave, when suddenly you hear a light rustling at the door—the gendarme has looked into the peephole and has covered it with the slide. It seems as if the wire of an electric battery were stretched from there. The current has touched your body for a minute, and the shock runs through your frame and strikes your hands and feet; fine needles plunge into the ends of your fingers, and your whole body, your foolish, silly body, after one violent shock, keeps trembling long and painfully. It fears something, and your heart quivers, and refuses to lie still.

And the dreams by night! Those mad dreams! You see flights, pursuits, gendarmes, fusillades, arrests. Somebody is being led to execution. The crowd is agitated and angry; red faces are distorted with malice. But most often you see torture. They torture with hot steam which escapes through hundreds of thin pipes in the wall, the ceiling, the floor; it burns, it beats, it is terrible, and there is no escape from it. The cell is locked, it is empty, quite empty, it is filled only with hot streamlets. Or they torture you with electricity. You sit on a wooden chair, like those they have at the guardhouse, and you cannot rise; some invisible jailer is sending a current through you. Once, twice—you wake up—your nerves all along the arms twitching, or a convulsion has bound the muscles of your leg into a lump as hard as iron.

There is only one sound place in your soul, and it repeats to you:

"Have courage, Vera, and be firm! Remember the Russian people, and how it lives! Recall all the world's unfortunates, recall their crushing toil, life without the light of joy; recall humiliation, hunger, sickness, and poverty.

"Be resolute. Do not weep if your mother has been taken away from you, though they do not inflict such punishment even on an infamous seducer or a greedy murderer. Do not weep over the failures of the struggle, over the comrades who have perished. Do not weep over the ruins that have covered the field of your life!

"Do not fear. Do not fear. In this mysterious stillness, behind these deaf stones your friends are invisibly present. It is not you alone who are oppressed here; they too are suffering. Think of them. They are invisible, but they are here. You do not hear them, but they are here. They watch over you and guard you, like disembodied spirits. Nothing will happen, nothing will happen. You are not alone, you are not alone!"

II

THE FIRST YEARS

WE had been deprived of everything: of our native land and
humanity; of our friends, our comrades and families; we were
cut off from every living person and thing. The opaque panes
of the double windows dimmed the light of the day, and the
Fortress walls shut out the far horizon, the fields and hamlets.
Of all the world they had left us but a prison courtyard, and
of the broad expanse of the heavens, just the little strip of sky
that hung over the narrow, cramped enclosure where we took
our walks. And of all people, only gendarmes remained, and
for us they were as deaf as statues, and their faces as immobile
as masks.

Life flowed on, without impressions or contacts. Though
complex in its inner experiences, it was outwardly so im-
measurably barren, so simplified, almost transparent, that it
seemed like a dreamless sleep; while dreams, in which there was
movement and a shifting of faces and colors, appeared as
reality. Day after day, week after week, month after month
went by. Confused and vague they piled up, one upon another
like photographic negatives, indistinct in outline, exposed on
a cloudy day.

There was no clock, but we knew when the outside guards
were relieved. With heavy, measured steps they would walk
around the prison and pass on up to the high wall where the
sentinels stood. My cell, which was white at first, was soon
transformed into a gloomy box. The asphalt floor was painted
with a black oil paint; the upper walls, with gray, and the
lower walls, almost to the height of a man's head, with a very
dark lead color. Every one who entered one of these repainted
cells, said to himself, "This is a coffin!"

Indeed, the whole interior of the prison was like a tomb.
Once, when I had committed some offence, and they were leading me down to the punitive cells, I saw it as it looked at night,

with its lights burning. Small lamps hanging on the walls illuminated the two floors of the building, which were separated only by a narrow balcony and the net. These lights flamed like those ever-burning little lamps in the small shrines of a churchyard. And the forty tightly closed doors behind which prisoners were pining in loneliness, looked like a row of coffins standing upright.

Mystery and uncertainty enveloped us. We were not allowed to see any one, or to correspond with our relatives. No word of any kind was allowed to reach us, nor were we permitted to send messages to any one. News of every kind was withheld from us, and no one was permitted to know where we were, or how life went with us.

"You will hear from your daughter when she is in her grave," remarked Assistant-Minister of the Interior Orzhevsky to my mother in answer to her inquiry about me.

Our very names were to sink into oblivion. Instead of using our surnames, they identified us by numbers as though we were books, or things owned by the state. We knew nothing of the region surrounding the Fortress; we had never seen it. The building in which we were made to live was a mystery to us. We could not walk through it and examine it. The prisoners who lived within it under one roof, but separated by thick stone walls, were strangers to each other. Everything familiar and customary, everything near and dear and comprehensible, disappeared; and the unfamiliar, the strange, the foreign, and the incomprehensible remained. And over us all there brooded an oppressive silence, not the silence of the living that rests the nerves. No, this was the silence of the dead, that eerie stillness which clutches at one's heart when one remains for a long time at the side of a corpse. And days would pass, one like the other, and nights would come, one like the other. The months came and went; a year came and went, the first year; and the year was like one day and one night.

Prisoners brought to Schlüsselburg were not expected to live long. During the very first years, fifteen of them died. Minakev and Myshkin were shot for making a protest; Klimenko hanged himself; Grachevsky burned himself to death; while Yuvachev, Shchedrin, and Konashevich, went insane. Shebalin was mentally unbalanced for a time, but regained his sanity. In later years, Yurkovsky died, and Pokhitonov went insane and died. In the eighth year of our imprisonment, Sofia Ginsburg cut her throat. She could not bear more than one month of the isolation that we had endured for years. Even prisoners discharged from Schlüsselburg found it impossible to go on living. Yanovich and Martynov shot themselves while in Siberia; Polivanov committed suicide abroad. Their Schlüsselburg experiences had dried up all their vital forces; they had lost all their ability to resist life's mishaps and misfortunes; they had no reserve force on which to live.

My own spirit was stifled and crushed during these years. And whom would Schlüsselburg not stifle and crush? What comforting thought had we, members of The Will of the People, brought with us to Schlüsselburg? The revolutionary movement had been defeated, its organisation destroyed, and the Executive Committee had perished to the very last member. The people and society had not supported us. We were alone. The noose of autocracy had been drawn more tightly, and we, passing out of the life of the world, had left no heirs to carry on the struggle which we had begun.

Schlüsselburg gave me something, however, which I had not foreseen, for which I had not prepared myself. The very last joy in my life had been my mother, and they took her away from me—the only person in the world who made life real and worth living, the only one to whom I, fallen into the depths of the abyss, could cling. Joy died within me, but, dying, left behind it a keen and bitter grief. While I was free, I had not lived with my mother, and had thought of her only occasionally. But then I had had my country to think of; my revolutionary activities occupied my mind; there were strong attachments and friendships; there were my comrades. And now there was no one, nothing. And my mother, that final loss, the loss of the very last thing dear to me, became, as it were, the symbol of all my losses, large and small; of all my deprivations, both great and petty.

Never did I regret that I had chosen the path that had led me to this place. It was *my will* that had chosen that path—there could be no regret. Never once did I regret the fact that I was deprived of delicate underclothing and fine garments, wearing instead a coarse rag and a convict's gown with a brand on the back. I did not regret but I suffered. Only the thought of my mother filled my mind—her image and no other, and my overwhelming grief at being separated from her. But that grief absorbed and included all of my sufferings, all of my griefs; the grief of my crushed and wounded spirit, and the grief of my oppressed and humiliated body. And thus, symbolised in the loss of my mother, it assumed the caustic bitterness of all my losses, all my deprivations, and became vast and uncontrollable, as do all feelings which are never freely expressed but lie hidden in the dark depths of the subconscious. Destruction threatened my darkened mind.

But when one step more would have carried me to a point beyond all chance of recovery, an inner voice said, "Stop!" It was not my fear of death that spoke. Death was quite desirable; it was linked with the idea of martyrdom, which in my childhood Christian traditions had taught me to regard as sacred; while later the history of the struggle for the rights of the oppressed had strengthened this idea in me. It was the fear of insanity, that degradation of the individual, the degeneracy of his spirit and flesh, that halted me. But to stop at this point meant an effort to regain a normal outlook on life, to become again spiritually whole. My friends helped me to do this.

A dim light began to dawn in me, like the little flames of the wax candles on Palm Sunday. The dumb walls of Schlüsselburg began to speak; I was able to communicate with my friends.[40] They spoke tenderly, sent me loving messages, and Schlüsselburg's icy crust melted in the warmth of their affection. Other influences were brought to bear, stern words, lessons. Once my neighbour, a man whom I had not known before, asked me what I was doing.

[40] A reference to the system of communicating messages by tapping on the walls.—*Translator.*

"I am thinking of my mother and weeping," I replied.

My neighbour rebuked me in strong terms. He asked me
if I had ever read the *Memoirs of Simon Meyer*, the Com-
munard, and I remembered the scene on board ship, when the
ship was rolling badly, and they began to shave the heads of
the Communards. He put before me as an example this Simon
Meyer, one of many thousands of Communards. He read me
a lecture. I was startled and hurt and angry. I had read the
Memoirs of Simon Meyer, and I remembered the scene on board
ship, and many others. "Why this sermon?" thought I. "I
don't need his sermons!"

But that was precisely what I did need. If my neighbour
had sympathised with me, had begun to console me tenderly,
his words would have been of no avail; they would have coincided with my mood. But he censured me in no uncertain
terms; he showed me plainly what my duty was, and he vexed
me. And this vexation was salutary; it was in contrast with
my customary frame of mind, shattered it, made it incongruous.
In solitude a trifle sometimes grows to unwonted dimensions; it
sticks in your consciousness, and will not be dislodged. So it
was in this case. I could not get my neighbour's words out of
my mind. The wall between us every day reminded me of our
conversation; and each time I recalled it with an unpleasant
feeling of irritation and annoyance. In this way my grief
and longing were interrupted, and the annoyance served a
useful purpose.

But there was something else, infinitely greater, which raised
me out of my depths.

The trial had been the last, conclusive act of the revolutionary drama in which I had taken part. My social activity had
ended there. After receiving my sentence, I had felt myself
no longer a public character but only a human being. The
strain under which I had lived during the years of freedom,
and while awaiting the trial, which had heretofore been subdued
and repressed, now collapsed; there was no task for my will,
and the human being awoke within me. This human being
might now suffer without check or self-control, and thus yield
to the onslaughts of sickness and death. I forgot that once

having undertaken a public career I could not again be just a human being; that I was both more and less than a human being, and that the public task I had chosen was not yet solved. The fact that we as a revolutionary body had inscribed the name of The Will of the People on the history of our time, and that Schlüsselburg, the Russian Bastile, would play its part in the minds of our contemporaries, and cover us with its glory, never occurred to me, or to my friends. We were too humble to imagine it. But in the fifth year of my imprisonment, after a hunger strike which had ended unsuccessfully and before the set time, when I came nearer death than ever before in my life, and longed to die, but was forced to live in spite of myself; when my spirit was full of despair and disappointment, and my nerves utterly shattered, I heard these words, spoken by one of our comrades there, a man more gifted than any of us. He was speaking not to me, but about me, and I chanced to overhear him. He said, "Vera does not belong to her friends alone, she belongs to Russia."

These words raised me to a height that one cannot contemplate, a terrifying height; a height that is oppressive, and imposes obligations above one's strength. But these words, spoken and overheard, placed an ideal before me, an unattainable ideal, but for all that, one to which I was bound to aspire. They gave my will a task: to strive to be worthy, to work on myself, to struggle, and to overcome myself. To strive, to overcome, to conquer myself! To conquer sickness, and madness and death!

But how was I to struggle, how prevail? To prevail meant to disperse the darkness hanging over my spirit, to drive away everything that kept the light from my eyes. That meant to forget. I tried to forget. I drove away recollections; I buried them all in a grave. For ten years I buried them, for ten years I tried to forget. For ten years in my consciousness my mother was dying; and my longing for my native land, for activity and freedom, was dying. Grief was dying, and love too. The snow fell, and covered the past with its white mantle. And I? I was alive. I was well.

III

EXECUTION AND SUICIDE

DURING the first six months after the opening of the Schlüsselburg prison, two executions by firing squad took place. I
have before mentioned Minakov and Myshkin, whom they shot.
Both of these men had had long careers in the revolutionary
movement.

Minakov had been sentenced in 1879, in Odessa. He was
sent into penal servitude at the Kara River [in Siberia], but
after an attempt at escape, was sent back to European Russia,
and imprisoned at first in the Fortress of Peter and Paul, and
later transferred to the Schlüsselburg prison, as soon as it
was rebuilt. Schlüsselburg meant the end of all hopes, and
Minakov did not want to die slowly in this new Bastile, "to rot
like a block dropped into the mire," as he expressed it in one
of his poems. He demanded the right to correspond with his
relatives, and to receive visits from them, asked for books and
tobacco, went on a hunger strike, and finally struck Zarkevich,
the prison physician, in the face. Minakov suffered from taste
hallucinations, and he suspected the physician of mixing poison
with his food, with the purpose of killing him. It was revolting
that a man of abnormal mind should have been turned over to
the court-martial and shot within twenty-four hours. Minakov
refused to ask for clemency.

That was in September, 1884, a month before my comrades
in the Trial of the Fourteen and myself were brought to the
Fortress. In December, on Christmas Day, the whole prison
was shocked by a scene that took place in one of the cells. As
our suppers were brought to us, we heard the crash of metal
dishes falling on the floor, sounds of scuffling, and a nervous,
half-strangled voice crying, "Don't beat me! Don't! Kill
me, but don't beat me!" This was Myshkin, one of the longest-
suffering figures of the Russian revolutionary movement. He

had been a burgher of Moscow, and ran a small printing press
in the Arbat district. The compositors were intelligent young
people. All of the workers, together with Myshkin, lived in
a friendly, communal group in the same house where the
printing press was located. Myshkin was a socialist, and had
connections with those who were preparing to join the Populist
movement. They began to print illegal publications. The
police discovered that illegal work was being carried on in the
printing shop; a search was made, and the workers were arrested. However, they succeeded in warning Myshkin; he escaped and went abroad. There he conceived the plan of going
to Siberia and liberating Chernyshevsky [41] single-handed. In the
guise of an officer of gendarmes he appeared at the town of
Viluysk, where Chernyshevsky was held, and presented to the
chief of police a forged order from the Third Division,[42] to
turn Chernyshevsky over to him for the purpose of conducting
him to St. Petersburg. But the chief of police became suspicious, suggested to Myshkin that he go to Yakutsk to see
the governor, and sent with him two Cossacks, ostensibly as
bodyguards. Myshkin saw that the game was up, and decided
to get rid of his companions; near Yakutsk he shot one of
them, but the other succeeded in making his escape.

Myshkin was caught, sent to St. Petersburg, and stood trial
in the Trial of 193. The defendants at that trial decided to
appoint one speaker, and to entrust to him the task of deliver-
ing the revolutionary speech, composed by all of them. The
choice fell on Myshkin, and he fulfilled his duty with all possible energy and ardour. Myshkin, who had already been imprisoned three years before coming to trial, was sentenced to
ten years of penal servitude. From 1878 until 1880, he lived
under horrible conditions in the Kharkov prison, then he was
transferred to Kara. Two years later, several prisoners escaped from Kara in a body, among them Myshkin; he succeeded in getting as far as Vladivostok, where, in the absence

[41] N. Chernyshevsky, brilliant economist and leader of the radical youth
in the early sixties. He was exiled to Siberia.—*Translator.*
[42] The all-powerful Imperial chancery in charge of political cases.—
Translator.

of proper connections, he was recognised, caught, and sent back to St. Petersburg. He was confined in the Alexey Ravelin, where the members of The Will of the People were slowly dying. There Myshkin attempted several times to instigate a general revolt against its murderous régime, but his proposals met with no sympathy. The Ravelin remained inert. Later all the inmates were transferred to Schlüsselburg.

Myshkin had spent almost ten years in going from one place of torture to another, and now, after all his trials and wanderings, he had fallen into the most hopeless of the Russian Bastiles. This was more than even his sturdy spirit could bear. He decided to die—to insult the prison inspector, and be brought to trial, so that in court he might reveal Schlüsselburg's cruel secret, strip it bare before all Russia, as he thought and at the price of his life purchase an easier lot for his comrades in captivity. On December 25, 1884, he carried out his purpose, and was shot on the same plaza of the old citadel where, three months before, Minakov had been shot.

Through his nearest neighbour, Myshkin had charged his comrades to sustain him by a general protest. But the prison made no sign; it was silent; we were so isolated that his solemn bequest reached only one solitary cell.

After his execution, the Assistant-Minister of the Interior, Orzhevsky, visited the Fortress and made the rounds of all the prisoners. His visit, which was, as we surmised, connected with Myshkin's case, resulted in permission being granted to six of the frailest and most ill among the prisoners, to take walks in pairs. Those who were thus favored were Morozov and Butsevich, who had been transferred from the Ravelin (Butsevich, by the way, died from tuberculosis not long after this) ; Trigoni, and Grachevsky, who set fire to himself and died; and Frolenko and Isayev, the latter of whom was in the first stages of consumption. These walks in pairs were the first breach in our stony grave. Up to this time, although the prison rules which hung on the wall spoke of walks with a companion as being a reward for good conduct, this privilege had remained a dead letter. And yet, after Orzhevsky's visit, the privilege was not extended further; during the entire year of

1885, no one received it except the six mentioned above, and substitutes appointed to take the place of those who had died. Such was the will of the inspector; our conduct had evidently not been "good."

In the autumn of the year 1887, M. F. Grachevsky, my comrade on the Executive Committee, died a cruel death.

In his early youth he had engaged in social work, later joining the Tchaikovsky group in St. Petersburg. Twice arrested and imprisoned, he was at length exiled to the province of Archangel, whence he later succeeded in escaping, and returned to St. Petersburg, where he joined the newly organised Will of the People. He later became a member of the Executive Committee of this organisation. In 1882 he was arrested and tried for his activities in organising and managing a laboratory for the manufacture of explosives. He was condemned to death, but his sentence was commuted to penal servitude for life, and he was imprisoned, first in the Ravelin, and later in Schüsselburg.

Here, in Schlüsselburg, he waged indignant and unceasing warfare against the prison administration, for its petty and arbitrary acts of malice. In 1886 he even went on a hunger-strike and fasted for eighteen days. Inspector Sokolov, to conceal this fact from us, had him removed to the old prison, and there, in desperation, Grachevsky wrote a letter of protest and appeal to the Police Department. Naturally the letter never reached its destination, and Grachevsky was deprived of pen and paper, and also of sedatives, as punishment for his rebellion.

At last he could endure it no longer. He resolved to commit an act of violence that would bring him before the court-martial, at which he could testify as to the inhuman régime in Schlüsselburg. He struck the prison doctor, and was removed to the old Fortress, pending his punishment. The months dragged on, but no trial was given to Grachevsky. Having lost all hope for action along the lines he had previously purposed, and despairing of ever appearing in court (they did not grant him this privilege on the pretext that he was mentally unbalanced), but desiring at any cost to make public all the sufferings and abuses that he and his comrades had endured, he carried out a plan formed earlier, and on October 24, 1887, poured over his body kerosene from the big lamp that lighted the cell and burned himself to death.

Three days later General Petrov visited Schlüsselburg, and shortly afterwards Inspector Sokolov disappeared; he was discharged for *neglect of duty*. The sacrifice bore fruit, and a break occurred in our prison life. The dead did not come to life, but the living began to breathe more freely. Schlüsselburg remained, but Malyuta Skuratov [43] was gone.

After Sokolov's removal in 1887, for a full six months there was an interregnum in the prison. For some reason they did not appoint a new inspector. Possibly there was some doubt as to just the sort of person who should replace Sokolov. At last, in April, Fedorov, the newly-appointed inspector, arrived. He was an annoying old fellow, as we learned in time, but not harsh, a great stickler for discipline, and a tale-bearer.

[43] Malyuta Skuratov was the chief executioner under Ivan the Terrible. —*Translator.*

IV

I ACQUIRE A FRIEND

EARLY in January, 1886, knowing that Ludmila Alexandrovna Volkenstein, one of my co-defendants in the Trial of 14, was also in the Fortress, I asked the inspector why they did not permit me to take my walks in company with one of the other prisoners. The inspector was silent for a moment, and then said, "We can grant you this privilege, only you mustn't. . . ." He bent his forefinger and tapped on the door jamb, imitating our fashion of carrying on conversations by tapping on the wall. I replied that I did very little tapping.

The interview went no further, and I was left in solitude as before. But on January 14, when they took me out for my walk, and the door into the little enclosure which we called "the first cage," opened, I beheld an unexpected figure in a short cloth coat, with a linen handkerchief on her head, who swiftly embraced me, and I recognised with difficulty my comrade Volkenstein. Probably she also was as shocked by the change in my appearance, due to my convict garb. And so we stood, embracing one another, and not knowing whether to rejoice or to weep.

Up to this time I had seen Volkenstein only during the trial. We had not met previously, and had known each other only by hearsay. Ludmila Alexandrovna's sincerity, her simplicity and warm-heartedness at once enchanted me. It did not require much time for us to form such a friendship as was possible only under the conditions under which we were living. We were like people shipwrecked on an uninhabited island. We had nothing and no one in all the world save each other. Not only people, but nature, colors, sounds, were gone, all of them. And instead there was left a gloomy vault with a row of mysterious, walled-in cells, in which invisible captives were pining; an ominous silence, and the atmosphere of violence, madness and death. One can see plainly that in such surroundings two friendly spirits must needs find joy in each other's company, and ever afterwards treasure a most touching remembrance of the association.

Any one who has been in prison knows the influence that the sympathetic tenderness of a comrade has on one's life while in confinement. In Polivanov's memoirs of his imprisonment in the Alexey Ravelin, there is a touching picture of Kolodkevich, hobbling up to the wall on crutches to console him with a few tender words. A brief conversation through the soulless stone that separated the two captives, who were dying from scurvy and loneliness, was their only joy and support. The author of the memoirs confessed that more than once Kolodkevich's kind words saved him from acute attacks of melancholy, which were tempting him to commit suicide. And indeed, loving sympathy works veritable wonders in prison; and were it not for those light tappings on the wall, which destroy the stone barrier separating man from man, the prisoner could not preserve his life or his soul. Good reason was there for the struggle to maintain the system of tappings, the very first struggle that a captive wages with the prison officials; it is an out-and-out struggle for existence, and every one who is walled up in a cell clutches at this device as at a straw. But when those sentenced to solitary confinement are permitted to meet their co-prisoners face to face, and to replace the symbolic tapping with living speech, then the warm-heartedness and kindness expressed in the tones of the voice, in an affectionate glance, and a friendly handshake, bring joy unknown to one who has never lost his freedom.

I do not know what I gave to Ludmila Alexandrovna, but she was my comfort, my joy and happiness. My nerves and general constitution had been completely unstrung. I was physically weak, and spiritually exhausted. My general state of mind was entirely abnormal; and lo! I found a friend whom prison conditions had not affected so profoundly and painfully as they had me; and this friend was the personification of tenderness, kindness, and humaneness. All the treasures of her loving spirit she gave to me with a generous hand. No

matter how gloomy my mood when we met, she always knew
how to dispel it in one way or another, and how to console me.
Her smile alone, and the sight of her dear face dispelled my
grief, and gladdened my heart. After a walk with her I would
come away reassured and transformed; my cell did not seem
so gloomy to me, nor life so hard to bear. Straightway I
would begin to dream of our next meeting. We saw each other
every other day; prison discipline evidently found it necessary
to dilute the joy of our meetings by making us pass a day in
complete solitude. But perhaps this fact only made our longing to see each other more keen, and accentuated our "holiday
mood," which was so pleasant to recall afterwards.

Whenever some misfortune occurred in the prison, such as
the deaths of our comrades, whose groans and death agonies we
distinctly heard within the walls of our prison, which echoed
back sounds with remarkable clearness, we would find each other
pale, agitated, and silent. Trying not to look each other in
the face, we would kiss and embrace, and then, silently, stroll
up and down the little path, or sit on the ground (there were
no benches) with our backs up against the wall, as far away
as possible from the gendarme, who observed our every movement from the summit of his little watch-tower. On such days
the mere fact of being physically near to each other, of being
able to touch the shoulder of a friend, was an immense comfort, and alleviated life's burden. There was one month in the
year 1886 during which Kobylyansky, Isayev, and Ignaty
Ivanov died one after another: the first from scurvy, the second from consumption, while Ivanov died, I think, from both.
Moreover, he was insane.

While Isayev was still on his feet, and taking walks out of
doors, his loud, hoarse cough, which sounded as though it came
from an empty barrel, tore our hearts as we listened. Sometimes they led us out to the same cage that he had occupied
just previously. On the snow, to right and left, one could see
the bright red blood which he had just coughed up. Those
drops of blood which no one had removed, or even covered with
snow, wrung our hearts. They were symbolic of a life that
was wasting away, the life of a comrade, whom no science, no

human power could help. And there was no place to which
we could turn our eyes so as to avoid the sight of them. The
small space within the cage was filled with snow; only a narrow path was left, along which one must perforce walk. It
was revolting, that cruelty, which cynically left the bloody trail
there for the torture and instruction of unwilling visitors, when
a few shovelfuls of snow could have hidden it. In those days
we were not even given shovels. Isayev's last sufferings were
terrible. That was perhaps the worst of the agonies we had
to endure. A little morphine or laudanum would have probably made his struggle with death easier, and spared all of us
suffering. But nothing of the kind was done. There would
be a deathlike stillness in the prison; we would all sit motionless,
tense, and with baited breath listen to the silence.
. . . not a sound . . and then, suddenly, in the midst
of this tense strain, we would hear a groan, more like a wail.
It is hard to stand by and see some one give up his life, but
it is still harder and more terrible to be a passive, entombed
auditor of such a leave-taking. Only in a prison or in an
insane asylum—which corresponds in many ways to a prison—
could such heartrending and terrible things happen.

In the spring they gave Ludmila Alexandrovna and me two
little plots (about nine by two and a half feet each) in the
vegetable garden. The administration had fenced off six
small gardens, which adjoined the high Fortress wall, and extended to within fifteen or twenty feet of the prison itself.
They had brought up on barges loads of earth which they had
bought somewhere at a high price, and had scattered it over the
big garden in mounds.

Our plot proved to be a small, oblong, and most ill-favoured
spot, almost entirely devoid of sunlight. On one side was a
stone wall, on the three remaining sides, a board fence over nine
feet high; there was always something to cut off the sunlight!
And yet, even this well-like space with its four walls seemed
like paradise to us. There was earth there, real earth, the
earth of the fields and the villages, black, crumbly, and cool.
Until this time we had seen only the unfertile space within
the enclosure where we took our walks, dead and stony ground,

unpierced by a single blade of grass. This, of course, was arranged with the purpose of keeping an easier watch over us, to see that we did not communicate with each other by letter, hiding our notes in some clump of green foliage. In the year 1886 they brought up sand from the banks of the river and emptied it into these small courtyards, and put a wooden shovel into each one; "to give the prisoners exercise," so the inspector said. One was supposed to take up the sand on this shovel and throw it about, distributing it from one place to another, and thus increase one's strength. Indeed, those who did not have gardens (for they gave these to very few) used to throw this sand about to kill time; but this became terribly dull, and we dubbed this futile pastime as the work of the French National Workshops of 1848.

When they were assigning a garden, the inspector and the sergeant would lead the prisoner to the place and point out to him one or two beds. Then, still silently, the sergeant would hand him a package of seeds (radishes, carrots, turnips, peas, cabbage, and poppies) and, taking up a pinch of them, he would without speaking show the other what to do. Stooping down to the ground, he would make a little hole with his finger and drop a seed into it, after which he would silently withdraw with the inspector, who had been a witness to all this procedure. The gendarmes were strictly forbidden not only to converse with the prisoners, but in most cases even to give the ordinary, necessary instructions and orders. In case of utmost necessity the sergeant would use signs, and hence, as a joke, we later gave him the nickname of "Pantomime."

When the young plants began to come up, their little green shoots pushing through the ground everywhere, gave us untold satisfaction; and when in summer the flowers bloomed that the gendarmes themselves had planted along the wall, we went into childlike rapture. We longed for the grass, for the fields and meadows, and a tuft of green called forth an utterly unexpected wave of emotions from our starved spirits. Every little blade of grass was dear to us.

I remember how once, coming out into the garden where the day before one of our comrades had been, I found that a young shoot of hops, joyfully flourishing near the wall, was buried under a whole mound of earth that had been thrown upon it. If a mother had seen her child choking under clods of earth, she could not have dashed it away with more anger and exasperation than did I. This was the first time since my arrest that I had been angry, and with whom was I angry? With a comrade! And yet I had thought that in the conditions under which we were living it was impossible to be angry with a comrade, or even to think ill of him.

This was my attitude towards plants; but Ludmila Alexandrovna showed especial tenderness to insects and the few animals that came within the range of our daily life. The sparrows became so tame for her that whole flocks of them would sit on her knees and eat crumbs of bread from her prison gown. Often, when we were walking arm in arm, I would suddenly note that she was going a few steps out of her way, and drawing me aside. Several times I was puzzled at this, but when she explained her reason I could not help laughing, and later being deeply touched. This terrorist had noticed a crawling caterpillar or beetle, and was afraid that she might crush it! It had never entered my head to notice whether or not some little creature was running across our path. When, later, we had raspberry bushes, and a little caterpillar began to eat the foliage, in no way could I persuade my friend to take the destructive creature and drown it in the watering pot. Far better that the raspberry and the whole bush perish—she could not kill a living thing. Another time, her treatment of a bedbug that she found in her cell, and which had probably been brought in by some gendarme, aroused much laughter. Ludmila Alexandrovna carefully wrapped it up in a piece of paper, and took it out with her when she went for her walk, there she carefully released the bedbug from its paper wrappings, and set it at liberty!

Such treatment of animals interested me greatly, and I asked her if she had always felt this way about them. She replied that she had always respected life in all its forms. And with her such an attitude was indeed no temporary prison "sentimentality," but a sincere emotion, completely in harmony with all her loving nature. It would have been difficult to find a person more kind and tender in her relations to people; and during the first years, before the petty struggle with the prison officials had darkened her spirits, this humaneness and warm-heartedness shone with a marvellous radiance. Ludmila Alexandrovna knew life and knew people, and she did not idealise either the one or the other. She took them as they were, a mixture of light and shadows. She loved the light and forgave the shadows. She had the happy ability to find, and never to lose from sight, the good side of a person, and unfalteringly believed in the fundamental goodness that lies hidden in every one. She firmly believed that goodness and love could conquer every evil; that not stern reproofs, or repressions, were the most efficacious means of correction, but kind words, and sympathetic, friendly criticism. A boundless leniency character-ised all of her personal relations. "We must all live and let live," was her favourite proverb.

My own outlook on life was very different from this gentle one of hers, but during the first years of my imprisonment, which were so remote from social strife and that excited atmosphere in which I had lived during my years of liberty, my spirit softened; and my contact with such a noble expression of love, not only for humanity, but also for the individual, wrought a marvellous change in me. I experienced a moral, and at the same time esthetic, pleasure: this was love and beauty, a beauty quite unlike that energy and stern, unyielding will, crushing all things that stand across its path, of which I had seen so many examples during my earlier years. Observing Ludmila Alexandrovna and listening to her words, appreciating her personality, one asked oneself involuntarily how her humaneness and tender-heartedness were to be reconciled with the violence and bloodshed of revolutionary activity. To radiate light and warmth, to make people happy, seemed the natural career for such a loving nature. And yet it proved otherwise; the monstrosity and injustice of the political and economic order of things had forced her to choose another path. The atrocious exploitation of the working classes had made her a socialist. The impossibility of free, public activity in

Russia, and the barbarous oppression of the individual, transformed her into a terrorist. Her loving, self-sacrificing spirit found in revolutionary protest the only form in which it could express its altruistic aspirations with a clear conscience, so that, at the price of her own life, she might clear the path of life for generations to follow.

In spite of the joy I took in Ludmila Alexandrovna's company, we were obliged in the fall of that same year, 1886, to give up our walks together, although they were our only pleasure and solace. It happened in this manner: according to the prison rules, these walks and the use of the garden were a reward for "good behaviour." Naturally, no one could enjoy being punished for one's "conduct"; and it was the prison inspector who appraised our conduct; or rather, he dispensed privileges as the spirit moved him, and was usually atrociously unjust. There were comrades of ours whose daily conduct never deviated from the general regulations, and who still never enjoyed any privileges. Sometimes they tapped on the walls to their neighbours, but that was a sin common to all of us.

In prison, people must have communication of some sort with each other. Only those who are mentally unbalanced do not tap messages. But if one breaker of the prison rules received permission to walk in the garden with a friend, then it would seem as though all should have the same privilege. This was not the case, however, and some of our comrades, like Kobylyansky and Zlatopolsky, died without having seen one friendly face. Others had to wait whole years for this privilege.

It was hard to come back from one's walk, and think of one's neighbour deprived of the last joy, to meet with a comrade. It was hard to stroll in the yard with a friend, when so close at hand some comrade was listlessly pacing, just as eager to see a friendly face, and in just as great need of companionship, of sympathy, of a friend. But no plan of escape from the situation occurred to me. The prison rules seemed to me as fixed and unyielding as the stone walls, the iron doors and gratings. It seemed as impossible to break up the prison régime that was crushing us, as it would have been to destroy the walls and the bolts.

But Ludmila Alexandrovna held a different opinion. She thought that one ought to protest against the prison régime by one means or another. The inspector was arbitrary and unjust in his distribution of privileges, and therefore we should not countenance them. Ludmila Alexandrovna suggested a passive protest in this case, that is, a voluntary rejection of privileges on the part of those who were enjoying them at that given time. Our refusal, of course, must have a motive. In it we should refer to the more or less similar conduct of all the prisoners, and to the feeling of comradeship and sympathy which would not permit us calmly to enjoy something of which the rest were deprived. For a long time I could not resolve on such a sacrifice. Of course, I was unhappy at the thought that I was enjoying a benefit for the lack of which many of my comrades were grieving. But I felt that I was living "in the depths," and my meetings with Ludmila Alexandrovna were my only joy. If I could only have believed that this sacrifice would bear fruit, and that our voluntary refusal would succeed in wresting from the inspector the weapon which he was using to oppress our comrades! But it seemed to me improbable that they would yield on such an important point; and in this case, would it not be merely a case of self-flagellation, and a permanent deprivation at that, since, having once taken our stand, it would be impossible to withdraw? Besides this, several of those who were enjoying this "privilege" of walking with a comrade, were so ill that they stood in absolute need of friendly help.

Seeing how I feared the thought of separation, Ludmila Alexandrovna would not mention it for some time. But the disturbing question broke out again and again in our conversations. Ludmila Alexandrovna persistently pointed out to me new aspects of the question. She said that we must keep in mind not only the immediate results of the protest; that, apart from its direct aim—to make the garden and walks with a comrade the common heritage of the prison inmates, its normal state, and not special privileges—our protest would have a significance in itself. In the midst of general silence and submission, the administration would see that we did not passively endure the things that were being done around us, that we thought not of ourselves alone, as those in power constantly demanded, but that we also sympathised with our comrades, and raised our voices in their defence. "Talk only about yourself," was the inevitable retort when any of us used the word "we." And in this case, prisoners would be refusing in the name of comradeship a thing that the authorities considered a reward. Nothing was so dear to the authorities as humble assent and passive submission to all the orders they issued. And here, people who had been deprived not only of all civil, but of even simple, elementary human rights, and against whom every measure that might crush their spirits had been taken, these people would place themselves higher than their jailers and executioners, though only for a moment; they would stand in judgment on the administration's management of the prisons, and point out the necessity of a change in the régime that had been established to keep in an iron vise these same critics.

Gradually Ludmila Alexandrovna convinced me that her arguments were just, and with a few other comrades we refused to make use of our privileges until they should be granted to the entire prison. At first quite a few agreed to stand by us; but later, as is often the case in prison, the movement lost support; and instead of a more or less general protest, only Ludmila Alexandrovna, Yuri Bogdanovich, Popov, Shebalin, and myself, carried it out to the end. For a year and a half we had no use of the garden and took no walks together.[44]

[44] Under the new inspector, Fedorov, these privileges were granted to all the prisoners, without exception.—*Translator.*

V

THE PUNITIVE CELL

Like most of those who are newly-imprisoned, and find themselves in unfamiliar and malevolent surroundings, during the first years I was crushed and seemed to find my only refuge in silence, resigning myself to the lot of one who has been tied hand and foot. But this attitude of mine was not due merely to a realisation of the impossibility and fruitlessness of any resistance or struggle; another element mingled with it. Whoever, like myself, has at some time been influenced by the spirit of Christ, who, in the name of His idea has endured abuse, suffering, and death; whoever during his childhood and youth has made of Him an ideal, and regarded His life as an example of self-sacrificing love, will understand the mood of the newly-condemned revolutionist who has been flung into a living grave for the cause of liberty. After his trial, the sentenced prisoner experiences a peculiar emotion. Calm and radiant, he does not clutch convulsively at that from which he is departing, but looks firmly ahead, fully conscious of the fact that what is coming cannot be escaped or averted.

The ideas of Christianity, which are implanted in all of us, consciously or unconsciously, from our very cradles, and also the lives of all martyrs for ideas, create in such a prisoner the consoling consciousness that the moment of his test has come. A trial is given to the strength of his love and the hardiness of his spirit, as a fighter for that good which he has longed to attain, not for his own transitory self, but for the people, for society, for future generations. One can understand that in such a mood we can have no thought of engaging in a war of words or of action with a band of jailers and executioners. Did Jesus resist when they abused and struck Him? Any thought of such an action seemed a profanation of His pure spirit and gentle dignity.

And yet, notwithstanding this mood of non-resistance, after

six months of separation from my friend Ludmila I came into conflict with the prison régime, which might have had tragic results.

A few days before Whitsunday, at nine o'clock in the evening, when the inspector was making his customary survey of the prison, looking through the peep-hole in every door, Popov called to me with a loud tap from his cell, which was below mine and several doors removed. I was tired. The day had been long and wearisome and empty. I wanted to lie down on my cot and go to sleep, but I did not have the heart to refuse, and I answered. But when Popov began to tap, his sentence broke off in the middle of a word. I heard a door slam, steps rang out in the direction of the exit, and everything was silent again. I understood. The inspector had taken Popov to the punitive cell.

The punitive cell was the place to which the inspector threateningly referred when he said: "I'll take you off to a place where not a living soul will hear you." Not a living soul—that was terrible to think of.

Here we prisoners were all together under the Fortress roof; all around were friends, each in his stone cell, and that was protection and defence. If you should cry out, your cry would be heard. If you should groan, they would hear it. But "off there?" There "not one living soul will hear you."

I knew that not so very long ago, Popov had been taken "off there," and that they had beaten him cruelly. The thought that he would again be put in that terrible place, that he would be alone, and that a whole pack of gendarmes would again fall upon him, an unarmed man, this thought flashed through my mind and seemed so horrible that I made my decision: I would contrive to be put there too; he should know that he was not alone, and that—if they were going to torture him, he had a witness.

I knocked on the door, and asked them to call the inspector. "What do you want?" said he, angrily, opening the little window in the door.

"It is unjust to punish one, when two were talking," said I. "Take me to the punitive cell also."

General View of the Schlüsselburg Fortress

Main Entrance to the Fortress

"Very well," said the inspector promptly, and unlocked the door.

Then it was that I first saw the interior of our prison as it looked lighted up at night: the little lamps along the walls of our tomb; the forty heavy, black doors standing there like coffins set on end, and behind every door, a comrade, a captive, suffering alone; dying, sick, or waiting his turn to die. Hardly had I passed along my "Bridge of Sighs," and approached the stairway, when my neighbour called out: "They're taking Vera to the punitive cell!" and scores of hands began to beat madly on the doors, and voices shouted, "Take us too!"

In the midst of the gloomy surroundings that stirred me so deeply, the sound of the familiar and unfamiliar voices of invisible people, the voices of comrades, which I had not heard for many, many years, awoke in me a certain morbid, flaming joy: we were separated and yet united; our spirits were one.

But the inspector flew into a fury. When we came out into the courtyard accompanied by three or four gendarmes, he raised his fist, which clutched convulsively the bunch of prison keys. With his face distorted from rage, and his beard quivering, he hissed at me: "Over there, just make a sound, and I'll show you!"

I was afraid of this man. I had heard of the cruel corporal punishments that the gendarmes had inflicted at his command, and the thought came to me: "If they beat me, I shall die." But I replied in a voice that sounded so calm that it seemed to belong to somebody else: "I am not going there to tap messages."

The broad wooden gate of the citadel yawned open before me, and my fear was replaced by ecstasy. For five years I had not seen the night sky and the stars. Now this sky was above me, and its stars shone down on me. The high walls of the old citadel gleamed white and the silvery radiance of the May night poured into the deep, square, well-like space enclosed by them. The whole plaza was overgrown with grass. It lay thick and fresh and cool, lightly brushing one's feet, and it had the allurement of the dewy expanse of a *free* field. From wall to wall stretched a low, white building, while in the corner a single tree loomed dark and tall. For a hundred years this splendid creature had grown there alone, without comrades, and thus solitary had spread about it, unhindered, its luxuriant crown. Keys grated, and with difficulty, as though the lock had grown rusty, they opened the outside door of the prison, which led into a dark, tiny antechamber. I smelled the musty odour of a cold, damp, uninhabited building. Before us stretched the naked stones of the broad corridor, at the far end of which glimmered a little night lamp. In the cold twilight the dim figures of the gendarmes, the indistinct outlines of the doors, the dark corners—everything looked so ominous that the thought suddenly flashed into my mind that this was a real torture dungeon, and that the inspector had spoken truly when he said that he had a place where no living soul could hear one. A moment later they opened a door on the left, and thrust in a small lighted lamp; the door slammed, and I was alone.

I was in a small, unheated cell, which had never been cleaned. The walls were dirty, and here and there crumbling from age. The floor was of asphalt; there was a small stationary wooden table with a seat, and an iron bench on which there was no mattress, nor any kind of bedding.

Silence.

In vain I waited for the gendarmes to come back and bring a mattress, and something to put over me; I had on a thin, cotton chemise, a skirt of the same material, and a prison gown, and I began to shiver from the cold. How could one sleep on the iron lattice-work of that cot, thought I. But no bedding ever arrived; I had to lie down on this Rakhmetov bed.[45] However, it was not only impossible to sleep, but even to lie for long on the metal bars of the bench. The cold wafted up from the floor, from the stone walls, and penetrated one's body in contact with the iron bars.

The next day they took even this away. They raised the cot and fastened it with a padlock for the rest of the time. At night one had to lie down on the asphalt floor, in the dust. It

[45] Rakhmetov is one of the characters in Chernyshevsky's novel, *What Is To Be Done?*, who advocates and practises an extremely Spartan mode of living.—*Translator.*

was impossible for me to lay my head on the floor, which was very cold, not to mention the filth that covered it. In order to save my head, I had to sacrifice my feet: I took off my rough boots and made a pillow of them. My food was black bread, old and hard. When I broke it, all the little holes within were filled with bluish mold. I could eat only a little bit of the crust. They gave me no salt, to say nothing of towels or soap.

When I went to the punitive cell, I had not planned to speak at all; I had gone there only that it might not be so terrible for Popov to be alone. But Popov had no intention of remaining silent; the very next morning he began to call me, and I was weak enough to answer. But hardly had he begun his tapping again when the gendarmes forestalled him by snatching up staves and beating furiously on our doors. A din beyond all imagination arose. One who has not spent many years in the silence of a prison, whose ear has not grown unaccustomed to sounds, cannot imagine the pain experienced by an ear grown tender through the constant stillness.

Unable to stop their furious beating, I became angry and hysterical, and began myself to beat with my fists on the door behind which the gendarmes were raging. This was beyond one's strength to endure. And yet again and again Popov attempted to send messages, and evoked torturing battles with the gendarmes through the door. At last the patience of the gendarmes was exhausted. All at once the hellish din broke off abruptly. The heavy footsteps of the inspector rang through the corridor, and some mysterious preparations and an ominous, whispered conference broke the eerie stillness.

"Now they are going to open Popov's door," thought I, "and begin to beat him. Can I possibly be a passive witness to this savage punishment? No, I can't endure it."

I began to call for the inspector.

"You want to beat Popov," said I in a strained, hard voice, as soon as he opened the little window in the cell door. "Don't beat him! You've beaten him once already—they may call even you to account!"

"We didn't beat him at all," said the inspector, quite un-

expectedly beginning to justify himself. "We tied him, and
he resisted, that's all there was to it."

"No, you beat him!" I retorted vehemently, feeling firm
ground beneath my feet. "You beat him. There were witnesses, too. He will not do any more tapping," I continued.
"I shall tell him, and he will stop."

"All right!" blurted out the inspector.

I called Popov, and told him that such a struggle was more
than I could endure, and begged him to stop tapping. . . .
Silence again.

The next day they brought me tea and a bed, but gave none
to Popov, and I dashed the tea on the floor at the feet of the
inspector, and refused to use the bed. But I broke off a piece
of bread, and pointing to the mould, said to him: "You're
keeping us on bread and water; just take a look then at the
kind of bread you feed us."

The inspector flushed. "Give her some other bread," he
ordered the gendarmes, and within five minutes they brought
me a piece of fresh, soft bread.

For three more nights I lay on the asphalt in the nasty
filth, in the cold, with my prison boots for a pillow. I lay
there and thought, and thought. . . . What should I do
next? It was evident that in the future there would be frequent
occasions for collisions with the authorities. Under what circumstances, then, ought I, under what conditions would it
be possible and expedient for me to resist the prison administration? By what methods should I struggle against it, how
voice my protest? Must I always defend a comrade? My first
impulse said, "always." But was one's comrade always right?
I had lived through a test and it had been severe. I surveyed
everything that had happened during the past few days; I
examined my own conduct and Popov's, and asked myself: Do
I wish, and have I the strength, to use Popov's methods in
my struggle? He was a man with a constitution of iron, great
self-control and an immense capacity for resistance, tempered
in the Kara mines and the Alexey Ravelin; a cool, obstinate
warrior of steel. When his jailers insulted and abused him, he
repaid them in like coin. Rough treatment by the guards,

noisy scuffles with the gendarmes, did not bother him at all. They bound him, and beat him; several times they beat him cruelly; and he bore it all, and took no revenge; he could still go on living. But I? I could not have done so. Plainly our ways were bound to diverge. I did not have enough strength, enough nervous energy, for the kind of warfare that he was waging; and from a moral point of view, I did not want to start a protest that I could not consistently carry out. Now was the time for me to map out my future conduct, to choose a firm position, to weigh all the conditions, both within and without, and to decide once and for all how I should act, so that there might be no opportunity for weakness or wavering. Petty daily quarrels, rough skirmishes ending in humiliation, were repellent to me, and I decided to reject such methods of warfare. I had learned the measure of my strength, and knew exactly what I could, and what I wished to do. I decided to endure everything that could be endured; but when some cause should arise worth defending with my life, I would protest in its defence, and protest to the point of death.[46]

On the fifth day of my imprisonment in the punitive cell the inspector said to me: "Prisoner Number Five has been given a bed, and a few other things."

Exhausted, and weakened as though by a wasting illness I was able at last to lie down on my bed, and it was high time; there was an incessant roaring and ringing in my ears, and I felt dazed and dull, half asleep and half awake. As I lay there in the twilight in a half-lethargic state, I suddenly heard singing. A pleasant, rather light baritone voice of unusual timbre was singing, and its quality reminded me vaguely of some one or something, I did not know which. It was a plain little folk song, and its motif simple and monotonous. Who was singing? Who could be singing in this place? I wondered. Could some workman have been admitted to the building on a repair job? That was impossible. And where did the sound come from? It seemed to come from the outside. Were they repairing the roof of the building?

The mystery of this unknown singer confronted me for a

[46] Fifteen whole years passed before life offered me such cause.

long time, even after I had been released from the punitive
cell. It was some time after this that I suddenly recalled his
name, Grachevsky, after he had passed out of this life by committing suicide. And indeed, I learned afterwards that he was
in the old prison at the same time that I was there.

Two more days went by.

"Time for your walk!" said the inspector, opening my door.
My term of punishment was over.

"I will not go if you are releasing only me," said I, withdrawing into the corner, and added fearfully: "You surely
wouldn't drag me out by force?"

The inspector appraised my frail, bowed figure in the corner from head to foot, shrugged his shoulders, and said with
a contemptuous air: "What is there to drag!" And he added:
"Number Five has left already."

And so I followed.

When I came back to my old cell after my walk, I moistened
the slate board, and looked at myself in its small, mirror-like
surface. I saw a face that in seven days had grown ten years
older: hundreds of thin little wrinkles furrowed it in all directions. These wrinkles quickly disappeared, but not the impressions of the days which had just come to a close.

VI

PAPER

FIVE years had passed since the time of my arrest, and the first three most difficult years of my imprisonment in Schlüsselburg, when they first gave us paper. This was an event. But after the first impulsive gladness, we began to doubt and to wonder: how should one use this paper? What should we write on it? The inspector had said as he handed out a copy-book with numbered pages, "When you have filled it, you must hand it in, and they'll give you another one." This meant that the prison officials, and later the Police Department would read what had been written. Our holiday spirit again became one of everyday drabness.

There were no belles lettres, either in prose or verse, in our scanty library. I remember that the first thing I wrote in my notebook was an extract from Nekrasov's poem, "Who can be happy and free in Russia?" Other poems that I knew by heart, followed. But soon a new source of material was disclosed. Via a few friendly stages, Lopatin tapped out this poem to me:

Accursed be the day that lighted up my way
To these grim walls, where I have said farewell to Freedom's shade;
And curst the day of birth that brought me to this earth,
And would not wisely let my mother kill the child she made.

The remaining five or six verses began with the same refrain of curses.

My own state of mind, and, as I later learned, that of the majority of my comrades, was so far removed from these furious complaints, that I was extremely surprised by them. During my years of freedom, I had never written poetry, but now it suddenly occurred to me to reply in verse, through these same friendly mediators, and I wrote:

Fortunate are we to give our strength that Liberty may live;
And though we suffer, though we die, we shall not shrink from destiny.
We shall endure, and not reproach, but humbly, peacefully approach

The kindly darkness waiting near. . . . Our strong young brothers,
they will hear
Our silent call to battle new, for freedom, and for justice too.

All our comrades approved this reply of mine, while Lopatin sent back the word that it had touched him to the point of tears.

After such success, the desire arose in me to express in verse the emotions that I had been obliged constantly to suppress. I wrote the poems, *To My Mother*, *To My Sister*, *My Old Home*, and others. My comrades followed my example, and poems appeared in quick succession. Verses poured in from all sides. Sixteen poets appeared, and each one tuned his lyre to his own pitch and played; Schlüsselburg was transformed into Parnassus. Every one tapped away so busily on the prison walls that Morozov, who was living in one of the lower cells, did not know what to make of it: it sounded, so he said, as though the whole place was possessed of spirits. The most sober of us became inspired. Even Popov and Frolenko, our realists, each wrote a poem. Only Lukashevich, Yanovich, Aschenbrenner, and a few others refrained. We wrote various forms of poetry: acrostics and sonnets, odes and lyrics. Pankratov described in his stanzas the life of the Rostov underworld; Lagovsky celebrated in verse the revolutionary flag and other lofty subjects. Some wrote in an heroic vein, some in elegiac, according to each one's propensity and ability. The themes were for the most part reminiscent. Such a note harmonised with the lyrical mood peculiar to one's first years of imprisonment. I shall not consider the question of the quality of the verse; one thing was certain: writing verses lightened the burden of our life by giving an outlet to our pent-up emotions. On the other hand, our mutual exchange of verses brought a certain variety and pleasure into our solitude, and sometimes gave us great happiness. On birthdays or name-days one would sometimes receive touching offerings, like the one that Lopatin sent me on September 17:

Though buried in this fiendish tomb,
Our love surrounds you, close and dear.
And though deprived of light and room,
And kindred, yet your friends are near.

You are not utterly bereft,
For friendship's loving words are left.

If the privilege of using paper made it possible for us to pour out our feelings, and to assuage our sorrow, it rendered us at the very beginning a service of an entirely different sort.

During the first three years we were subjected to a personal search on the Saturday of every week. Nothing was ever hidden; there was nothing to hide, and yet every single week we were forced to undergo this humiliation. The men were brutally searched by the gendarmes, while I was taken to an empty room, where a woman summoned especially for the purpose awaited me. One after another she would remove my garments and pass them to the gendarmes in the corridor, through the half-opened door. At first this office was performed by that elderly person who resembled the housekeeper of a "respectable house," of whom I spoke in the first chapter describing my life in Schlüsselburg. She would pass her hands from my bare shoulders down and over my entire body, even my ears and fingers. Once another woman, young, and, judging from her exterior, more refined, took the place of this first one. She wore a stylish black wool dress, and on her breast a gold chain. When the inspector brought me in to her, he touched his ear and his mouth, and said, "She is deaf and dumb," thus giving me to understand what was evident without words. This woman was visibly embarrassed by her rôle. She blushed. I did not see her more than this once. She was replaced by some Finnish or Esthonian woman, probably a cook, an ill-bred, rough, peasant woman with white eyebrows. She would examine my hair, strand by strand, with her vile fingers, and fling my head roughly from side to side as though it were a big wooden ball. I would leave the room in tears.[47]

And so it happened that while our poets were practising their anapests and iambics, Martynov, the workman, expressed himself in prose. He wrote a diary, and after he had filled his

[47] Justice forces me to say that once when the Inspector noticed that I was crying, he asked me what the trouble was. "That woman is very rough," I replied. "I will speak to her," said Sokolov curtly; and from that time on she did not pull my hair any more.

notebook, he handed it in to the inspector, who sent it to the Police Department. In his diary Martynov described among other things the Saturday searches. The description must have been colourful. At any rate, either on account of it, or else because the period during which we were to be subjected to searches was over, they ceased suddenly. But we firmly believed that the diary was responsible for their abandonment.

VII

THE HUNGER STRIKE

Two years passed after my imprisonment in the punitive cell. During these years there were many days so colourless and drab that my memory bears no recollection of them. And there were also others when my soul struggled and seethed; and still others when it was melancholy, and I suffered silently. There were also collisions of one kind or another with the administration, and more or less outstanding facts of prison life. But I shall relate only the story of our collective protest in the form of a ten-day hunger strike.

Like all state institutions, our prison was subject to periodical visits of inspection. These usually took place twice a year, and always disturbed and irritated us. In that monotonous environment in which we lived, every break in the orderly routine of the day was oppressive. Everything that broke up the normal course of things was painfully exciting; we were tense and uneasy, suffered from nervous headaches, and could not regain our composure for a long time. One after another the doors of the cells would be opened, many footsteps would resound noisily in the corridor, and voices would boom out. There, now they're coming into your own cell. They come in, a whole crowd of them, surrounded by the gendarmes, strange, distant people, sometimes indifferent and sometimes hostile, but always failing utterly to understand you. They ask questions, and perhaps awkwardly touch on something painful— an annoying, official catechism, to which you hurriedly and in confusion reply "yes" or "no"; while the gendarmes drawn up on either side of the dignitary, glare at you, ready to protect the distinguished visitor from you with their breasts, as though you were some wild beast. . . . There, they are gone—but the prisoner, uneasy and restless, forced out of his daily rut, with a quickened realisation that he is a captive, paces his cell, and attempts to quiet his agitation.

Ah, those visits! That inspection! That intrusion! And
every time, just as in all state institutions, the prison officials
were secretly informed by some obliging friend of the impending
arrival of the authorities; they knew, and made their preparations, secretly during the first few years, but later more openly.

So it happened that in the fall of 1889 Inspector Fedorov
was warned, and made the rounds of the cells, telling each one of
us not to leave extra books out in sight: either to turn them in
to the library, or to hide them. He had in mind the books
which we had brought with us upon our commitment to the
Fortress, and which, after many requests and petitions on our
part, had been accepted by the prison library, possibly without
a list of them having been first sent to the authorities in St.
Petersburg. His advice was good, and we all followed it, all
save one.

The Director of the Police Department, Durnovo,[48] was
going serenely from one prisoner to another. He entered the
cell of Number 28, who was Sergey Ivanov. On the bunk,
which was lowered, lay a book. Durnovo picked it up. "Hm.
. . Hmp!" he mooed. *The History of the French Revolution,*
by Mignet! And after they had left the cell, he expressed his
astonishment to the inspector that such books were allowed
to circulate in the prison. He then ordered that the library
catalogue be examined and all books removed which were in any
way related to the social and political views of the prisoners.
Thirty-five books, the best in our little library, which alone
furnished us with mental activity, were thus removed from
use: Motley's *Rise of the Dutch Republic* (two volumes);
Gervinus' *History of the XIXth Century* (five volumes); Spencer's *Principles of Sociology* and *Social Statics;* Mawdsley's
Body and Soul (in English); a *Life of Lincoln;* a *History of
the Civil War in the United States;* Pisarev (one volume); and
others. These were the very books that we had brought with
us, and the ones which we treasured the most. Now these beloved books, which had already been accepted, had fallen into

48 As Minister of the Interior in 1905-1906, he succeeded in crushing
the revolutionary movement by means of ruthless military suppression.
He was later killed by the Terrorists.—*Translator.*

disgrace and were forbidden us. They had deprived us of our only spiritual possession, and there was no assurance that other seizures would not follow this first raid. This was a moral catastrophe, and it deeply shocked and stirred the whole prison.

A short time previous to this, a few comrades who especially longed to converse with the rest, discovered that the sewer pipes in the cells were not isolated, but were all inter-connected except in four places. As a result of this, when the pipes were empty, the prisoners in each group of cells were able to hear each other, and to converse, as they did in St. Petersburg in the House of Preliminary Detention. And so four clubs were formed, and when the books were taken away from us, we were able to discuss the matter together. The clubs communicated with each other by tapping messages on the cell walls next to the corridor, a most imperfect method of conversing, although at that time, under Commandant Fedorov, the practice of tapping no longer provoked punishment. As soon as the loss of these books became known, we began to consider what course to take. All agreed unanimously that it was impossible to let the matter go without a protest. There were few books in the library, we were unable to secure more; and now they had taken away the most precious ones among the few that we had. If we should acquiesce silently in this action, would they not rob us still further?

A few suggested that we protest by refusing to take our outdoor walks. It was not difficult, of course, to sit in one's cell; but who would ever pay any attention to this? Surely not the Police Department, the head of which had issued the decree. To deprive ourselves of our walks, of the possibility of breathing the fresh air, though it were for the space of a brief hour during the day! To stay perpetually behind walls, and wearing ourselves away with this self-torture, to become convinced of its fruitlessness, and crawl out of our solitude without having attained the end! No! Let our protest be passive, but less prolonged and more serious, said the others and I with especial insistence; and we proposed that all of us refuse to eat, and fast, not for a matter of three or four days, but until we died. Even supposing that there should be not only one

sacrifice, but that several should die; we should have defended
our right to our books, the only things that brightened our
lives.

Thus there arose a difference of opinion. The majority,
among whom were L. A. Volkenstein and her neighbours, united
in refusing to take outdoor exercise. But the minority, to
which I belonged, believed that theirs was a half-way measure,
and insisted on a general hunger strike. When it became evident that a unanimous decision was impossible, our acting minority, numbering five persons, decided to begin their fast,
irrespective of the opinion of the majority. And so we did.
In this we made a great mistake. It was only many years
after (on the occasion of Karpovich's hunger strike in 1901)
that I understood the full significance of what we had done.
I realised that our decision was impracticable and unjust. One
must not begin such a protest individually or even in a group,
so long as the rest of one's comrades fail to sympathise and
refuse to join in. The fact is that during the course of a hunger strike, others are invariably drawn into participation,
drawn in against their will. No one could endure the feeling
that nearby, comrades were depriving themselves of food, to
attain some purpose. Whether he wills it or not, sooner or
later his feeling of comradeship and sympathy will force him
to join the protest. But one cannot expect constancy in a
protest that is actuated by such motives. Yet, in my opinion,
a hunger strike either should not be attempted at all, or else
should be undertaken with the serious resolve to carry it out
to the end. Of course, no one would consciously drag people
to their death against their will, using merely their sympathy
for the fasters as a pretext; while temporary support and
eventual retreat invite defeat from the beginning.

Unfortunately, at that time I did not think of this point at
all, and so disregarded the feelings of the rest that I was angry
with those who did not agree with our view. I believed that
they resisted our plan out of sheer weakness, and I was indignant at their spirit of self-preservation. "They don't want
to risk their lives," thought I, "but one must make the venture;
it's worth the risk!"

The consequences of our action were most disastrous, and especially for me. As soon as we had begun our hunger strike, all those who had before disagreed with us, immediately joined it. We learned that they had secretly decided to resist our plan as long as they could, but to join us if we should begin to fast. Incidentally, it was resolved to accept tea but no sugar; also that the women should start the fast two days after the men. Almost the entire prison united in this protest. Those who refrained were: Lopatin, who never took part in our protests, and refused on general principles to support any attempts at joint action, regarding such a course as not feasible in prison; Antonov, because he believed only in active protests; Aschenbrenner, who frankly confessed that he was afraid he would not hold out to the very end, and Vasily Ivanov and Manchurov, who disapproved of the hunger strike, and did not openly take part in it. (Both of them made a pretence of taking food, but dropped it into the water-closet. They were afraid that they would not be able to maintain their fast, but would give in, and thus injure the general cause by their defection.)

The comrades in our division all lay on their bunks, and hardly conversed at all. But in Ludmila Alexandrovna's division there were constant queries as to each member's sensations. After a few days one of them became dizzy; another could not stand up; Butsinsky vomited blood, and absurd as it may seem, they asked the prison physician, Naryshkin, to attend him. The latter replied, quite reasonably, that it was a strange procedure to doctor people who were killing themselves by starvation, and refused to help him.

This incident took place on the ninth day of the hunger-strike. Shortly afterwards, one of his neighbours suggested that we bring it to a close, and his proposal was accepted by the majority of the prisoners on the north-east side of the prison. Popov informed me of this, and added that in view of the decision of the majority, he was not going to fast any longer. Martynov, a healthy, strong man, did not stand the test at all, and began to eat on the third day. I, in my rigour, broke off all communication with him. Starodvorsky, who said that he would die like Seneca, by opening his arteries, made an awkward attempt at committing suicide in this manner. The gendarmes noticed what he was doing, and took him off to the old prison, where, under the influence of an overwhelming desire to live, as he called it, he began to eat. There remained only Yurkovsky and myself. He tapped a message to me, saying that he would do whatever I did. I replied that I was accustomed to finish whatever I started, and did not regard myself as bound by the opinion of the majority, and that I was going to continue the protest.

The defection of my comrades was a heavy blow to me. Of course, the feeling that I had been abandoned, left solitary, was bitter. But there was something else that stirred me far more painfully. Five years ago I had entered this prison, bringing with me an ideal conception of the revolutionist as an individual, and of collective revolutionary solidarity in particular. Zhelyabov, Frolenko, and other members of the Executive Committee had given me the basis for this concept of the revolutionist who never faltered or drew back. And the absolute cohesion and solidarity of the Executive Committee of The Will of the People had furnished me with my idea of a collective revolutionary conscience. But now I was forced to abandon these conceptions. A test had occurred, and it crushed my spirit to the ground.

Those around me were all revolutionists. And they had spoken and expressed their readiness to die. They had spoken of sacrifice, of carrying the protest through to the end. What did it all mean? Had they spoken sincerely or not? Had they deceived themselves, or did they wish to deceive others? But whom, then? Was it the prison officials, who knew from the gendarmes everything that we said in our conversations through the pipes, which were plainly audible? Were these conversations intended as a verbal demonstration, to influence our jailers? Could these really have been empty threats, and did those who uttered them know well that no one would die, and that nobody would risk his life in this protest? But why then had not my comrades warned me? If all this had really been nothing but a farce, surely it was unworthy of a revolutionist.

He should not abuse his word, even when an enemy is involved. If, on the other hand, their words and intentions had been serious, then their retreat was weakness, a lack of courage to fulfil that which they had begun. And yet, my comrades were people of strength and determination, the very strongest people in Russia. Otherwise they would not have acted as they had during their years of freedom, before they had come to live in that stone tomb. Yes, they were strong people, and *ought* to be strong. And yet, they had spoken, and not acted on their words.

This was a burning disillusionment, and filled me to the brim with uncontrollable anger. Unworthy, dark suspicions passed through my mind, and it seemed to me that I hated every one. They, my comrades, had been the only thing left to me in life; and now, having betrayed themselves, they seemed like strangers to me. I had believed in them, in their steadfastness, in their inflexible will; I now saw before me not the firmly united collective which I had pictured to myself, but vagrant personalities, weak, unstable, and as prone to abandon a cause as ordinary people. My whole soul was racked and distorted by these thoughts. My hunger strike had lasted for many days, and my decision to carry it through to the end had grown correspondingly. After all that I had lived through, it was easier for me to die than to live. My entire being longed for death. Yes, I would fast until I died. I would carry through to the finish the thing I had begun. Let "them" abandon their purpose, that was their business, but I would fulfil the purpose on which I had resolved! And then, when I had already passed the boundary line beyond which the firm will cannot turn back, when I wished for nothing more than to leave this life behind me, to pass out of this pitiful, humiliating, ephemeral life, two of these same comrades of mine dealt me a new blow.

For a person who is master of himself, and who, in full consciousness of what he is doing, has resolved upon a definite course, there can be no greater offence than an interference which prevents him from expressing his crystallised will, and shatters it. Such interference, such an onslaught on one's strength, is an assault on one's spiritual integrity, on his inherent right to determine his own conduct, to express his own individuality, and to create his own form of life, which no one else can duplicate. And my comrades infringed upon this resolution of mine, and broke my will.

Yurkovsky and I had already fasted for two more days, when Popov, and later Starodvorsky, each one separately, without having conferred together, announced to me that if I died they would commit suicide. This was moral violence, and it enraged me. To think of it! These men, who had before agreed with me, and who had deserted our cause without even asking for my opinion, dared now to demand the same thing from me. Their masculine vanity would not permit that a woman should prove herself more consistent and steadfast than they themselves. They were ashamed, and wished to bring me down to their own level; they did not want to *die*, and so they were forcing me to *live!* Perhaps I should have laughed at this declaration, and given no credence to it, but there was something in it that forced me to believe it. Was it really possible for me to lead to their death two men who had just demonstrated that they valued their lives, and desired to live? No, I would not drag them to their graves against their wills. I did not want them to die, not for a common cause, but because of me. I abandoned my fast, but did so in utter despair. It was then that I broke my spiritual contact with the entire prison, and made myself a solemn promise, which I communicated to my comrades, that from now on I refused to be one of their organised group; and that I would not take part in any serious general protest whatsoever; that I would protest, but protest individually, on my own initiative, because our hunger strike had demonstrated to me that there were not even two people whose pulses beat in unison. In the future I would go my own way, and decide for myself what I should do, and how I should do it.

I need not say that, so far as decisive results were concerned, the hunger strike, which apparently did not disturb the prison authorities in the least, was a failure; and the books were not returned to us. It even resulted in additional repression. On one of the days while I was still fasting, Dobro-

deyev, the Commandant, who had held the position for not more
than a month, I believe, made the rounds of the cells. He read
a document stating that the money which each of us had
brought when we entered the prison, was to be confiscated, and
would be given to our relatives.[49] A short time before the
hunger strike, we had obtained permission to use these small
sums for the increase of our library. This had been partially
accomplished; Morozov had ordered the voluminous set of
Reclus' *Geography of the World.* The rest of us had not succeeded in taking advantage of this possibility, and now we were
entirely deprived of it.

So ended this chapter of our prison history, which caused us
all much bitterness, and left me on the brink of the grave. The
moral catastrophe which I had experienced, destroyed the silence and peace that had pervaded my mind while I was fasting
and waiting for death. I was shocked to the very depths, and
many years passed by before I recovered in spirit. But the
remembrance and the results of what I lived through, are vivid
to this very day.

During the nine days in the course of which I took no food,
I did not suffer at all from hunger. I did not experience any
of the pain which my comrades (who were stronger physically
than I, and less nervous) endured on the second and third days.
I, on the contrary, had not the slightest longing for food, and
did not notice anything abnormal in my own sensations. I lay
peacefully on my bunk, and read. My head was perfectly clear,
and I read with pleasure Molière's plays in the original French;
I read and laughed at Harpagon and his chat with the cook,
but *The Shopkeeper Turned Gentleman* amused me especially.
Only gradually did I become conscious of weakness, and after
the ninth day darkness arose before my eyes when I moved,
just as is always the case when one has been lying in bed for
a long time. And so it did not require any great effort, or
power of endurance, for me to persevere in my decision to continue the fast. In this respect my position was far easier than
that of my other comrades, who were of a different state of
mind. Probably my complete freedom from physical suffer-

[49] As a matter of fact, it was just confiscated.

ing was due in part to that calm, steadfast resolution which abode with me from the very beginning. But though my system did not succumb to the great test during the actual fast, the after-effects were terrible. In addition to my mental depression, my nerves were completely disorganised; every controlling centre refused to act. In many ways my will power seemed not to have become weakened, but to have disappeared entirely. My reaction to sound, which had before been keen, became unbelievably more poignant. Instead of shuddering nervously at every sudden sound, as I had done before, I would scream, and later even burst into sobs, which disturbed and excited the entire prison; and worst of all, I had not the slightest desire to restrain them. I do not know to what point this disordered state would have brought me, had I not heard those words which Lopatin said about me, and of which I spoke in the second chapter of this book—words which revolutionised my spirit.

A social duty! A social mission! Could it be that here, beyond the borders of life, there still existed for me a mission of some kind? that I was necessary to some one, and did not belong only to myself and my friends? I had believed that society had eschewed me, that life had rejected me and cast me overboard. Was it really possible that there was still some reason for my existence?

It had seemed to me, as I have said before, that my social task had come to an end, my rôle played to the last word. During my years of freedom, I had regarded my part as unimportant, and had never thought that our names would be remembered. It had seemed to me that we were still so far from the goal of our aspirations that the period in which we were living might be regarded as only an early, geological stage, so to speak, and that we, the members of The Will of the People, might be compared to those minute organisms, to those microscopic foraminifera, which in dying day after day, year after year, drop to the bottom of the sea, and in the course of centuries, form with their skeletons mighty strata of limestone. One separate organism is invisible to the naked eye, the tiny, brittle shell is insignificant, and only the collective whole, the limestone stratum, is mighty, and forms whole mountains.

Pondering over the words that I had overheard, I began to feel, to believe that I had not yet died to everything that lay beyond the boundary of our Fortress walls; it was as though the walls had parted and opened, and my eyes looked into the distance, to that distance where I had been before, and for the sake of which I must remain upon a certain height.

VIII

MY MOTHER'S BLESSING

Among the things which I treasure there is a cheap little porcelain image. It was with this that my mother blessed me after the trial, before our separation; and I guard it more carefully than any of my other possessions. They did not take it away from me; I had it with me in Schlüsselburg, and even now I still cherish it. On one side there is a quaintly engraved figure kneeling before the likeness of the Mother of God, and on the other side the inscription, "*Most Holy Virgin of Joy Unexpected.*"

As she blessed me, my mother said: "Perhaps sometime even you will know a joy unexpected."

What did my mother have in mind when she spoke precisely these good words, these and not others, before we parted? Was it a change in my fortune, the joy of seeing her again, to which she referred? Or did she wish to strengthen and encourage me with her words of blessing? To impress upon me that, however cruelly life be crushed, existence could not be entirely without joy?

Year passed after year, but joy, the joy of seeing her, my mother, did not come. And as I retreated farther and farther from the present, no longer looking forward, but always backward, I sought in the events of our prison life for a fulfilment of the blessing my mother had uttered, and of which the little image constantly reminded me. Were there joys in Schlüsselburg? Yes, there were. Indeed, had there not been any, could we have endured and survived? During the first years, the most difficult for a beginner, our only joy was mutual intercourse: a quiet greeting tapped on the wall; a poem transmitted in like fashion; congratulations on one's name-day; a few tender lines in a note passed secretly in a book—how all these things

excited us and gladdened our hearts! But there was something bitter in these joys, something that brought tears to
one's eyes. They aroused one, when it would have been better
to forget. . . . The years passed and brought other, un-
mixed joys.

And the first of such joys was a newspaper—*one* copy of a
newspaper. A tall, handsome officer at one time had charge
of the shops in the old, historic prison, where we used to work,
driving away with the sound of hammer and jack-plane the
memory of the long succession of those who had once pined
away their lives here in silence. Once, when we were working,
the officer came in with a newspaper in his hands, and, having
read it through, laid it down, perhaps not unintentionally, so
that any one who wanted it might pick it up as he passed by
without being seen, and take it away. And such, indeed, was the
result. Passing from hand to hand, the paper made the rounds
of the entire prison.

Nansen, on his *Fram*, frozen amidst immovable icebergs on
his way to the North Pole; Stanley, charting the first path
through the virgin forests in Central Africa, would hardly
have rejoiced over a fresh newspaper page, miraculously flying
into their hands, as did we, hopelessly locked up within the
walls of a Fortress. The newspaper included a dry account of
the internal life of the country, which had been sterilised by
the censor. Apparently not one little bush, nor one new sap-
ling had sprung up in the vast wilderness of our native land.
But then we came upon an article on Germany, and it revealed
to us a broad and distant horizon.

In connection with Emperor Wilhelm's intention to summon
an all-European Conference on labour legislation, the newspaper spoke of the revocation of the discriminating measures
against the Socialists; it spoke of how the Social-Democratic
movement, after breaking free from the fetters of its underground existence, had swiftly and irresistibly spread through
the country. With joyous excitement we read of meetings and
congresses, of the development of a workers' and socialist press,
of the rapid growth in membership of the Social-Democratic
party. It mattered not that all this was happening in Ger-

many and not in Russia. To us, Socialists, brought up under the banner of the International, the interests of the working classes in all countries were near and dear.

We were in an ecstasy of joy; for the first time the walls of our prison opened up and moved apart. Light appeared for a moment, and in a flash it brought a breath of freedom.

The second joy was—a book.

The prison library was at first hardly worth mentioning. It consisted of one hundred and sixty titles, among which, excepting books of ethical and spiritual content, could be found only older works belonging to the first half of the nineteenth century: *Notes on India, by an English Officer*, published in 1846; Basil's *A Journey to Constantinople*, and *A Journey to Greece*, published during the forties; *A Journey to Mongolia and Tibet*, in German; *The Geology of Belgium*, in French; *The Caucasus; its Manners, Customs, and Legends;* Tengoborsky's work on Russia's productive forces, dating from the fifties. After three or four years of earnest effort and solicitation, the few books which some of us had brought with us when we entered the Fortress were also admitted for general use. But they too were quickly read. Additional grants of books from the Police Department came in microscopic doses, and finally ceased altogether.

In the year 1894, when the absence of useful reading matter rendered our lives especially dreary, I made an attempt to escape from this situation, and applied to Commandant Gangart [50] with this request: Did he not think it possible, in view of the extreme scarcity of books, to put in a few subscriptions for us in some of the St. Petersburg libraries, and have the gendarmes bring out and later return the books secured on these subscriptions? The request was almost hopeless, for its fulfilment would establish a bond between our stony, embalmed Fortress, and a free institution. And yet Gangart said, "Good. I will arrange it!"

[50] Gangart was exceptionally broad-minded. He obtained numerous privileges for the Schlüsselburg prisoners, and in every way endeavoured to fill their existence with meaningful work, both physical and mental. The author devotes a grateful chapter to Gangart, omitted in this edition. —*Translator.*

Within a few days we received a catalogue, and later, a whole box of the books that we had selected. Our joy was great. The first book that fell into my hands was a small volume on England by Madame Yanzhul. Even under normal conditions of life this book would have produced a good impression; while to me, imprisoned as I was, it was a spring of fresh water, a complete revelation. Only in the withering atmosphere of captivity could one become so enraptured as I did in reading about the mighty English trade-unions, the brilliantly managed coal-miners' strikes, the extraordinary development of co-operative organisations in England, and that movement among the English intelligentsia which was expressed in the organisation of popular universities and of university settlements.

Into the industrial sections of London, Manchester, and Liverpool, the English intelligentsia, like the Russian youth of the seventies, had borne their knowledge and their love— could that fail to encourage, to warm one's soul, grown frigid? I forgot *my* prison, *my* inactivity, *my* personality—in the face of that throbbing life and its fresh, new offshoots for the good of the masses.

The newspaper came—one copy—flashed up through the darkness, and vanished. The book came, pushed asunder for a moment the walls of the prison, made it radiant, and vanished. . . . The Police Department firmly forbade our taking books from a free library.

But soon a new source of courage and strength opened up to us, and with it came joy. Morozov had chanced to hear through the prison doctor of a circulating museum in St. Petersburg which possessed rich collections, embracing the various branches of natural history. The doctor even brought him a few cases of petrified specimens from this museum. Lukashevich, Morozov, and Novorussky were especially interested in the natural sciences, while I had for years been endeavouring to make up for the topics that I had omitted from my course of medical studies at Zurich. The thought of securing from the museum the loan of these various collections, so necessary to the study of natural history, allured us, and we decided to try to gain permisison to make use of them. Morozov applied to Gangart, who always helped us whenever he could. But this time Gangart said that we should have to apply to the Police Department, that he himself did not have authority to act on this point.

How should we explain this request to the Department? Morozov thought and thought, and finally came to a decision: having stated his request, he wrote that he needed the stones because he was engaged in writing a treatise on the Composition of Matter.

We were utterly unprepared for such an absurd explanation, and laughed, thinking that nothing would come of it; and yet, the Department which had not permitted us to borrow books, let us borrow stones.

From that time on, for almost four years, Dr. Bezrodnov did us a memorable service, acting as mediator between us and the museum. Every two weeks he would bring out whole boxes of scientific apparatus and specimens, returning them later. We were able to look over at our leisure the museum's rich collections on geology, paleontology, and mineralogy; its apparatus for the study of physics; its herbariums and specimens for the study of histology and zoology—in short, we enjoyed all the riches that the museum possessed.

Gradually the extent of our privileges increased to a marked degree. The doctor began to bring back from the museum books on scientific as well as on general subjects. Later the museum began on its own initiative to make use of us as workers. It would send us raw material on entomology, botany, and mineralogy, and commissioned us to prepare it into collections and herbariums of different sizes, for primary and secondary schools. At that time we ourselves possessed rich material for herbariums close at hand. We were growing several hundred different varieties of plants in the garden plots; while the soil of the island on which we lived abounded in ancient strata of igneous rocks, examples of alluvial deposits of the Silurian system. One had only to lean down in order to collect as many specimens as one wished of granite, gneiss, and other minerals. The prison hummed with work: the joiners, the turners, the basket-makers planed and ground and polished; they made wooden boxes and invented various devices and improvements for mounting specimens. They glued cardboard boxes and turned out little plates for the minerals, while the lovers of natural history made up rich herbariums, classifying according to system and structure, collections of mosses and lichens, seaweeds and mushrooms, collections of fruits and seeds. They prepared hundreds of glass plates demonstrating the various parts of a flower, assembled collections of igneous rocks, minerals and ores; gathered together many specimens of insects, and so on. And all these things, as well as dozens of boxes of physical apparatus, were sent to the museum through the doctor.

Those were memorable years. Something real and tangible occupied the days; difficulties and problems appeared which had to be solved. The work for the museum, which we were enriching with our labour, wove a bond between the dead and the living. The smart from the consciousness of our uselessness, our fruitless existence, subsided. Our ever-present unconsolable sorrow at being torn away forever from the world, at knowing that there was no social task, no social goal in store for us, was assuaged. Later they deprived us of this work also. Gangart and Bezrodnov left the prison staff. There was unrest in the prison, the regulations were changed. The work that had satisfied our moral craving was snatched from our hands.

The joy of seeing my mother failed to come—it never came! And yet, the promise had been fulfilled: life had not been utterly devoid of joy. In the black skein of grief and sorrow, there were threads that shone with the radiance of a sunny day; there were joys—great ones, the "joys unexpected," of which my mother had spoken encouragingly, and of which my little image now consolingly reminded me.

IX

SOME COMRADES LEAVE US

"From here they are carried out, but they never walk out," said a certain official, upon visiting our Fortress. And indeed, many, very many were carried out; but there were in the prison not only persons condemned to penal servitude for life, "forever and evers," the Russian people called them; there were also some who were incarcerated for a definite term, and who left us when their appointed time had been served.

The first one to be freed, long before his term had been served, was the naval officer, Yuvachev, who had been tried at the same time as I. Yuvachev had been recruited to the military organisation of The Will of the People by Aschenbrenner, and belonged to the Nikolayev group of naval officers, who frightened the far more phlegmatic Aschenbrenner by the ardour of the revolutionary propaganda that they carried on among the sailors. At the trial Yuvachev made no definite impression and denied any share in the revolutionary activity of the party. However, he was condemned to death with other members of the military groups, his sentence being commuted to fifteen years of penal servitude, after he had presented a petition for clemency. Shortly after his arrival in Schlüsselburg, he lapsed into an abnormal state of religious frenzy. In their attempt to save our souls, the authorities distributed Bibles to all of us, and Yuvachev used to kneel for whole days reading his, or praying. On Wednesdays and Fridays the prison administration required a partial fast, but Yuvachev, not satisfied with such half-way measures, took no food at all on these days. His religious zeal was, of course, noticed by the administration, and reported to the Police Department. In 1886, two years after his imprisonment, he was removed from the Fortress, exiled to Sakhalin, and made use of as a naval officer. Upon his return to Russia, he occupied an official position on the prison board in Petersburg.

The next person to be released from Schlüsselburg was Vasily Andreyevich Karaulov, who had been condemned in Kiev in 1884 to four years of penal servitude, at the Trial of 12 (members of The Will of the People). Karaulov was condemned in November, and after a month was transferred to Schlüsselburg, together with his fellow-comrades in the trial. In 1881, while I was still free, I had met Karaulov once or twice in St. Petersburg. He was, as the saying goes, a "fine, stout lad," immense of stature, broad-shouldered, full of the joy of living, with cheeks the colour of "blood and milk." And yet, during all of his four years in the Fortress, he was constantly ill; he had hemorrhages, and more than once was on the point of death. Either because of his illness, or possibly because of his short sentence, which gave him hope of release from prison, Karaulov conducted himself quietly and unobtrusively. He did not participate either in our struggle to establish our right to communicate by tapping on the walls, or in the passive protest over our walks with one another, and never once disputed a point with the authorities.

Before Karaulov's release in 1886, we began to entrust small commissions to him, asking him to tell our relatives some small news of us. I dictated to him my poem, *To My Mother*, which he promised to learn by heart and send to her by mail. But, to our astonishment, he did not fulfil one of the things entrusted to him, although he lived in as large a city as Krasnoyarsk. We sought to explain this by the dark rumours that the authorities had threatened to return Karaulov to the Fortress, should he utter even a word concerning one of us. He himself refuted this in print, several years afterwards, saying that no threats whatever were made.

Karaulov's political convictions did not survive his imprisonment. He was elected to the first Imperial Duma on the ticket of the Constitutional-Democratic Party.[51] He no longer stood for the universal suffrage, which The Will of the People

[51] The Russian liberal party formed by Milyukov and others after the revolution of 1905.—*Translator.*

had demanded; according to his revised opinion, the people were not intellectually prepared to make use of suffrage; and his attitude towards the agrarian question, that central point of our program, was determined by the bourgeois demands of the party which sponsored his candidacy. Karaulov was a notable figure in the Duma, and won general respect as a fiery and talented defender of religious freedom. Boldly and skilfully he parried the taunt of "convict," which the Black Hundreds cast in his face in the Duma. "My drop of blood, too, has been shed that you might hold session in this chamber!" he cried in reply. And this was true, and not one, but many drops of blood did he give for the cause of popular representation, for which The Will of the People had waged its war. This athlete, who had entered prison full of health, left Schlüsselburg with the face of a corpse. He regained his health in Siberia, and died in 1907.

After the year 1888 a long interval ensued, during which no one was brought to the prison, or removed therefrom. To be sure in 1890 they were under obligations to release Lagovsky.

The fate of this man had been tragic. All of us had been tried—form had been observed—while he had been imprisoned in Schlüsselburg without even a trial, and confined in the Fortress by administrative order under the direction of the Minister of the Interior, for five whole years. An infantry officer, he was sent into administrative exile in the province of Tomsk in 1883, but escaped, and joined The Will of the People. In March, 1884, he was arrested in St. Petersburg on the street. The formula for a new explosive was found on him, and this was enough to send him to our Fortress without a trial in October, 1885. His behaviour at the Fortress was most provoking, and he suffered many penalties. When his five-year term came to an end, the Commandant came to his cell and read a decree from the Minister of the Interior that Lagovsky remain in Schlüsselburg for five years more, "for bad conduct."

These five years passed also. They released Lagovsky. He had a mother and a sister whom he loved with especial tenderness. For a long time he could not find them; during all those ten years he had had no word whatever from them, for at that time we did not have the privilege of correspondence. Lagovsky was at first exiled to Karakol, and later, in 1898, he moved to the province of Saratov, spending the last years of his life in the city of Balashov. On May 19, 1903, he was drowned while bathing in the Khopra.

The ten-year sentence of one of our beloved comrades, Ovanes Manucharov (whom we called "Man" for short), expired the same year. When Manucharov was arrested in Kharkov, he offered armed resistance, not with the idea of killing any of the police, but by the uproar to warn his friends of the ambush which might have been laid in their dwelling. In the prison at Kharkov he was clever enough to contrive his escape, but was caught and sent to our Fortress after his trial in 1884. An Armenian by descent, he had neither a brilliant education nor a prepossessing exterior, but it would have been difficult to find a person more affectionate, or of kindlier impulses. He was just, keen, and patient towards the opinions of others; and one could not wish for a better comrade in the difficult conditions of our prison life; so attentive was he to the interests of each one, so patient in his attitude towards individual problems, that frequently he performed services that no one else could have duplicated. He had become so attached to us all that he did not want to leave us when the term of his imprisonment was ended; and only Gangart's flat statement that he would be removed by force, obliged him to yield to the inevitable. He was exiled to Siberia, where he married, but died as early as 1909 from a heart attack, leaving a little son behind him.

A year or two after Manucharov's release, I unexpectedly found one of my own poems in an issue of *Russkoye Bogatstvo* (Russian Riches) [52] for the year 1896, which Gangart had given us:

> Tell me why, beloved friend,
> When springtime suns are warm and bright,
> And bathe all creatures in their light,
> My sorrow knows no end?
> Why does this clear and azure sky

[52] An important monthly review of Populist tendencies.—*Translator.*

Which tenderly returns my gaze,
With dull pain fill the weary days
That endlessly pass by?
And why do I, so dull, so drear,
Stand motionless, in weary wise,
And never lift my languid eyes
To see the living sunlight here?
And if you know, I pray you, tell
Me why I go so swift away
From all this warm and radiant May
To rest within my stifling cell?

I turned the page; on the other side was the reply:

When your heart is wrung with pain,
And against your will the tears
Flow so bitter-hot again,
Lie upon your pallet then,
Think of those who love you well,
Living in your mother land,
Living through the lonely years—
And when Sorrow lays its hand
Hope and hope still—bravely quell
Brooding fears—you are not dead.
Life and love may still be yours;
Tender friends will press your hand.
Surely some bright dream endures,
Saved from Shipwreck's angry strand.
And the grave cannot hold all,
Nor all lovely things be slain,
Nor the angry thunder call,
Smiting all your hopes again.
And the darkness is not deathless,
And the day is almost here.
See—the shadows pale in breathless
Wonder, for the dawn is near!

Beneath this poem was written the initial "M." The name flashed into my mind—Mikhaylovsky! Need I speak of the joyous emotion that flooded me to the point of tears? From behind the Fortress walls my voice had gone forth to my friends, and from beyond the stone barrier their words of love had flown back to me. And it was dear "Man" that had given me this joy [by transmitting the poem to Mikhaylovsky].

The next exodus from the Fortress occurred in the year 1896, when five comrades were taken away at once.

In 1894 Nicholas II ascended the throne. His father did not die a violent death, but passed away as the result of an illness. A wave of excitement passed over us; no doubt there would be an amnesty—we might even be freed. The prison

administration believed that Schlüsselburg would be entirely
emptied. Inspector Fedorov congratulated us on our approaching freedom. "Pretty soon you'll live like a lady again,"
he announced to me with a pleasant smile, evidently thinking
that there was nothing on earth better than that. However,
a year went by without any change in our condition and we
concluded that no amnesty would be granted us.

But early in November of 1896, while we were at work in the
shops in the old prison, a sergeant suddenly appeared and led
out several persons, one after the other, among them Ludmila,
saying that the Commandant wished to see them. Every one
was perplexed and agitated, not knowing what this meant.
However, they soon returned. With much excitement they related the Commandant's words, that the coronation manifesto
had commuted to twenty years the life terms of Vasily Ivanov,
Aschenbrenner, Starodvorsky, and Polivanov; while the sentences of Pankratov, Surovtsev, Yanovich, and Ludmila Alexandrovna Volkenstein had been cut to one-third, on the
strength of which the last three were to leave the Fortress at
once. This partial amnesty, leaving the situation of the other
comrades unchanged, did not bring any happiness to those pardoned, while Ludmila Alexandrovna received it even with anger.
When we, happy in the thought that at least a few were to
leave our tomb, hastened to congratulate her, she would not
listen to any congratulations and rejoicings, and only gradually became reconciled to the fact. Then began hurried preparations for the departure.

It was hard for Ludmila Alexandrovna to leave us, after
having spent so many years with us, filled with vicissitudes of
every kind. She loved us, and knew that to some of us she was
as indispensable as light or air. Time and again she expressed
tender concern for these comrades during her last talks with
me, begging me not to forget that for some of them her departure was particularly hard. On November 23rd, she and four
other comrades, Martynov and Shebalin, whose twelve-year
sentences had just come to an end, and Yanovich and Surovtsev, who had been pardoned, were to be taken away.

The last hour before her departure Ludmila Alexandrovna

spent in my cell. She wept continuously, and I comforted her. At parting, she said with deep emotion that she was leaving behind her in Schlüsselburg, the finest people she had ever known.

At one o'clock our departing comrades were led out of their cells, one after the other, and thence conducted from the prison. Upon leaving the prison walls and entering the yard of the Fortress, each one of the discharged halted, in order silently to bid us his "last farewell." From the windows of our cells we looked at their retreating figures. Each of them, turning toward us, made a low bow; each man took off his hat and waved it in sign of greeting, while Ludmila Alexandrovna stopped two or three times and waved her handkerchief. We also held white handkerchiefs in our hands, which could easily be seen through the double windows and gratings of our cells. Our glances followed them—those friends of ours who were returning to life—while at the same time a new, dark void seemed to well up around us. They reached the gates, and disappeared. For us they ceased to exist, as though a deep ocean had yawned and swallowed them up; not a single message could reach us as to what might further happen to them. A dark uncertainty, the spirit of Maeterlinck's *Les Aveugles*, settled down upon us.[53]

Vasily Pankratov was released in 1898. He had been a cabinet maker by trade, and was arrested in 1883 as a member of the Fighting Organisation of The Will of the People. At his arrest he showed armed resistance, and wounded one gendarme. He was sentenced to twenty years' penal servitude, and sent to Schlüsselburg together with Karaulov and Martynov. By the partial amnesty of 1896 his term was reduced by one third. At the Fortress he was my first neighbour, and as we were both novices in the art of tapping, it took us some time to get well acquainted. He was only twenty, and as his senior by twelve years I treated him with motherly tenderness, which was expressed also in two or three of my poems dedicated to

[53] In January, 1906, Ludmila Volkenstein was killed in a street demonstration, at Vladivostok, while marching with rebellious sailors. Machine-guns were used against the procession.—*Translator.*

him. I encouraged his desire to study, and helped him as much as I could. The knowledge he accumulated at the Fortress enabled him later, in Siberia, to take part in scientific expeditions and to make geologic discoveries.

In 1902, Trigoni and Polivanov were released. Of Trigoni I have written in my book *Schlüsselburg Prisoners*. Pyotr Polivanov was the son of a wealthy landowner in the Saratov province, and when still in high school he displayed his devotion to the common people. His romantic vein prompted him, in 1878, to take part as a volunteer in the Serbian war of independence. In 1882 he was arrested while attempting the liberation of a fellow member of The Will of the People. At the Fortress he proved the most voracious reader. "I see and read fifteen lines at once," he explained to me. At the same time he retained his reading matter marvellously; thus he would relate almost literally the contents of a weekly London *Times*. Beside his linguistic facility, Polivanov showed also a fine literary talent. After his release he was exiled to Siberia, whence he fled abroad. In 1903, he shot himself under mysterious circumstances, while in France,

X

CHAUTAUQUA

In 1892 or 1893, Commandant Gangart had us bind for him a magazine of unusually large size, *Virgin Soil*, published by Wolf. In it I found a short article, which gave a new direction to my thoughts, and led me to studies that formed a special phase in my prison life, a phase full of brightness and wholesome gladness. I gathered from the article that, since in the hurly-burly of life and practical activities people of middle age forget much of what they have learned during their school-days, in the United States a movement had arisen which inaugurated review courses for adults. Although simple in itself, this idea appeared as a revelation and was taken up by multitudes. The headquarters of the movement were in a small town on one of the large lakes in America, Chautauqua, which was soon invaded by a throng of adult men and women, eager to renew and increase their knowledge. "I am forty years old," thought I; "I, too, shall apply myself to a systematic review of the things I have studied at the university, and supplement my education with subjects which I have so far neglected."

Up to then I had read everything I chanced upon in our library, but had not studied anything systematically. I had had medical training, but like other Zurich students, I had paid scant attention to the natural sciences, which were taken up during the first two years of our course. I had attended the lectures on mineralogy, botany, zoology, physics and chemistry, because they were compulsory. But of all these subjects, chemistry alone attracted me. I studied Mendeleyev's text book and in Berne I enjoyed working in the laboratory of Professor Schwartzenbach; the other subjects I neglected. Furthermore, at that time I had absolutely no curiosity to learn more about nature, though as a source of esthetic pleasure, I valued nature highly, and was most sensitive to its beauties. The pitiful fragments that were taught at the Institute were adapted to kill all interest in the subject. The narrow outlook of the medical course fostered this indifference, while revolutionary activity strangled all interests other than those pertaining to the movement. Only in Schlüsselburg, where there were no people, no society, and where the whole universe was reduced to a bit of sky and a small piece of ground, did my attitude toward nature change, and I realised that I was practically ignorant of all its phenomena: I knew neither the history of the skies nor the genesis of the earth, nor the formation and evolution of the rocky strata from which our Fortress wall was formed, and the fragments on which our feet trampled. If I bent down to a mound of sand and took up a handful of its grains, warmed by the spring sun, I did not know what those transparent particles were, those tiny, pink fragments and beautiful spangles that poured from my hand in a thin stream. Here was the grass, the very same kind that grew in our village cemetery; here was a flower of the sort I used to see in the forest when we gathered lilies-of-the-valley, but I could neither name nor identify them. Many questions occurred to me, and I had no answers for them.

This tardy consciousness of ignorance was definitely borne to me when I read the announcement of the Chautauqua project, but at first I began to follow a wrong course. Upon entering the Fortress, I had brought with me all the medical books which I possessed, and now I resolved to review them. However, I realised at the very beginning that this procedure was a mistake. Why should I reread pathology and therapeutics when I had no hope of ever applying my medical knowledge to practical life? Why review the past, which does not expand my horizon, when there are domains quite unknown to me? Such a domain was natural science, and I turned to it. In our library, which at that time was very poor, there was a splendid book by Auerswald, *Botanical Discourses*, with coloured illustrations. I read it through with enthusiasm, and then began to study plant tissues under the microscope. We had a microscope. Gangart had bought it for us with the fifty roubles earned by our comrades for constructing a fence around the common grave of the soldiers who were killed while storming the Schlüsselburg Fortress at the command of Peter I. The necessary reagents were obtained by the prison physician, Remisov, who was very attentive to all our needs.

At this time also I began to study chemistry. I again read through the large and informing manual of Mendeleyev, *The Foundation of Chemistry*, which had given me such a wealth of information during my university years. But all this did not satisfy me—I wanted the living word, the direction of my more competent comrades. Among us there was a naturalist, I. D. Lukashevich, who had been arrested in 1887, shortly before his graduation. As a student he inspired his professors with great hopes, and they intended to retain him at the university. Familiar with the methods of scientific investigation, he possessed such full and precise information that he could give absolutely definite answers to all questions in his field. Modest in regard to his own attainments, he was not hasty in making generalisations, and cautious in accepting hypotheses. At the same time he readily shared his knowledge with every one who applied to him for help. I, too, turned to him, asking him to deliver a series of lectures, and to direct our practical studies in natural science. Lukashevich undertook this, and Novorussky, Morozov, and occasionally Pankratov joined me as auditors. Novorussky did this because he was absolutely unacquainted with the natural sciences, having received his education in theological schools; while Morozov came because he had been interested in the study of nature from his childhood, and never tired of listening even to matters that were already familiar to him.

Lukashevich was paired off with Morozov in "cage number 5," where he had a large, improvised blackboard for drawings. I could hear him in the adjoining "cage number 6," where I came to take my walk, while Pankratov and Novorussky, who were working in the first vegetable garden at that hour, also caught his words. Thus we completed a course in invertebrate zoology, and a course in botany, for which we had several good texts in the library. The nimble hands of Lukashevich made, for the purpose of illustration, fine models from Japanese wax:

his sea-nettles and salpæ were admirable, while his histologic preparations and numerous drawings also served as object lessons.

Beginning with the year 1896, when we began to receive fine collections from the St. Petersburg Circulating Museum, we were able to pass on the study of mineralogy, geology, and paleontology, which we took up with great interest. When the museum promoted us from our first status of passive clients to that of active collaborators in the increase of its treasures in natural history, the practical work of preparing herbariums and collections of minerals helped us not a little in solidifying the knowledge acquired from books and from the lectures of Lukashevich. Once Novorussky made a list of the things we had sent to the museum through Dr. Bezrodnov, who replaced Remisov, and we ourselves were surprised at the amount of work that we had done for that enlightened institution in the course of three or four years. Afterwards, when we had left the Fortress, we learned with regret that not all of our contributions had reached the museum, and that many collections and specimens had apparently been lost. Lukashevich, Novorussky and I tried plants by the thousands for the herbariums, and they lay in great heaps in my workshop, awaiting the time when Novorussky and I should mount them on white pasteboard (ladies' pasteboard, we called it), upon which the well-preserved herbs made a lovely sight. We became so expert in preparing plants with delicate, fine leaves, afterwards mounting them on white cardboard, that the freshness of the colouring and beauty of the arrangement charmed not only our comrades, who demanded a demonstration of our work, but earned praise at the Paris exposition, to which the museum sent them, concealing the fact that they came from the Russian Bastile.

Considerable leisure, and the necessity of attaining great results with small means, so sharpened the ingenuity and inventiveness of my comrades, that they performed actual wonders. Thus, to assist in their study of physics, they contrived with the scanty materials at our disposal, a simple electrophorus, an electroscope, and even a small electrical machine. Novorussky became fascinated in preparing an entomological collection; and, in order to have material for all the stages of insect development, undertook to breed the insects. For this purpose he built "an isolated prison," as I called the two-story toy house, made of glass and divided into many sections—cells —into which he locked insects of both sexes, of various species. These laid eggs from which larvæ hatched. Fresh plant food was needed for each species, and Novorussky had the patience to devote about two hours every day to searching in all sorts of places for the necessary plants. His household prospered, and when all the stages of the insect's development were obtained, he prepared specimens of them. These consisted of nice little boxes, covered with coloured paper, each with a glass top. In the box was fitted both the entire insect and its dismembered parts, even to the tiniest antennæ and probosces, the work on which was done with the aid of a magnifying glass and tiny tweezers. In one box were shown all the stages of the metamorphosis of the insect, from the egg to the mature organism.

The ingenuity of Lukashevich was revealed in all its splendour when we needed material for the herbarium of the spore-forming plants; at his request, a pound of dried sea-weed was secured from a greenhouse, and from a drugstore a pound of lichens, from which slime cultures are prepared. After carefully separating them, with untiring patience he soaked them, painstakingly adjusted and pressed them, and then, with the aid of a magnifying glass, a microscope, and a pipette, classified them and turned them over to Morozov, Novorussky, and me to make up into an herbarium.

When we began to study geology, Lukashevich drew splendid charts in colour. One vertical column in the chart contained figures of animals and plants, graphically showing their evolution in the various epochs of the development of the rocky substrata. Another column showed the changes in the vertical surface of the earth during those same epochs, while a third enumerated the formation of the rocks belonging to each epoch. Not satisfied with that, he fitted in tiny specimens of those formations along with the drawings of the animal and plant life, in a long, upright box which also represented a vertical cross-section of the earth's core. For practical study we classi-

fied minerals and rock specimens according to their surfaces,
comparing them with specimens which the museum sent us, with
the help of a polarising microscope which also belonged to the
museum. For our study of crystallography, Lukashevich prepared many wooden models, simple and complex, and we practised identifying various forms from them. This task was easy
for Novorussky, but I often provoked laughter by my hasty
and wrong classifications. It was curious to note how one's
eyes gradually became trained. Just as a traveller, newly arrived in Japan or China, fails to distinguish characteristics in
individuals, but thinks them all alike, so did I at first make out
only one form in all those complex specimens. Only gradually
did my eye learn to catch the differences in the angles, ridges,
and surfaces.

One of the tasks given to us by the museum was the mounting
of flowers, and all their separate parts, under glass. That work
fell to Novorussky and me, and we prepared several hundred
fine mountings of this sort, together with descriptions of each.
Novorussky was particularly zealous in his labours for the
museum, and beyond doubt surpassed all of us. I think I held
second place, while Morozov came third, specialising in collections of moss and lichens, which he mounted carefully in neat
pasteboard boxes.

Chemistry was not forgotten amidst these studies. Under
the guidance of Lukashevich, Novorussky and I completed a
practical course in analytical chemistry, which was a review for
me, while for Novorussky the subject was entirely new. At
this time I had a private shop in the old prison, and we performed our analyses thus: I would stand at the little open
window in the door of my shop, while Lukashevich and Novorussky would stand in the corridor, outside. In this way we could
all see the chemical reaction which we wished to observe. Whenever we had finished some series of experiments, I would turn to
Lukashevich and say with a radiant face: "Luka, you will not
believe how happy I am at the light you have poured into my
mind!" Then I would add, "but here is another dark corner—
light that up also!" And we would make arrangements for
further study.

Thus in the course of several years we covered the most important branches of the natural sciences, one after another. For me, these lectures and joint studies endowed with significance the inactive life of the prison. Aside from the pleasure furnished by the mental labour, it was a continuous source of satisfaction to observe the infinite altruism of our incomparable lecturer, who begrudged neither his time nor his energy in helping us. And the products of our hands gave us great esthetic satisfaction, aside from the consciousness that we were taking part in work of cultural value. There was nothing beautiful in the prison, but we created things of beauty and craftsmanship, which one could not help admiring.

All these interests united Lukashevich, Morozov, Novorussky and myself into an intimate circle, and in this common work and continuous intercourse our friendship strengthened, and did not weaken even after we had left Schlüsselburg.

XI

CORRESPONDENCE

BELATED joy does not warm the heart, and so, when after thirteen years of imprisonment we were granted the right to correspond, I felt no gladness. In the course of these thirteen years, my relatives had gradually withdrawn into the distance. The roads of our lives had parted, and continued to diverge more and more widely. My relatives seemed dead to me. Is not a long, hopeless separation similar to death? If from the beginning we had not been deprived of the right to correspond —that would have been a great boon; contact with our relatives would have been contact with the living world. But that they did not want us to have; they designedly forced upon us conditions which, divorced from everything customary and normal, would create a fantastically outlandish world, a "Beyond."

The right to correspond might have revived the ties with our relatives, renewed our intimacy, but we were permitted to receive letters and send answers only twice a year. Twice! That alone stood in the way of intimate contact, and forced us to be cold. Then, too, we were not permitted to keep letters, but had to return them. Yet every one knows how pleasant it is at times, in a certain mood, to reread an old letter. I know not what the feelings of others may be, but for me it is a pleasure to see the handwriting of dear ones; when I glance at a letter, there arise in my mind not only the outward form of the writer, but by association also his spiritual aspect in its essential traits. Typewritten letters become impersonal, and I should not on any account wish to keep a collection of such letters, which cannot be distinguished by the handwriting, and the authorship of which can be determined only when you find the signature.

Living as we did, the arrival of letters did not gladden us, but brought forth anxiety; we were agitated, but not with the feeling of agreeable anticipation. No! It was the painful agitation of people who had better forget, and whose peace of mind was disturbed by the intrusion of a reminder from the outside world.

In Oblomovka,[54] Goncharov tells us, the arrival of a letter was an unusual occurrence. It disturbed the routine of the Oblomovs and brought confusion. To them a letter seemed a messenger of unpleasantness and trouble, no good could be expected from it, and they were in no hurry to open the letter, but let it wait a while! They had to accustom themselves to its appearance, prepare themselves for its contents—and the letter would be opened after three or four days. So among us, Lopatin, whenever he received a letter before dinner, would put it aside so as not to spoil his appetite, being certain that it would depress him; and then did not read it when he had eaten, so as not to disturb his after-dinner rest. To be sure, not all of us were so calmly sensible.

Of what did our relatives write us? Their letters never contained a word on public affairs—the Police Department took care of that. During all that time the only exception was the first letter which came to us in prison. That was a letter of sixteen pages sent to me by my youngest sister, Olga. Without any preliminaries which might have agitated or moved me, she addressed me as though we had just parted under the most ordinary circumstances, or as if that were not the first, but at least the three hundred and first in a series of letters, that she might have written in the course of the thirteen years of separation. She described the Russian industrial exposition of 1896 in Nizhni-Novgorod and the Conference which took place at the same time, and which showed an enthusiasm quite unusual for that period. In connection with this, my sister wrote of Witte's financial policy, and of the flourishing condition of Russian industry resulting from it. She told of the Social-Democratic movement, which received a strong forward impulse from Russia's industrial progress; of the conflict between the Populists and the Marxists, who were living through their

[54] The village in Goncharov's novel, *Oblomov*, the epitome of Russian inertia and lackadaisicalness—*Translator*.

first period of storm and stress; of the heated battles and venomous disputes which raged amongst our young people, in literature, in the home circles, where economic materialism excited differences of opinion, arguments, and almost quarrels. The entire content of the letter was of a social character; one felt in it the breath of life, one heard youthful, challenging voices. The letter went the rounds of the whole prison, and we each read it with gasping interest. But that—that first swallow—was, as I have said, the only one of its kind. We never had any other such letters. If that one was overlooked by the Police Department, it was only because my sister cleverly interwove social matters with scenes of domestic life, family talks on Marxism, and the like.

Usually one's relatives wrote about the weather; of the drought, storms and damage done by hail. They spoke of the wheat crop, of the fruit crop, and so on; a good deal of space was taken up by the family chronicles—marriages, births, and deaths. Regardless of their contents, these letters went the rounds; we read them as in the first years we used to read anything that came to us, as we read the insignificant *Pilgrim*, a theological journal, seeking everywhere, even there, a hint of life, of contemporary events. But while these letters did not gratify our wish to know what was happening out in the world, the permissible theme of domestic affairs brought to many of us grief and sorrow; in that domain the news was at times violently distressing. One comrade received word that his old, lonely mother was left without shelter. She had apparently become melancholy; at night she had left the house and aimlessly wandered about the city. Once they surprised her when, having gathered all her belongings, she was on the point of setting fire to them. Possibly the people with whom she lived were annoyed by the necessity of always being on guard, for the old lady was obliged to go to another city. There, without relatives or acquaintances, and without any means, she was forced to go to the poorhouse. Every one knows what sort of an establishment a poorhouse is. This mother was an ordinary, uneducated, but proud woman—all her life she had hated these philanthropic shelters for the homeless. Vainly did our comrade request that he be permitted to send his mother his prison earnings. The Department refused, but sent her fifty roubles of its own accord. However, the money was returned, and the Department informed the son that the money failed to reach his mother before her death.

In the family of another, things came to an even worse pass, resulting in complete disintegration. The mother, mentally unbalanced, had been for many years a patient in a psychopathic hospital. The father, a landowner, was dying in loneliness in a dull, provincial town, on his estate, from a severe illness. Strangers surrounded him, scheming for the inheritance. Two of his sisters were on hostile terms and did not speak to each other, while a third, who was estranged from them, had descended to the very depths of society. All this had been happening gradually through the space of years, but now it all fell in one blow, like the stroke of a hammer, on the head of the prisoner.

Simple and sincere were the letters of the illiterate mother of Antonov: she had to dictate them. She complained of her loneliness, grieved over the separation from her son, spoke about the helplessness of her old age, and after each expression of sorrow, inevitably added: "But may Thy will be done, O Lord!"

And we? What had we to write of? We were forbidden to write about our comrades, of the prison buildings, of our own cells or the régime of the prison. The censor of the Police Department regarded the contents of our letters with a suspicion which bordered on the ridiculous. Once, in a letter to his brother, speaking of insomnia, Lopatin quoted the verse of Pushkin: "On the bayonet of the sentinel glows the midnight moon." The Department returned the letter, demanding a change of text. A guard paced the wall of the Fortress, and over the Fortress, as over the whole earth, a moon shone! That was enough for the police censor to find in the verse of Pushkin a hint at the arrangement of the cells in the prison buildings. If the Department, in prescribing us to write only of ourselves, expected to find in our letter a reflection of our frame of mind, to note a change in our views, they did not have that satisfaction; we were silent as to our own experiences.

Now, since the outward side of our existence was poor, and our intense inner life was sealed, what was there left to write about? Since we were anxious not to disclose any corner of our souls, and since we were forbidden to mention this and that—it is not surprising that our letters showed little freedom or cordiality of spirit. They were strained, artificial; often one had to work over them for a long time, so as to squeeze out at length enough material to fill the pages of the large-size letter paper. Surely it could not be sent out half empty! Luckily, the officials grew tired of reading the long missives, even though they were sent out only twice a year, and soon they began to give us paper of ordinary size.

In thirteen years the ties of relationship had weakened, memories grown dim, feelings toward relatives had changed, had become somewhat distorted, I may say. When I learned that my favourite uncle had died, I felt merely regret. It is difficult to admit what a cold, purely rational regret that was! But when the little bird that lived in the cell with me had a convulsion and died, I experienced a great and genuine sorrow. The bird was tame, it sat on my shoulder, pecked at service-berries from my hands. I could cover its soft, warm body with the palm of my hand; it chirped on my table and happily splashed water in all directions when it bathed in the basin of the water pipe. When it died I cried for a whole fortnight. I could not look without weeping at the peg where it had usually perched to sleep. In order to stop this flow of tears, I had to ask the inspector to transfer me to another cell for a time. No, one did not feel like writing short, deeply felt letters!

Once, to make sure that there was nothing in his message that might give cause for its return, Morozov read me a long letter to his mother and sister, while we were taking a walk. When he had finished, I said: "Well, it is splendid material for your obituary." So we laughed. We laughed when we should have wept. Similar laboured passages, devoid of spontaneity and simplicity, filled the letters that I sent in the period between 1897 and 1901. My benumbed soul was aroused only in 1903, when after a lengthy and enforced interval, I received news that my mother was sick, that she was dying, and I realised that I should never, never again see her.

Yes, letters were not a joy, but a burden. The Department did not realise what they were doing. The officials thought that they had made it easier for us, but in reality the relief was a mockery. If the authorities, before permitting us to correspond, had asked me whether I wished it, I should have said "No," only I should have asked them not to mention it to my mother.

XII

WORKSHOPS AND GARDENS

FROM 1893–94, when so many workshops were opened
that all those who wished had the opportunity of using them,
physical labour began to play a great part in our lives. In
this we now received the support of the authorities. The
government appropriation for every kind of material was
generous, and we ordered great quantities of boards, blocks
for turning, veneerings often of very expensive wood, lacquer,
cardboard, pasteboard, and paper. Some of us made fine
furniture, while others turned out a cruder sort: cabinets,
whatnots, easy-chairs and tabourets. A few specialised in
making caskets from maple, walnut, chestnut, and so on; or
turned dishes, vases, and plates that were ordered by the
Commandant and various officials for our own use. Our work,
being that of cultured people, was distinguished by its beauty
and often was quite graceful, although except for our three
workmen (Pankratov, Martynov, and Antonov), none of us
had ever held a chisel or a jack-plane in his hand, and we
learned to work merely from Nekyts' manual. Trying out
various methods and making small inventions, a thing impossible for persons who labour for bread and from necessity,
we sometimes created masterpieces that gave us no little esthetic
pleasure. Particularly beautiful things were usually exhibited
in the corridor, so that every one might see them. Thus, for
instance, a carved buffet was exhibited, upon which Antonov
had toiled for half a year. For his labour he received twenty-
five roubles, which were divided among all of us.

For many years Antonov endeavoured to secure a forge
for metal work. Finally, in 1900, by "imperial permission"
its installation was sanctioned. Our comrades themselves
erected a whole building for this purpose, in the large yard
of the citadel, across which many of us, including myself, had
once walked on our way to the punitive cell in the mysterious

old building that so resembled a torture-chamber. But now, since 1893, in the ten cells of this former torture-chamber, from fifteen to twenty people cheerfully worked; and finally the men were hardly ever locked in the workshops. The wide corridor of the old prison, which had formerly worn so deserted and ominous an aspect, was now obstructed with lumber for all sorts of carpentry. In the blacksmith shop our comrades themselves built a forge, and the work began to hum as they turned out all sorts of things: razors, knives, carpenters' tools, sugar tongs, fine hatchets, and so on. Antonov assured me that he could even build an engine for a motor boat and make a piano for me.

Our gardening flourished. We sent for seeds of all sorts of vegetables and flowers, ordering through catalogues. We developed four hundred and fifty varieties of flowers. In this occupation Lukashevich was particularly apt, having been from childhood a connoisseur and a lover of botany. As for the vegetables, we even had an exhibit in one of the gardens. On a wide platform, decorated with sheets that were fastened by coloured bows, were displayed Lukashevich's ponderous turnips, Antonov's gigantic onions, my own strawberries, Vasily Ivanov's roses, Popov's tomatoes, and so on. . . . The visitors consisted of the prisoners, Commandant Gangart, and the doctor. When writing for seed Lukashevich, mindful of the smokers who suffered for want of tobacco, smuggled in, under the Latin name *Nicotiana*, a fine grade of tobacco and later seeds of makhorka [a very strong and coarse tobacco]. When the plants grew up, the leaves were gathered and dried and smoking began, at first secretly, later openly. Having no matches, we went through all the stages through which the human race had passed in the history of fire-making. Novorussky made a friction device, a revolving rod which smoked, but did not produce a spark. V. Surovtsev suggested a flint and steel; he burned rags, supplying the smokers with punk; and there was any amount of flint in the soil of the gardens; he even made sulphur matches out of chips and sulphur. The authorities, worried by the smoke and the odour of tobacco, tried to legalise smoking. In 1896, during the visit of Minister of the Interior Goremykin to the prison, Bezrodnov made a plea for tobacco as a prophylactic against scurvy—and tobacco was forthwith permitted. Since the allotment of matches was small, many smokers divided each into two, and thus satisfied their passion.

Many of my comrades felt such enthusiasm and love for gardening and horticulture, that the place allotted for vegetables, six gardens in all, and the six cages, where during the second decade of our imprisonment we had raised flowers, seemed small territory. They obtained Gangart's permission to open up two more gardens, the seventh and eighth. Later the same enthusiasts, Frolenko and Popov, managed to secure the large yard in the old citadel. Together with other comrades they cultivated it, destroyed that virgin meadow which had so charmed me when I went to the punitive cell, and destroyed all signs of the severity which had surrounded that mournful place where Myshkin and Minakov had been shot, where later Rogachev and Stromberg had perished in 1884, and Ulyanov,[55] Shevyrev, Andreyushkin, Osipanov, and Generalov, in 1887. In front of the historic prison building, where the workshops were now located, our comrades planted vast beds of tobacco, tomatoes, cucumbers, and many hot-beds, in which they even grew melons, which flaunted such blatant names as Golden Perfection. But Frolenko, who loved horticulture, planted fruit trees and berry bushes in every corner in the cages and gardens.

Thanks to the workshops and to the land allotted to us for cultivation, the prison, by a slow process of evolution, was gradually converted into a secluded working community, resembling an anthill in its energetic activity. The majority of us wearied of reading without a definite aim and system; wearied of studying without hope of applying the knowledge to some purpose; wearied of thinking continually within one and the same cycle of ideas and dreams; of grieving over the same, always the same sorrows. Unable to devote ourselves

[55] Alexander Ulyanov, brother of Lenin, was executed for complicity in a conspiracy against the life of Alexander III.—*Translator.*

to social work, to create or produce something for the benefit of others, we found in physical labour a relaxation from nervous strain, an outlet for our energies, the only field in which it was possible to be active. We found a real purpose in transforming by our labour the unproductive, rocky soil into soft greenery, in converting the joyless desert into an orchard nook. At times our comrades did wonders in this respect. Vasily Ivanov cultivated all sorts of roses on his small territory. Here were tea roses, moss roses, Irish, yellow, maidenblush, and others the names of which I cannot recall. Lukashevich and Novorussky made tin pipes and conducted water to their garden, where they constructed a small fountain about five feet high. Its thin stream fell into a small round basin, inlaid with tiny, parti-coloured pebbles, and framed by water plants, thin-branched alyssum and others. The water murmured and splashed quietly, as streams in the open murmur and splash. I used to call it The Fountain of Bakhchisaray.[56]

Novorussky, who, along with Lukashevich, was particularly anxious to beautify my surroundings, planted perennial birdweed along the entire fence of the first cage, which was considered my especial property. It grew luxuriantly, and its twisted stems, climbing up the cords, covered the entire fence every summer, forming a solid green wall upon which here and there bloomed large, white bells. At the slightest stir of the air this living wall rocked like a lovely emerald curtain. Through a tin pipe Novorussky led the water to the triangular flower-bed, which was in the centre of the cage, and made for me also a Bakhchisaray Fountain, like the one I had admired in the garden where he and Lukashevich worked. This green wall, entirely masking the prison fence, and that murmuring fountain, so unusual in prison surroundings, entirely transformed this nook, in which I had taken my strolls during the first years. Then it had been a bare waste, upon which not a blade of grass grew, and the earth lay melancholy, flat and hard, like a rock; it had been put to death, this earth, literally and figuratively, and lay dead and hard in its enforced sterility.

[56] The title of a poem by Pushkin.—*Translator.*

XIII

A WIRY COBWEB

Our agriculturists were not content with acquiring two new gardens and exploiting the spacious yard in front of the old prison in the citadel. Like the peasant in Tolstoy's tale *How Much Land Does a Man Need?* they wished to extend their domain ever further and further. They could not see a single clod of uncultivated land without dreaming of conquering it. Their minds were disturbed by the thought that the yard behind the old prison was filled with weeds, when this barren space could be converted into a garden with blossoming apple trees, honeysuckle and lilacs. They spent much eloquence and persuasive effort, until finally, in 1898 or 1899, their obstinate and energetic persistence met with success. "Well, go on! Work, cultivate the ground; only let there be peace and quiet in the prison," so it seemed the prison authorities said or thought.

The yard behind the old prison was a worthless wasteland, a long, narrow space, on three sides shaded by the Fortress walls, overgrown by an almost tropical profusion of nettles and burdock, and cluttered with a mass of chips and pieces of bark, which we had stripped from the wood destined for the lathe. The upper layer of the ground, for nearly three feet in depth, consisted of ponderous clods of limestone and gravel, for which reason only the most ordinary plants could grow there. A century-old mountain ash, just as lovely as the one which grew in the front yard of the old prison, stood in the corner of the yard and was the only thing that gladdened the eye amidst this abomination of desolation, further emphasising the neglect of this sorry place. Such was the spot that our gardeners decided to convert into a lovely nook of paradise.

The problem was a hard one, and all their pent-up energy was needed in this matter. They dug up the entire surface of the yard and cleared it of stones; they carried the gravel

away and used it for paving the gardens and cages. In order
to prepare the garden for planting, it was first necessary to
secure fertile soil. Our comrades dug a deep, wide pit, reached
the blue, Silurian clay, brought it up, and by mixing it with
sand and mulch, prepared an excellent soil, while into the
empty hole they threw the clods of lime, the useless gravel,
and the rubbish that had cluttered the entire space.

After this preliminary, truly cyclopean labour, the creative
part of their programme began, and I was not permitted to
look into the scene of operations; my comrades wanted to
surprise me. The moment arrived. They called, "Vera!
Come!"

Dusk was approaching when the guards brought me to the
appointed place, which I had seen previously in its most chaotic
state. I entered and stopped still: near the mountain ash I
saw a garden, a beautiful little garden with bushes and flower
beds. The flowers were in bloom. Tall lilies opened their
yellow, scalloped chalices; the columbines their fluted purple
crowns; by the side of the white nicotiana glowed crimson car-
nations, and a splendid dahlia bent its raspberry-coloured
head. Everywhere the honeysuckle shaded with its dull, soft
green leaves the dark, lacquered green of the lilac, and the
whole was crowned by the old ash with its lovely, feathery leaves
and large bunches of red berries. O, miracle! As in a real
garden, this patch was separated from the rest of the space
by a light wire fence.

In the soft light of the waning day, breathed upon by the
warm air and the aroma of mignonette, I stood and looked in
thoughtful meditation. It was so beautiful . . . so lovely!
Before my eyes were a garden, flowers, a wire fence and all
around the high walls of the Fortress. A wave of vague emotions rose in my breast and unexpected tears flowed from my
eyes. "Whence these tears? Why do I weep?" I involuntarily asked myself, not seeing any reason for sadness. I questioned and felt puzzled.

Back "home," as I had become accustomed to call the prison,
when I was calmer, I understood. That garden, created by
the labour of my comrades within the walls of the Fortress,

with its bushes, its flowers, that fence, so primitively woven
into an irregular web by the hands of the prisoners, reminded
me of other gardens, other fences. Pictures from the past
swam out of the depths of memory where they had been hidden
away by the effort of my will. These images had been buried,
and now they arose again out of the depths where they had
been entombed; and with tears they were protesting against
being regarded as dead.

XIV

BOOKS AND MAGAZINES

I HAVE already mentioned how poor the prison library was at the time of our arrival at the Fortress, and yet reading was at that time our only possible diversion. With years the library became enriched. Aside from all the books which Gangart passed on to us, some material, however desultory, was given us by the gendarmes to be bound. In the main these were supplements to the cheap magazines to which they subscribed, absurd novels with the most sensational names and descriptions of romantic and criminal adventures. In order to take advantage of free binding, they often loaded us with so much of this rubbish that we refused to expend our labour on it. During the first ten years we vainly compiled from time to time lists of books that we wanted to have in the library. The prison authorities dispatched them to the Department heads, who either ignored our requests or answered ironically that our extravagant demands would require an expenditure of one or two hundred roubles. When, during the inspection of our cells by a high official, one of us asked for books for light reading, the answer came that belles-lettres were not given to us, to avoid exciting us. However, thanks to Morozov's appeals to those visiting "personages," our scientific material gradually increased. But an especially large number of good books was bought after 1895, when, under Gangart, we began to earn money, and were able to use it for the enrichment of our library. As soon as we had a certain amount of money, we would present lists of the books that we needed, and these were procured after they had been approved by the local and government censors. To be sure, curious things happened in this connection. Once they refused to send for Mertvago's *Not on the Beaten Path*—they failed to realise that this was a work on agronomy. On another occasion they declined our request for Collins' *A Compilation of Spencer's Sociology,* although they had restored to us Spencer's *Sociology*, which they had confiscated in 1889. In later years the works of Gorky and Chekhov were forbidden.

In 1896, after Goremykin's visit, the Department granted us an allowance of one hundred and forty roubles a year for adding books to our library, and permitted us to prepare lists of new books, to be approved by the censor, of course. At that time there were twenty of us, and the question arose, what considerations should guide us in making up the lists? Some thought that the best way would be to decide by the majority vote. In that case the individual needs of such specialists as Lukashevich, Morozov, and Yanovich, would be totally ignored, since only the books desired by the majority would be sent for. Others suggested dividing the one hundred and forty roubles by twenty, thus permitting each of us to use his share for whatever he wanted; if his portion should not be big enough to make the purchase, he might get others to go shares with him in the acquisition of that particular book. This system permitted us to give up one's individual portion, or part of it, to help those in need of especially expensive works; and after many arguments this plan was adopted and we began to club together and present one another with gifts. Thus in Morozov's interest we subscribed for *The Journal of the Physico-Chemical Society;* and later for the English journal, *The Chemical News;* for Yanovich we subscribed for an excellent English annual. By clubbing together we subscribed for a German weekly, *Naturwissenschaftliche Wochenschrift* and for an English journal, *Knowledge*, and others. I must acknowledge that we were all interested in scientific novelties. When we read of radium and helium the whole prison was astir, and there was no end to our talks on radio-active substances. Does the ether exist or not? This was a question upon which Morozov and Lukashevich disagreed, and it stimulated heated debates.[57] The first news of aeroplanes was greeted with en-

---

[57] During our strolls we talked about the brilliant prospects of aviation. Our guards became alarmed, and informed the inspector, who at once demanded back the supplement to the magazine, *Field,* where the article on that subject appeared. The gendarmes took it into their heads that we were going to fly away.

thusiasm. Morozov's treatise, *Revelation in Thunder and Storms*, written in Schlüsselburg as an explanation of the Apocalypse on the basis of the astronomical chart of the heavens, plunged the entire prison into excitement. Shaking his head, Lopatin asked compassionately: "Is Morozov sane, immersed as he is in study of the Bible and the writings of the Fathers? Is he not tending toward *mania religiosa?*" But Antonov announced with ecstasy that Morozov was a genius, and would become a celebrity throughout all Europe.

We received Russian liberal monthlies, usually a year after their publication. The current news was sometimes torn out, sometimes not, and we became aware of Russia's awakening, the student movement, disorders, demonstrations, and so forth. We also learned of the development of Russian industry, and we had lively discussions on economic problems.

In the winter of 1895-96, Gangart sent the journal, *The New Word*,[58] to our bindery. The New Word! We had not heard any new word in all the fifteen years during which we had gradually withdrawn from the outside world, and the last ones to bring us "new words" were those who had been brought to the prison in 1887 and 1888. And now, from the pages of this magazine a whole avalanche of new thoughts poured forth upon us and agitated our passive life. Youthful, ardent thought challenged all the Populist ideas, so dear to us. The peasant commune was furiously attacked, and in its place was advocated free, personal initiative. Writers glorified the beneficent influence of thriftily acquired capital, by way of inevitable usury and exploitation. The peasantry were declared to be petty-bourgeois; they were to be made proletarians, so that the peasant, after "getting cooked in a factory kettle," might become a socialist. All these "new words" of the nascent Russian Social-Democracy had the effect of an ideological bomb which unexpectedly exploded in our midst. The first roots of the Social-Democratic current had been scarcely perceptible in 1884; the very development of capitalism in Russia was still questioned in the literature of the time; the prevailing opinion of the revolutionary youth

[58] The first Marxian monthly magazine in Russia.—*Translator.*

as to the possibility of its development, was rather negative.
Now, the new tendency, grown stronger, was eager for con-
quest and victory. Questions arose, acute and categorical.
. . . Beyond the walls of the Fortress a furious quarrel had
been raging along the entire revolutionary front, while not a
single echo of the battle had reached us. Now a journal was
put into our hands, which skilfully and brilliantly reflected
the fight that was being waged. The "factory kettle," in which
the peasant "was to be cooked," boiled in our heads. There
was much that hurt and offended us; there was much that was
biting, that seemed an insult to our ambition, and to our
respect for beloved ideas and persons. This journal left a
profoundly disturbing impression upon us; its contents dealt
blows to our most precious ideas and convictions. At once
different camps sprang up among us: some were triumphant,
others wounded. Lukashevich and Novorussky, those terrorists of 1887, who had attempted to repeat the First of
March, announced that they were Social-Democrats, although
they approved the tactics of The Will of the People. They
were supported by Shebalin and Yanovich; Morozov joined
them later. The remainder of our comrades, the Populists,
members of Land and Freedom and of The Will of the People,
opposed them. And now began discussions, heated arguments,
which reproduced on a miniature scale what was going on at
that time outside the prison. Each one defended his inner-
most opinion, and lent to the dispute either the bitterness of
insult or the challenge of faith in victory, in the support of
life itself. Strangely enough, our scholar, our objective and
painstaking naturalist, Lukashevich, was the most virulent and
pugnacious combatant. The matter finally took such a pas-
sionate turn that I once said: "Comrades! Living as we do,
peace among ourselves is more important than theoretical disputes. Let us cease our polemics!" Whether these words
proved a drop of oil on our tiny, turbulent sea, or whether we
already understood that for the moment we could not persuade
one another, and that it was better to let time compose in
our minds the new ideas that the journal had brought us, I do
not know; but henceforth our disagreements began to lose their

sharpness, although they did not disappear; and the militant mood died out. The same disputes with our Social-Democrats, which Ludmila Alexandrovna and I had carried on in cages 5 and 6, took place in other parts of the prison. Later we recalled laughingly how our passions had flared up, and how furiously Lukashevich had attacked me for my support of the communal ownership of land.

As our store of books became richer, particularly in works on scientific subjects, the paper that they had begun to give to us in 1887, began to play an ever more important part in our lives. Earlier it had cheered our utter loneliness, permitting us to express ourselves in poetry. But now those comrades who had chosen some special field had an opportunity to accumulate the necessary scientific material, to fix it in writing, and to do creative work, profiting from their collected data.

Working systematically from day to day, Morozov was able to create one of his chief works, *The Structure of Matter*, which was written in such an attractive manner that it was a real pleasure to read it. He used up whole reams of paper sketching out a multitude of articles and notes, and made brilliant conjectures in chemistry, physics, and astronomy; and when he left the prison he took this material with him. Among other literary activities at Schlüsselburg I may mention Yanovich's valuable statistics on economic questions, on which he worked with zeal, at the expense of his health. Lukashevich undertook a large work on the elementary principles of scientific philosophy, of which he published two volumes upon his release, under the title, *The Inorganic Life of the Earth*, which was awarded a gold medal by the Geographic Society, and the Akhmatov Premium by the Academy of Science. Other comrades engaged in non-scientific writings, such as memoirs and fiction. Several attempts were even made at issuing "periodicals," in which the element of humour mingled with that of serious discussion.

Usually one does not appreciate health or light, until one loses them; nor does one value paper, which is always at hand in ordinary life. But one who is acquainted with the history

of state prisons, knows what a privation it is to be for years
without paper, without an opportunity to put down ideas, to
divert his mind, and record knowledge if any is acquired. Our
life in Schlüsselburg was devoid of all variety, of all cheerful
stimuli; and the contributions of our comrades, poems, calling
forth sympathy, criticism, or laughter, or serious articles rous-
ing new thought—all were welcome gifts, which would have
been impossible without paper and pen.

Our life was poor, quite wretched in every respect. When
Lukashevich drew his first geological charts, he used for black
the soot from his lamp; for blue he scraped the plaster of his
cell wall, and for red he drew his own blood.

XV

OUR BENJAMIN

In Bret Harte's story, *The Luck of Roaring Camp*, the author describes how, into a camp of gold prospectors, a rising mountain stream brought a mother, who died shortly afterwards, and a child; and how the helpless child became a source of unexpected joys and happiness for the gold-seekers. A similar happiness and a source of life-giving joy for us was the appearance in the Fortress, of Karpovich, whom we in a tender impulse, immediately christened "Benjamin."

His story is well known; on February 12, 1901, he arrived in St. Petersburg from Berlin, and on February 14, at the reception of the Minister of Public Instruction Bogolepov, he shot and wounded in the neck this strangler of the university youth. It was during Bogolepov's time, after the student uprising in 1900, that college students were forced into the army by way of punishment; and that, by the professors' verdict, one hundred and eighty-three students of the Kiev University, and twenty-seven from the St. Petersburg University, were sent into the ranks of the army as privates. This measure, coupled with several cases of suicide on the part of students who had been thrown into the barracks, aroused all the intelligentsia and college youth, and produced an enormous impression on Karpovich, who, before going to Berlin, had taken part in university uprisings, and had been twice expelled during his university career. Because of this expulsion for taking part in the fight of the students against police orders and morals, installed by the Ministers of Public Instruction in the temples of learning, and because of his deep attachment to the student body by recognition of their common cause, his own sympathy, and the vicissitudes of his fate, Karpovich, who ascribed great political significance to the students' movement, decided to make an armed protest against the prime agent in the chastisement of the students. Not being a member of any revolutionary organisation, he decided to act for himself. He returned from abroad hastily and alone, without help from any one, accomplished his feat. Bogolepov died of the wound, while Karpovich, in March, 1901, was sentenced to twenty years of penal servitude, and dispatched to Schlüsselburg. By this act Karpovich successfully defended the university youth; after his shot the students were no longer forced into the army. Through his exploit he inspired the young people, who named him "Brave Falcon," and from among them came forth Balmashev, who one year later carried out in the name of the Socialists-Revolutionists a similar act of self-sacrifice.

Since the trials of 1887 and 1888, not a single person from the outside world had been brought to our Fortress. In 1901 only a handful of us were left—fifteen in all, nine of whom had been sentenced for life. In this small group we were doomed to live, without any ingress of new people, to revolve within the circle of our surroundings the self-same ideas, emotions, and moods, with no outlet into the free world. In the grey prison life, year after year, hopes vanished, expectations died, even memories faded. We had hoped that we would be replaced by new, young comrades, but in vain—there were no new fighters.

In the midst of this hopeless mood, Antonov announced to us one day late in March that the gates of the Fortress had opened, and that a "novice" had been brought in and taken to the office. When we were taking our walks, shortly after ten in the morning, there was a commotion among the gendarmes. They came to each one of us and stated that those wishing to go to their cells or to the workshops must do so at once, because later we should not be allowed to leave the yard. We surmised that the new prisoner was going to be conducted from the Fortress to the prison, and those who hoped to see the newcomer from their windowsills hastened to their cells. I did not go. I felt depressed, as though I had attended the burial of some one near and dear to me. Truly, was this not a burial? They were here entombing a young life, unspent energy, unused strength. So had we, seventeen years previously, entered this Fortress, to bear for long years the consciousness of our life's futility. He, too, would have to bear this consciousness.

According to Antonov's report, he came into this life of ours with buoyant steps, a tall, well-proportioned youth. He wore no chains as we did when we were brought in, nor the prisoner's coat with the diamond-shaped patch on its back; and, smiling, he waved his hat, saluting in the direction of the prison windows.

The appearance of Karpovich caused the greatest agitation among us: we of the old generation were to meet for the first time face to face a representative of the young people who had grown up and developed during the years of our absence from life. How shall we meet? What shall we find in one another? Will there be mutual understanding, a harmony of outlook? What will this messenger from the Beyond bring to the prison desert, what news, what moods? What shall we find in him—a real son, or an alien foundling?

In 1901 the prison régime was no longer that of 1884. To isolate Karpovich, who was placed near us, was now impossible. In passing his cell or the cage where he took his walk, we might stop and exchange a few words. These few words might easily extend to a lingering visit, and we at once took advantage of every opportunity to enter into intimate conversation. Communicating by knocks on the wall and conversing through the door, we received the first news of what was going on in the world. Longing to hear more, we begged Karpovich to write and bury the manuscript in the earth where he took his walks, so that some one could dig it up and hand the pages around for all to read. We wished to know about everything, all the details of the inner life of Russia, and also the events and happenings in Western Europe. Karpovich proved equal to the task, since as a student he had led an active life, in various places, and had spent some time abroad.

His good news revived our souls. According to him, all Russia was astir with life. The labouring class, which during the eighties had been hardly noticeable, was becoming similar to the western European type of industrial proletarians.

United, they noisily entered the public arena, demanded improvements in the economic situation, organised strikes that involved tens of thousands of workers, and demonstrated their coming strength in the city streets. The university youth, stronger in numbers, and no longer disorganised as they had been during the seventies, had united in one body throughout all Russia, and was rising in unanimous insurrection against the national police régime, which held the universities in its clutches. The wave of the student movement swept over the face of Russia, terminating in hundreds of arrests and thousands of banishments. There were illegal printing presses in every city, revolutionary leaflets were published, as well as newspapers and proclamations. For every press confiscated by the police, a new one straightway arose, and·the agitation continued with renewed energy and strength. "In five years there will be a revolution in Russia," Karpovich prophesied, and he was mistaken only in that the revolution occurred not in five years, but in four. But we, who had entered the prison amidst the silence of the masses, the speechlessness of all public elements, hesitated to believe such a prophecy—we feared to believe it. In our time society had been fixed, immobile; there were no protests other than ours. Everything slept. Could there possibly have been an awakening? Then why were we left lonely in our retreat? Why did they not send us new comrades, if the war was raging, if the people had awakened and were striving toward victory? There was a great deal of room in our prison, too much! Our dead had left great spaces behind them. Why did no one come to take their places? Was not Karpovich exaggerating? Was he not carried away by an illusion, natural in a person who had just been torn away from political strife?

Karpovich was not influenced by our experience, and acted impulsively, often provoking collisions with the authorities. Once, at the request of several comrades, the Police Department sent a dentist to the prison. To prevent any adverse reports on the part of the latter, we were naturally expected to maintain proper order. But Karpovich took it into his head to sing, and filled the whole place with the strains of some

aria, carolling at the top of his voice. In vain Inspector
Provatorov approached him, asking him two or three times to
stop. Karpovich did not heed him. Then the inspector led
him to the old prison building, where he remained two or three
days.

His attitude towards us was the attitude of a son, and his
downcast eyelashes bespoke the tender respect which he felt
for the prisoners of the Russian Bastile when he entered it.
We, the old inmates of Schlüsselburg, were Karpovich's seniors,
some by ten, and others by twenty years or more, and that
alone determined our relation to him, a friendly, parental relation. We had starved for new companions, and we treated
him with particular gentleness. His "youthful readiness," as
Lopatin called the impetuosity with which our Benjamin, without moving an eyelash, disturbed our prison discipline (once
he climbed like a cat over the fence, and jumped into the
neighbouring cage), had for us a certain charm, the winning
response to a boyish prank, a challenge defying all barriers
to which we had been wont to submit. Our hearts felt with
gladness that between us, the old revolutionists, and him, a
representative of the new revolutionary generation, there was
no chasm, no failure to comprehend one another's psychology,
as we had feared on learning of the unexpected arrival of the
new prisoner in the Fortress.[59]

[59] Shortly after the revolution of March, 1917, Karpovich sailed for
Russia from England, where he had been living most of the time since his
escape from Siberia, in 1907. A German submarine sank the boat, and
Karpovich was among those who were drowned.—*Translator*.

XVI

AFTER EIGHTEEN YEARS

As before, the white walls of the Fortress stood with their corner towers resembling clumsy Easter cakes; and as before the Fortress gates were tightly shut. As before, the river now lay smoothed as a mirror, now flung itself with a violent roar at the flat banks of our little island at the source of the Neva. But inside the prison everything had changed. Its formerly numerous inmates were reduced toward the end of 1902 to thirteen.[60] Some, the majority, had died of scurvy and tuberculosis; others had completed their terms; some had been pardoned, and three mentally deranged prisoners had been sent away in 1896 to a hospital. For the remaining thirteen the severe régime had eventually become softened. By means of persevering storm tactics the prisoners had step by step wrested various privileges, and continually enlarged and broadened them.

Here and there, in various cells, still hung the regulations of 1884, but in actual practice there was no more talk of "good conduct" or of its reward—joint walks and the use of the garden and shops. All these privileges had long become the common lot; all distinctions had disappeared. After our hunger strike for books, as if to give us a substitute for mental food, they improved the food for our bodies; they began to give us tea, sugar and wheat bread, and increased the daily allotment for food from ten copecks (5 cents) to twenty-three copecks (11½ cents). From this time on, death from malnutrition came to an end, and the health of the survivors began to improve perceptibly. The walks, originally of forty minutes' duration, were gradually prolonged. Now we could remain

[60] Frolenko, Morozov, V. Ivanov, Aschenbrenner, Antonov, Lopatin, S. Ivanov, Starodvorsky, Popov, Novorussky, Lukashevich, Karpovich and myself. Trigoni left in the spring, and Polivanov in the fall, of 1902.

outdoors nearly the whole day, and left only to go to the shops. One summer we were allowed outside even after supper, which was given us at seven o'clock in the evening. What a holiday this outing was for us, who had long forgotten the meaning of a summer evening! The interior of our cells had also improved. They were now less lugubrious in colour, and admitted as much light and air as we wished. Instead of monotony and solitude, our days were now filled with a variety of occupations, conversations•through the grated fences, and collective work, physical and mental. Save for the collisions of Martynov and Lagovsky with Inspector Fedorov (in the beginning of the nineties), the treatment of the prisoners became humane.

Towards 1900, the higher authorities of St. Petersburg seemed to have forgotten that some thirty-five miles away important political prisoners were incarcerated in a fortress; they had their hands full without thinking of us. The vigorous development of the Social-Democratic movement, the continual disturbances among the students, the appearance in the political arena of the recently organised industrial proletariat, which loudly proclaimed its existence, engrossed the entire attention of the government. The revolution was decidedly emerging into the open, and red flags were raised in the city squares of Russia. How could they think of a handful of Populists, whose activity belonged to the early eighties! Almost a quarter of a century had passed since March 1, 1881, and instead of the former dead calm, life was rising in ever higher waves. A buoyant breath of protest was felt over the whole land. Since the higher authorities had forgotten us, what motive would the prison administration have for oppressing us within the confines of the Fortress? The reins were loosened. If only nothing happened out of the ordinary! If only the higher authorities in St. Petersburg remained unalarmed, and nothing came to their ears which should provoke a reprimand! In the prison, within our enclosure, we were the masters of the situation. When the sound of voices arose in the prison buildings, a shout, or an occasional word of abuse, they did not come from the prison authorities, but from this

or that prisoner. It was not the inspector that shouted—
the prisoners were shouting at him!

I remember with what pain my mind reacted to the words
of Trigoni, uttered by him shortly before his departure.
"None of us is any longer capable of an energetic protest."

Yes, doubt might steal in, misgivings as to the growing dim-
ness of our spirit. But how could we manifest this spirit of
war against oppression? Against what should we protest?
What should we demand, for what should we fight? Life furnished us with no pretexts whatever for this. Everything that
we could fight for and obtain through our own strength,
through the force of time, while remaining within the prison
walls, we had won and attained. The painful acuteness of our
feelings had become dulled, and we were like people storm-
wrecked on an uninhabitable island lost in an immense ocean.
There remained for this handful of new Robinson Crusoes,
with no hope of rejoining the rest of mankind, only to sustain
as much as possible their mental strength, and to cultivate
a peaceful field of labour. The veil of forgetfulness descended
on our minds.

In 1902, about twenty years had passed since the arrest of
many of us, and among them, of myself. Some had been imprisoned for even a longer period. If during that time our
memories had remained as keen as they had been twenty years
previous, we should not have been able to survive. One's
spirit began gradually to adjust itself, in self-preservation.
The long period of adjustment had ended; he who did not die,
commit suicide, or become insane, had attained equilibrium.
Time drew a scab over the bleeding wounds. Things were forgotten, or if not forgotten, were repressed by the strength of
one's will. Pain, burning and sharp, was subdued. And since
one's mind had become stilled, and forgetfulness had come into
its own, it seemed as though the whole universe had forgotten
us. Not only the authorities at the capital, but every one on
earth. We could not believe that our relatives remembered us,
since even we had forgotten them. It was unbelievable that
our names remained in the minds of those who followed us, but
who had not known us personally. After twenty years our

memories retained no record of personalities, and not one single name.

> Cast out by storm and by all forgotten. . . .
> Outside a new generation has arisen;
> It remembers me not, it laughs.
> I have given them fire,
> I kindled the sun for them,
> Myself now in the dark,
> Moaning, always, always.
>   (BALMONT)

XVII

SHOULDER STRAPS

AMIDST the quiet and absolute calm which had come to prevail by the year 1902, trouble suddenly arose in the prison, and the apparently firm structure of our privileges, acquired bit by bit, fell apart like a wretched toy.

On the second of March we returned from our walk about five o'clock in the evening, and were locked in our cells. Then I heard the noise of doors being unlocked in turn, which was a sign that some unusual inspection was taking place. The key in my door also sounded; the inspector and two or three gendarmes entered.

"The commandant is dissatisfied with the disorder in the prison," he stated, in his low, dull voice, with a grave expression on his face. "There must be an end to it, and from to-day on the regulations will be applied in full force." He ended and prepared to leave.

"What is the trouble? What sort of disorder?" I asked. "We have not been reprimanded for anything. I do not understand at all the reason for this announcement of yours."

"The commandant is dissatisfied. The regulations will be applied from to-day on," he repeated. "I am not permitted to say anything more."

"Has something happened outside the prison?" I asked, knowing that what occurred outside usually was reflected by repressions in the prison.

"I do not know."

"But from whom does this order come: from St. Petersburg or from local authority?"

"From local authority," replied the inspector, turning to the door.

"We cannot obey the regulations," said I to him as he was

leaving. "They bind us hand and foot. They don't let us even breathe; violations are bound to occur. You will have to prepare punitive cells immediately."

"That we will," quietly retorted the inspector.

Similar short dialogues were going on in the other cells also. We were agitated, excited and bewildered. Whence came this calamity? The situation in the prison did not warrant it in the least. We were living peaceably, did not annoy any one, and were not ourselves annoyed. Why then were we threatened by the restoration of the old régime, the abolition of all the small improvements wrested from the authorities during so many long years? We had been in prison for eighteen or twenty years, and some of us longer. We had grown tired and old there. It seemed that they might give us rest and peaceful work. But it was not to be; again they sought scandal, violent clashes and collisions.

We could no longer live by the old regulations. We were not novices; our state of mind had changed since those early years. Our nerves were laid bare, and could not help reacting with unrestrained violence. That evening we were troubled and restless. Some feverishly paced back and forth in their cells; others lay motionless on their cots; we could not read— the book dropped from one's hands. Some talked, first with one and then with another neighbour, tapping on the wall in our old, traditional code. Our nerves were taut, like tightly drawn strings. What would happen to us? What had caused this repression? Again the uncertainty. Again we are Maeterlinck's *Les Aveugles*.

About ten o'clock one's ready ear heard how at the far end of the corridor the little window in the door of one cell on the second floor opened, and then slammed shut. About ten minutes later the same noise was repeated and a few words were heard. A third time the same thing occurred. A commotion started on the lower floor; then the door of that faraway cell on the upper floor was unlocked and the gendarmes dragged something heavy out of it. They were evidently carrying the body of a man; a band of gendarmes was carrying some one by the hands and feet. A hoarse groan was heard.

In a moment the whole prison was at the doors and listened intently. Every one thought that some one had committed suicide, and each began to call the guard, asking what had happened. A gendarme responded to the call, opened the "peephole," but said not a word.

Suddenly the voice of the commandant was heard, and the words, "Untie him!"

So some one must have hanged himself. . . . Every one began to beat at the doors with hands, feet, books, mops, shouting, "What has happened?"

The voice of the commandant answered, "Number 28 has violated the regulations." Number 28 was Sergey Ivanov.

What! A man attempts to take his life and they call that a violation of regulations! All the doors began to rattle. Some one's voice rang out through the prison, "Help!" Deafening knocks were heard to the right and left, below and above. The prison was in a bedlam.

For the third time the authoritative, loud voice of Commandant Obukhov was heard: "Fetch the doctor!"

A furious frenzy seized us; the prison was converted into a violent madhouse.

At eight o'clock in the morning, wearied, nervous, we came out for our usual walk. The nearest neighbours of Sergey Ivanov explained what had happened. Infuriated by the frequent watching through the peephole in his door, he placed a paper against the pane, and refused to remove it. In vain did the inspector try to persuade him not to do this. Ivanov would not obey. The inspector ordered Ivanov to go to the punitive cell. Ivanov did not move. Then the gendarmes put a straitjacket on him, bound him, and to the accompaniment of the commandant's mocking remarks they carried him to the adjacent empty cell, which was to serve as a punitive cell for that occasion. When the gendarmes carried him out, he had an attack of epilepsy, as was later explained by the prison physician. It was then that the commandant called out, "untie him!" while we decided that some one had hanged himself. Sergery Ivanov lay unconscious, and the gendarmes tried to bring him to, but after futile attempts it was necessary to

shout for the doctor. For some reason or other the doctor
did not come immediately, and he had difficulty in reviving
Ivanov. He was unconscious for about forty minutes.

Crushed, we listened to this story. What could we do?
Such scenes might be repeated to-morrow or the day after—
it was impossible to bear them. We did not have either the
physical or the mental strength to endure them. We must
resist, but what form should this resistance take? It was
unthinkable to drop the matter without a protest. We would
be crushed, stifled—we had to act, at any price. A day of
torment passed. Every one racked his brain over the question: What will happen? What shall we do? Toward evening
I conceived the idea of writing a short letter to my mother, of
such a nature that the Police Department would under no
condition permit it to go through. They would, however,
become interested in the recent events at the Fortress, and of
course would not leave the matter without investigation.

I wrote:

"Dear little mother: I was on the point of answering your
letter, but something happened which turned everything topsy-
turvy. Request the Minister of the Interior or the Director
of the Police Department to conduct an investigation immediately.

March 3, 1902.   Your VERA."

I communicated the contents of the letter to my nearest
comrades, and that evening gave it to the inspector.

"They will not forward your letter to the Department,"
said Morozov. Others also doubted. I alone did not doubt.

In the morning nearly every one stayed in; only a few
persons, including myself, came out for a walk. I was brought
to the sixth yard, which was regarded as my own. In the
adjoining yard, number five, Polivanov was taking his walk.
All was silent around us; no voices were heard. We stood
sadly at the grating, and conversed quietly. In the watch
tower a gendarme stood listening.

"Here is a case worthy of the protest of Vera Zassulich,"

said I, reflecting aloud. "It is worth giving one's life for such a
protest." And I went on: "It is not fearful to die, it is only
fearful to be isolated from every one. What if they confine
me in the old prison, maybe forever? Alone . . . alone with
the gendarmes . . . without books . . . that is worse than
death. One cannot live over again what we lived through those
first years. Our vitality is no longer the same. I should go
mad. . . . Madness, madness—that's what terrifies me." But
the image of Vera Zassulich continued to hover before me.

I told Polivanov about the letter that I had given to the
inspector. He looked at me with his large, sad eyes, like those
of a gazelle.

"And what if your letter is not forwarded?" he asked.

But I did not even think of that.

"That is· impossible," I cried out, angrily. "The inspector
does not dare to withhold it; he does not dare not to send it on
to St. Petersburg. I don't want even to think of that possibility, or to talk about it."

Scarcely had I returned to my cell, permeated with the sad
poesy of the snow-covered field, the delicate white flakes, when
the inspector came in and announced: "Your letter cannot be
sent on. Write another."

"Why?" I asked angrily. "You *must* send it. Censorship
is the business of the Police Department, not yours."

"In your letter you may speak only of yourself. That is
the regulation."

"I know the regulation. You send the letter."

"According to the regulations. I cannot let it go out; I will
show you the rules," and he departed.

I was so confident that I was right that I did not doubt my
victory, and calmly continued taking off my wraps. The
inspector returned with the official book in his hands and read
the relevant passage. Raising my voice I said commandingly:
"Enough of this! I know—all letters must be sent to the
Department; it is their business to hold them or to send them
on."

"Don't shout," protested the inspector. "I am courteous.
You should be courteous, too."

"You are going to stifle us, and yet you demand that we be courteous," I replied angrily. "Send on my letter!"

"Please don't shout, but write another letter; then I shall send it."

"I will not!"

"In that case we shall deprive you of the privilege of writing."

It was only at this point that I realised the seriousness of the moment. I had to act. It was necessary to make up my mind *immediately, that very minute,* whereas I had not yet decided, nor *had I thought that such a moment would present itself to me.* I had to gain a little time, to collect myself, to regain self-possession and then. . . . Instinctively I prolonged the dispute and asked in a reserved tone: "How can you deprive me of my right to correspond? I have not committed any offence."

"You refuse to rewrite the letter, and for that we deprive you of the privilege of writing."

The words sounded, while my thoughts flowed impetuously: "The letter will *not* be sent . . . the Department will not know. The regulations *will* be enforced. The old régime *will* be restored—we shall not be able to bear it. My comrades— what will become of them?" Then my thoughts turned to myself. "Shall I be able to stand all the consequences? Court-martial and execution, or the horror of loneliness, madness and death. . . . Shall I not regret? Shall I not repent? Shall I have sufficient strength to bear it all?" And slowly, so as to make quite sure that the inspector was not merely threatening, my voice uttered, "So you will forbid my writing?"

"Yes," said the inspector with finality.

A thought flashed through my mind like lightning, and thrust aside all doubt: "Only in action do you come to know your strength."

Instantly my hands flew up; I touched the shoulders of the inspector and forcefully tore off his shoulder-straps. They flew to right and left. The inspector screamed in a thin voice, "What are you doing?" and sprang out of the cell. The bewildered sergeant crawled on the floor, picking up the shoul-

der-straps. Presently they would lead me to the old prison,
I thought, and with feverish haste I informed my comrades of
my act. A storm rose in the prison. But I asked them to do
me a favour. I needed absolute self-control. I could achieve
it only if they refrained from all disorders. They could do
nothing—everything was already done. "One thing I ask,
give me peace."

All became quiet. A gloomy silence reigned. Every one's
soul was shaken to its depths, and gripped by alarm. Uncertainty clutched our hearts. From the far end of the building came from time to time the terrible shout of Popov: "What
has happened to Vera?" It was not a shout, but a sort of
howl. It perturbed me to distraction,

XVIII

UNDER THREAT

[VERA FIGNER's daring act brought fruit. A representative of the Ministry of the Interior was sent to investigate the conditions in the Schlüsselburg Fortress. He interviewed Vera and other prisoners, and as a result of his report the commandant and inspector were replaced by Yakovlev, formerly of the Peter and Paul Fortress, and Provatorov, hitherto Assistant Inspector in charge of the workshops. The prisoners won their points, and the régime remained practically the same as had prevailed up to the sudden attempt of Obukhov to reintroduce the old regulations. The writing privilege was not restored to Vera, but this was no privation for her. Incidentally, Obukhov was provoked to restore the strict order by Popov's breach of discipline: Popov had tried to send a letter to his mother not through the prescribed channels, but by inducing a young soldier to mail the letter for him.

The affair produced a lingering effect on Vera's state of mind. The strain of the momentary decision, the fatal action, the expectation of court-martial and of a severe punishment, the prolonged uncertainty after the removal of the officials, resulted in a nervous tension which took the form of terrible dreams at night and exaggerated sensitiveness in the daytime. The sense of uncertainty was communicated to Vera's comrades, who lived in the constant dread of her pending removal or even execution. To continue]:

Once a whisper passed through our ranks. Into the court of the old prison the gendarmes were carrying planks and beams: something was being built there. Suddenly the report came that Frolenko had seen from the window, parts of a scaffold being dragged in by the gendarmes. The prison became alarmed. . . . "We must bid Vera good-bye," said Antonov.

In the prison mist everything assumes an exaggerated, distorted form; life is full of phantoms—ours was one continuous phantom. Again uncertainty; again we were *Les Aveugles*, without a guide, wandering, groping, with our eyes closed, arms outstretched, while at every step our feet might meet an abyss.

Yes, the gendarmes were building a scaffold, and no one knew for whom it was intended. Since there was a scaffold, there was to be an execution. Who was to be executed? For whom was this scaffold intended? The uncertainty ended at daybreak on May 4th.

XIX

AN EXECUTION

On May 3rd, shortly after seven o'clock in the morning, my neighbour, Antonov, gave a signal of alarm, "Look!" I rushed to the window. From the prison gate moved a compact group of men in military coats while in the centre walked one in a short, sheepskin jacket. We understood. A prisoner was being brought to the Fortress.

A mingled feeling of sorrow and glad expectancy seized me: sorrow for the young life which they would presently bury in our common grave, and excitement akin to joy, that a current of fresh air, air from the battle that was going on beyond our walls, would find its way to us. Nevertheless the keen pain for that other man was stronger than the gladness for myself. However, the prisoner was not brought to our prison; he was conducted to the office in the yard of the fortress.

After dinner Antonov solemnly said: "There is a priest in the yard. . . ."

"What of it?" I asked, without understanding.

"There will be an execution," Antonov explained gloomily.

Since 1884 more than one execution had taken place in the spacious yard of the citadel. What a terrible feeling to await an execution! A certain physical anticipation of the approaching, definitely fixed end of another human being. . . . He was brought about seven o'clock in the morning, and he now had less than twenty-four hours to live. . . . Now only twenty hours remained, now fifteen, now eight . . . five. With every hour the thread of life grew shorter, as though an elastic ribbon, stretched before one's eyes, shrunk gradually, diminished, becoming an ever shorter and shorter piece. The hours passed, but the minutes seemed to stand still, heavy and dragging; they were so long—these minutes, tense with attention and expectancy.

Under the windows of the prison the sergeant stole along with a rope, pressing toward the building, so as not to be noticed. A gendarme glided by, hiding under the skirt of his coat a saw and an ax. In the distance sounded the last strokes on the scaffold. "He" would surely be led past us in the night, but we would not sleep, so that we might accompany "him" at least with our glances. But the cleverness of the gendarmes foiled our vigil: not one of us saw in the dark night how and when the condemned was taken out. At three o'clock in the morning day broke. In the Fortress yard the white buildings became visible; the officers' dwellings, and separated from them by the wide, bare strip of path, the white church and the black trees, still entirely naked, grew clear in the faint light. Deserted and dead was this yard in the light of dawn, which threw a yellowish hue on the dismal space. But lo, one after the other there emerged the inspector, his assistant, the commandant, the chief of the garrison, the physician, the priest, and the gendarmes. They marched in single file along the brown strip in the direction of the gate of the prison-yard. And at one side, like an outcast and leper, with a gendarme in front and a gendarme behind him, walked a stout figure, in a thick coat, in appearance a workman—the executioner! The crowd passed the window, the solitary one passed on and disappeared through the gate of the citadel. Everything became deserted and dead in the yellow semi-darkness of the new day. The minutes dragged on—the last forty minutes in the life of a man.

With slow, weary steps the lonely, black figure of the priest emerged, bent by what he had seen, and dropped sorrowfully down on a bench near the church.

Again silence and dreariness, in which there lurks the menace of approaching death.

It is ended! The commandant appears, then the inspector, the gendarmes, and a man in the uniform of the Department of Justice. And again, like an outcast and leper, a stout figure in a thick coat. And when they came out of our gate, one of those who avoided the executioner, not wishing to associate with him, he who wore the insignia of the Department of Justice, turned his face towards us, to the windows, in which he could not help seeing our pale faces, pressed to the panes. He turned his broad, sleek, rosy face and smiled—smiled impudently, complacently, provocatively.

. . . But one of the gendarmes, whose duty compelled him to accompany the authorities to the place of execution, clutched at his chest when he was about to cross the threshold at the gate, and said, "Your Honour, I cannot! . . . Spare me! I cannot bear it. . . . I cannot. . . ." [61]

[61] This was the execution of Stepan Balmashev, who killed Sipyagin, the Minister of the Interior, by order of the Socialists-Revolutionists.—*Translator.*

XX

A BROKEN PROMISE

ABOUT a year had passed since the feverish days of March and April, 1902. The succeeding three hundred grey prison days had erased those acute experiences. On January 13, 1903, I sat peaceably in my cell and did not suspect that fate was approaching me with a heavy tread.

The tramping of feet was heard in the corridor; the bars of the door grated, the lock clicked, and the commandant came in with some gendarmes. Lifting his hand theatrically, and raising his voice, he announced with slow emphasis, "His Majesty the Emperor, in deference to the entreaty of your mother . . . has graciously ordered your term of penal servitude for life to be commuted to twenty years." Then, after a silence, he added, "Your term ends September 28, 1904."

At the words "His Majesty the Emperor," uttered with a grave intonation, I thought: "A belated penalty for the 'shoulder straps!'" And that would have been better than what I heard next. I stood stupefied; thinking that there must be some sort of misunderstanding, because knowing my ideas, mother could not, should not have begged for mercy, I asked an absurd question:

"Is that a general edict, or does it apply only to me?"

"Only to you!" said the commandant shortly and with displeasure, and continued: "Now you may write to your relatives."

But I did not wish to write. I felt indignant, insulted; my first impulse was to break all relations with my mother. With her, my loved one! With her, separation from whom had caused me so much suffering! Already a year and a half had passed since my last letter to my mother, and it was a year since I had received a letter from her. What had happened at home during this time? What did mother know of me during this last year and a half of enforced silence on my part? Still uncomprehending, I contained myself, and said: "Let my relatives write—I shall answer."

The cell was locked; I was left alone.

With bitter chagrin I rapped to my comrades the news of the misfortune that had come to me—for my pardon *was* a misfortune to me. Whence had this calamity come? How could my mother, my firm, valiant mother, "entreat" pardon for me? Without tears, without even the slightest weakness, she had seen two of her daughters depart, one after the other, to Siberia; and *when she bade me good-bye, had she not promised not to ask for any mitigation of my punishment?* What then had happened to her, on whom I counted as I would on myself? What had happened? What had forced her to break the word she had solemnly given me before parting? Tormenting, unanswerable questions. . . .

By appealing to the Emperor's mercy, mother had interfered with my wish; I did not want mercy; I wanted to drain the cup to the end together with my comrades of The Will of the People. Now, without asking me, without my knowledge or consent, mother was breaking up my life. Could there be a greater insult? How could she have done it? She, who respected the convictions of others, their individualities, and who had taught me a similar respect? So crudely, so arbitrarily to break up another's life! To shatter another's will! I felt humiliated by the imperial clemency. And who had humiliated me? My mother, my beloved, greatly honoured mother. . . . She had humiliated me, but she had also humiliated herself. How painful it was to hear my comrades say consolingly, "It is not your fault!"

After three days the explanation came. It was a letter from mother, a farewell letter: she was dying; she had been in bed for three months; twice she had been operated on—an operation for cancer, my sisters added. I had been painfully angry; I had been ready to break with the one dearest on earth to me—and at the threshold of death! What could be done? What bitter reproaches, what scornful complaints could a daughter send to a dying mother? I had to answer, and my answer might be the last letter that would find mother alive.

My cruel heart was humbled. In place of complaints and reproaches there rose in my memory all the transgressions that I had committed against my mother; all the good she had done me. I recalled my childhood, when she laid the foundation for my spiritual personality; the moral support which she exerted at the terrible time preceding my arrest; the joy of our rare meetings in prison before the trial, and the comfort that I had received from communion with her during the fateful days of the trial. I remembered everything. Much, much had she given me. And I, what had I given her, cut off as I was at first from her by an early marriage, then by revolutionary activity and its consequences? Nothing but sorrow, and much of that! Inattention, egoism, so commonly displayed by youth towards parents; lack of understanding, an occasional sharp word, an unpleasant smile, a petty prick due to my youthful pugnacity. . . . I remembered it all, and suffered in my awakened memory. Nothing, absolutely nothing, had I given her all my life long. Now the day of reckoning had come; all I could do was to fall on my knees in repentance, and in recognition of all that she had done for me; and kneeling, drench with hot tears the dear hands, implore forgiveness . . . and I implored it! And in reply came these unforgettable words: "A mother's heart does not remember any chagrin."

My mother died on November 15, 1903. After all sorts of conflicting reports, the authorities finally, in February, 1904, gave me some letters from my sisters, in which they informed me of having buried our mother at Nikiforovo, according to her desire.

XXI

FEAR OF LIFE

So, in twenty months, after twenty-two years of imprisonment, I was to leave the Schlüsselburg Fortress. Twenty months for reflection, for thought of the future. An ethical problem as broad as a boundless plain rose before me. Fate was giving me a rare chance, a second life, but I was entering it not as an infant, free from knowledge and experience; not as a child with all life's possibilities ahead of it; not as a youth. who had nothing behind him and everything in the future. I had a long, complex past; on my shoulders lay a heavy burden: a short, red-hot road of revolutionary struggle, then a long road of blood-freezing confinement. With such a load I was coming out into the field of life. I was fifty years old, and might live another twenty years. What use would I make of them? Wherewith would I fill them? It was painful, fearful to think of these questions, while an inner voice reiterated them day and night. No one could help me to solve them; no book, no comrade, no friend. They had to be solved face to face with myself, unknown to any one, unheard by any one. Ahead of me was life, but around me I saw no solid ground; it had receded from under my feet, step by step, during those twenty years, and in its place loomed emptiness. Whither, in what direction, had life turned its course during the last quarter of a century? What had died during those years, what had smothered? What had been rejected and destroyed? And what had germinated, thrown out branches, developed, and perchance, matured? What?

My position was like that of a person who must swim, but does not know how; at some time in the past he could do so, but he has forgotten, and now he does not know what to do with himself. Before him and around him stretches the endless sea, encroaching slowly upon the little spot of land on which he stands. . . .

At that time they were giving us all of Chekhov's works. He was dead, that was why they gave us his books to read, but while he was alive he had been forbidden. I began to read him, and devoured one volume after another, until, in utter distress I told myself, "No, I can't read another word." As I stood thus, on the threshold of a second life, there passed before me a world of weak-willed and will-less people, failures, hypochondriacs. Page after page presented scenes of discordant living, and of the inability of people to build their lives aright. "The Three Sisters" aimlessly wander through life, expecting salvation from moving to Moscow. But it is within himself that man bears corroding melancholy, or the buoyant spirit of creative life; and the "sisters" will wither as fruitlessly in Moscow, as they withered in the provinces.

Here were people who, instead of actively working for the betterment of life, instead of fighting for this aim, settled down on a couch and said: "Let's discuss what will happen two hundred years from now!" They did not sow, yet they would reap; they dreamed of it as though it would come of its own accord, without the effort of each and all. . . . And this passive dream of a bright, joyous, and happy life for mankind was the sole spark shining in the dusk of their existence.

Was it possible that such was the contemporary generation? Was life really so dull, inactive and dead? If so, then what was the use of going out into it? If such was life, then what difference did it make whether one languished in prison or out of it. One would simply come out from behind the walls of the Fortress to find himself in a larger prison. In that case, what was the use of coming out? Why change the dull certainty for the dull uncertainty? To be sure, in 1901 there came to us a messenger of good tidings—Karpovich. To be sure, he was the embodiment of courage, of assurance that our motherland was passing through a significant "on the eve." He said that all Russia throbbed with young, active ardour for freedom, for the reconstruction of life on new principles. All was turbulent, restive, and seething. He told us of the awakening of the city proletariat, of the growth of their class-consciousness and of their appearance in the political

arena; of the aroused college youth, who were proclaiming bold
watchwords of war for right and freedom. He impressed us
by citing as examples the organised artisans of the western
provinces. It seemed that a new spirit soared over the Russian plain, which we had left so silent, amorphous, and oppressed. Twenty years had passed, and Russia was like a
huge cauldron, filled to brimming with thick, seething liquid;
it was already beginning to bubble, streamlets of hot steam
were rising from the bottom to the surface. Soon, soon the
entire mass would begin to stir and boil.

I meditated. Had Karpovich given us a correct estimate of
the facts? Did he not overrate the revolutionary activity of
the moment? Had not Karpovich, that messenger, who had
come into our prison to sprinkle our dead souls with living
water, had he not lived in a very special milieu of heightened,
fervent hopes? Perhaps, that milieu was a small, hot streamlet
of lava on the ice-covered surface of the whole land? Where
were the peasantry? Where were the eighty-five million peasants? What was the attitude of the backward country dis-
tricts? Now Chekhov was the portrayer of this dull provincial
life. Karpovich pictured the revolutionary movement, the life
of the industrial centres, where the pulse of life beat feverishly,
the pulse of the intelligentsia and the city workmen. He drew
them in their general features. But Chekhov depicted a gallery
of people, of living, human individuals, individuals taken from
the very depths, from the main stratum of our land. And it
was this average inhabitant, the average Russian type, who,
amidst the nasty slush of everyday life, settled down on a
couch and offered to "talk of what would happen two hundred
years from now."

But I should be obliged to live not even in the backwoods,
described by Chekhov, with its physicians, agriculturists and
sermonising professors, but in a genuine, hopeless hole. I
should be sent to Sakhalin, or to the Yakutsk province, as
they had sent those who had left Schlüsselburg previously. I
should live amidst an outlawed population, convicts, on the
accursed island, where continual abuse, including flogging, was
the order of the day. It was fearful to live where on the one

hand was a ferocious, uncontrolled administration, while on the other hand were people whom society had cast overboard for their greedy acts, for murder, robbery and all sorts of violence. . . . Or I should be amidst snowy deserts near the polar circle, in a nomad village of a few Yakut wigwams, where besides the uncivilised natives there would be no one with whom to exchange a word.

What significance was there in such an existence? Was it worth while to leave the walls of the Fortress for such a life? How could one live beyond these walls? On what? And why?

XXII

MOTHER

I ANSWERED the letter of my family on the ninth of March:

"Dear ones! I shall not write you of mother, nor of my own mood. Why should I distress you? Grief and weariness fully describe my state of mind. Grief, because during these twenty-one years she had been the centre of my feelings; weariness, because for a whole year I have been standing before her open grave, in constant alarm, disquietude, and fear. I am consoled by the thought that all of you conducted her to the ultimate border accessible to man, and that she lies not in St. Petersburg [as it had been falsely reported], where it would be so cold, so unfriendly; but in Nikiforovo, which she so loved, and which was so dear to all of us, and has now become more dear, more beloved. I have always thought how fortunate one was to have in one's consciousness some specially beloved spot, associated with childhood's memories; where one first learned to love the expanse of sky and fields; where all sorts of family events have taken place, and where our beloved dead lie asleep.

"I often think of you and visualise your journey to Nikiforovo, and these thoughts always bring tears. And maybe it was on the very night when you drove there that I had a dream which has moved me deeply. I dreamed that we four sisters were riding in a sleigh, over a perfectly black road, bare of snow, and that we were driving through a village, now uphill, now downhill. We passed rows of fine peasants' houses, with sloping stone steps for pedestrians built everywhere, squares with leafless trees, and arbours with golden-yellow roofs. In the centre, on a hillock, rose a white church, a mass of stone, with many graceful, golden cupolas. And when I looked up, suspended from the sky I saw over the church and the whole hill a crystal canopy which amazed me by its beauty, and for

some reason reminded me of the Northern Lights. When we
had left the village there spread before us a limitless field,
covered with tender green, and above it shone a hot sun in a
blue sky. For some reason it reminded me of a picture I saw
some time ago: tired pilgrims are walking; and ahead of them
in the distance, as though hanging in the clouds a fine outline of
a city is visible, with an inscription: 'Hail, ye who seek the
city of the Lord!' I awoke in an unusually elevated frame of
mind. And now, when on February 11th, I received your letters
(written in December and January), and read how you had
journeyed to Nikiforovo, your description somehow coincides
with that November dream, and I should like to believe that
on the night when you escorted mother, my soul accompanied
you. . . ."

XXIII

POLUNDRA

On September 28, 1904, twenty years had passed since the trial and my sentence, and that was the day, the twenty-eighth, on which I was to leave Schlüsselburg. But on the preceding evening, the local authorities announced that I should be taken away not the next day, but the day after. Meanwhile, in anticipation of the departure, I had already taken leave of the nine comrades left in the Fortress on the twenty-seventh. We were reserved, and restrained our feelings, trying not to appear deeply moved by the parting, though we might never meet again. Some one's eyes filled with tears; some one's voice broke. "Don't! You mustn't!" said I, turning away so as not to weep.

"Surely you will weep at leaving Schlüsselburg," said one comrade, several days before my departure.

"What do you mean?" I protested warmly. "Weep! Why should one weep when leaving this place!"

Alas! Not at the moment of departure, but later, on the steamer, when the round towers and white walls of the Fortress were out of sight, I wept and sobbed in despair. When I spoke thus to my comrades, I was thinking only of the place, of the stone casing in which I had languished so many years, and did not think of the living people who were still to languish there. I did not think of my comrades, whom I had to leave against my will. And when my thoughts reverted to them, the feeling of revolt against that spirit-crushing stronghold vanished, and was replaced by sorrow and despair; sorrow for those who remained in the Fortress with no hope of ever coming out of it; despair because of the immeasurable loss which had befallen me. Yes, I was losing the people with whom I had spent twenty years in close communion, under the most exceptional circumstances. For twenty years these people had been the only ones with whom I had stood in a position of equality and solidarity, love and friendship. From them alone I received help, comfort and joy. The whole world was closed to me, all human ties broken, and they, they alone, took the place of family and society, of party, homeland, and all humanity. Unusual circumstances tied us with unusual bonds. And now these bonds were being torn apart under conditions that were particularly hard for one of the parties. There was cause for tears, cause for despair and weeping.

"Those others" remained to languish in hopelessness, perhaps to die there, while I—I, robbed of everything spiritual, was entering a path of life that might be called emancipation, resurrection, but which in its tardy and one-sided joy rang of irony and mockery.

On September 29, at four o'clock, the sergeant opened the door of my cell, and I stepped over its threshold for the last time. Serious, self-centred, without joy or even sorrow, I walked along the corridor, whose arrangement of net and balcony I had not been able to comprehend on my arrival. I walked over the bridge that spanned the net, separating the building into two floors—the Bridge of Sighs. Hundreds and thousands of times I had passed over this bridge leading to cell number 26, in which I was locked upon entering the Fortress. Over it I had passed on my way to take my daily walk, as I trod it now for the last time. The small space of the prison yard and the building in which was housed the corps of guards, made up the border-line at which our dead realm ended, and beyond which for many years only those who died were carried.

With a sure, habitual step I walked across the accustomed places, as I had walked before thousands of times. I walked as though my usual stroll awaited me, or the work in the shop, and not a great change in life—the return to "the world." . . . But as soon as I stepped over the border-line and entered a new, unfamiliar space, I became faint; my body lost its equilibrium, the floor gave way under my feet like cotton, while the wall, at which I tried vainly to clutch with my hand, swiftly moved away from me, like stage scenery. "I cannot go on!" I sobbed, "I cannot go on—the wall is moving!"

The accompanying gendarmes caught me, not letting me fall. "It's the fresh air that does it," the sergeant explained comfortingly. These words about fresh air in a room which was never aired, where twelve soldiers of the garrison were quartered, day and night, from year to year, and where they were now standing, lined in a row, sobered me at once.

A moment more and we were outside. I turned back, and bowed for the last time in the direction of the prison. My comrades were clinging to the iron frames of the windows that offered them support, and waving their handkerchiefs: "Goodbye! Good-bye!" The steamer which was to take me to St. Petersburg had not yet arrived, so that I had to wait for it in a stuffy office, where the commandant and his subordinates were hastily and needlessly bustling around.

"Would you like some tea, Vera Nikolayevna?" asked the commandant.

Vera Nikolayevna, indeed! During all those twenty years I had no name as far as "they" were concerned. For twenty years I had been only a number to them. Number 11, they always called me; some ten minutes ago I was still Number 11 . . . and now suddenly I became Vera Nikolayevna. No, I did not want their favours.

An hour passed, possibly longer. Finally the inspector appeared, an unpleasant, insignificant, stubborn man, whom we all treated with aversion. "Come, please," he said, and in a small group we moved to the gates of the Fortress. A few more steps, and the prison, in which my comrades remained, would be hidden from sight. But I did not turn back—I was afraid of turning; I wanted to control my feelings at any price.

Beyond the gates, to the right, was Lake Ladoga. The setting sun shone on it, and in its rays the water glistened, dazzlingly, like quicksilver in a flat plate. At the head of the small promontory at the end of the island, the waters of the Neva sparkled, eddying in tiny ripples of leaden sheen. In midstream, a small white steamer hung motionless, while on the opposite shore the vague outlines of a village settlement showed through a tender, pink mist. Everything was calm and beautiful. I realised this beauty, but did not feel it, it did not make

me happy, I was not carried away by it, and I marvelled at myself that I remained cold and only looked on. The sun was
poised over a *free*, boundless horizon. Well, what of it!

I was taken out to the steamer in a cutter, accompanied by
the inspector and the gendarmes; not a soul was to be seen on
it. *Polundra!* I read and memorised the name. *Polundra*, in
the jargon of the sailors means: "Beware!" my brother Nikolai
explained to me, several days later, when I met him. How
often later on did this word oppress my heart! On the threshold of a new life, after all that I had lived through, instead of
an encouraging word of greeting, fate menacingly stood before
me and hurled its harsh "Beware!" Did it mean to warn me,
"Do not nourish any illusions?" Did it mean to say: "You
have not suffered enough! There is more to come?" The
ominous warning tormented me, promising trouble and sorrow
beyond the walls of my prison.

On the steamer, not far from St. Petersburg, I asked where
I was being taken.

The inspector answered: "Yesterday I took two of your
comrades to the House of Preliminary Detention, but you are
going to the Peter and Paul Fortress."

My heart contracted. Still another fortress!

The magnificent quay along the Neva was brilliantly lighted,
when, about ten o'clock in the evening the *Polundra* docked near
the Peter and Paul Fortress.

"Come ashore!" said the gendarme, pointing to the place
where the gang plank was usually laid. But I did not see anything, and did not move from my place.

"Why don't you come?" urged the inspector.

But I was blind. "There is nothing there," I answered.

"What do you mean, nothing! Here is the gang plank; come
now!"

"No, no, that is water. How can I go there?" I insisted.

Two of the gendarmes took me under the arms and led me to
the land, where a carriage awaited us. The iron-grated gates
of the Troubetskoy Wing of the Peter and Paul Fortress were
familiar to me. Twenty years ago I had come out of here,
"abandoning all hope," and the pitying look of the "pledged"

soldier had with compassion followed my figure, clad in its grey coat with the diamond-shaped patch on the back. The stairway and long corridor were also familiar to me. Every two weeks I had passed that way for the twenty-minute visit with my mother and sister. And here was cell number 43, in which I had spent almost two years before the trial; but we passed it. I was assigned another cell, in another corridor.

This cell was large, but with a low ceiling. It was lighted with electricity instead of the former kerosene lamp.

New surroundings are always uncomfortable. I was hardly seated on the cot, about to collect my thoughts, when the lock clicked and with quick steps a tall, elderly officer came in. His face was thin and colourless; he had unpleasant, grey, protruding eyes.

"You will like it here," he said, praising my new quarters, and took in the cell with a broad gesture. "Everything is different now: electricity and all conveniences," he said, pointing to the light and to the toilet without a cover, taken off, as I later learned, to prevent the prisoners from rattling the covers by way of protest.

What did he mean? I became alarmed. Evidently this man was counting on my taking advantage of his hospitality for a long time. Was it possible that instead of being sent to Siberia I should be left here, and had only been moved from one fortress to another? But he began to shower me with questions about Schlüsselburg. What had my life there been like? Did I have books? Was I permitted to see my family? To top it all, he sat down unceremoniously, without permission, on the cot beside me, crossing his legs. I couldn't stand that. I had grown savagely shy in prison, had become unaccustomed to people, and was never left in a cell alone with any one. I was afraid of this impertinent stranger who settled on my cot, with crossed legs.

"Go away! Go away!" I said angrily, raising my voice, and stood up.

The inspector evidently had not anticipated such a reception; he jumped up from the cot and instantly disappeared. At last I was alone, but I could not compose myself. I had lived through so much that day, and there was still so much uncertainty ahead! Would they send me away, or leave me here? How should I meet my family? Mother had died—she could wait no longer! It was better so. What sort of a meeting would that have been? She was on her death-bed; I should have been brought to her by gendarmes. . . . What could we say to one another: the dying mother and the daughter returning from twenty years in prison! No one could bear such a meeting. And the gendarmes would have stood at the door. . . . I could not calm myself. How might I flee from my besieging thoughts? If I only had a book, to stifle my thoughts with those of others!

I knocked on the door: "Guard, please get me something to read. I cannot sleep in a new place."

"I do not know whether I can," answered the gendarme, "the library is closed, but I will ask."

In a quarter of an hour, a tall, slender non-commissioned officer, with a handsome, cultured face, handed me a book from which a page just then dropped to the floor. I picked it up. O wonder! Before me was a splendid portrait of Nadson. I turned the pages. The poetry of Nadson did not satisfy me. I felt in him too keenly a man of words and not of deeds, and that repulsed me. But my mood did change; the weak will of Nadson roused my strength.

I was no longer afraid—fear did not master me. Nothing more would happen to-day, and to-morrow—of to-morrow I need not think.

I placed the portrait in front of me on the table, leaning it against the pitcher; a friend was with me, I was not alone.

The chimes of the Peter and Paul Fortress were singing the same melody they had sung twenty years ago. . . . I fell asleep. The dark waves of the Neva roared; a white steamer, the *Polundra*, was speeding into the unknown. But I did not yet know that *Polundra* meant "Beware!"

XXIV

THE FIRST MEETING

THREE days passed, and still I was not permitted to see any one.

"You will see your family on the day when all the rest of the prisoners have visitors," said the inspector.

That was heartless, but wise. Anticipation, no matter how anxious, cannot last indefinitely. The weary tension relaxes; and on the fourth day my excitement and strain had almost vanished. I became absorbed in reading Carlyle's *Heroes and Hero-Worship*. Finally, about one o'clock on the fourth day, the inspector came in.

"Get ready," he said, "your brother and sisters have arrived; presently you will be taken in to see them." And, seeing my blanched, frightened face, he added: "I told them to act as though nothing had happened."

"As though nothing had happened!" That was heartless, but wise. That was a programme to follow, a programme not only for them, for my brother and sisters, but for me, too, and I had had no preparation at all. The programme said: Pretend. Don't play a drama, but act out the play. "As though nothing had happened!" Don't throw yourself on the ground, don't strike your head on the floor, don't sob in convulsions of soul and body. Put on a mask! Put out all the fires in your soul!

I was led along through corridors, stairs and unfamiliar passages; and again my steps were uncertain, and my hand sought support by clutching at the wall. A door opened.

There sat my brother and sisters. There sat a robust, mature man, a handsome engineer, who had paved for himself a wide path in life, my brother, whom I knew and remembered as a rosy-cheeked, beardless youth. There sat stout, sedate ladies, mothers of families, who had experienced decades of life's humdrum—my sisters, whom I knew and remembered as delicate young girls. While opposite them stood I, like that woman in

Dickens' novel—that mad old woman, in the rags of a wedding dress, who many years before had stopped the clock at the stroke of twelve, on the day when she learned that she had been treacherously deceived—the groom was not to appear. My life had stopped twenty years ago, and I had lived on in the mad illusion that the clock of life still pointed to noon.

My brother seated me in a chair opposite him. He took my hands in his. He held them thus all the time. Afraid to move, I tried to look at him only; he had changed less, and I eagerly tried to find the former, rosy-cheeked, beardless Petya. I had to find something familiar, near and dear, in these changed, strange, and alien figures. Little by little, through the thick veil of the present, broke delicate traits of the distant past. I began to recognise, to find that which I sought. It seemed as though in the dim distance, amidst the fog of confusion, chaos and obscurity, I found a fragile roadpost, and was trying to tie to it the cobweb strand of remembrance, in order to stretch it across the span of the past twenty years, and thus link the past with the present unhappy hour.

. . . Of what did we speak? I do not remember. There were words, empty, dull, untrue sounds, as though counterfeit coins fell and resounded, one after the other, on a marble table. The footlights were on, we were acting out the play, "as though nothing had happened."

"The visit is ended!" declared the inspector, rising.

That night, awakening often, I felt on the verge of insanity. My head was filled with words, impetuous and uncontrollable, a whole torrent of them, meaningless and incoherent. Names of objects—names and names. They poured forth, like white, crumpled papers, tumbling out of a bag that is being shaken; and they fell, swift as the sparks that one sees after a terrible blow from some one's fist. At the same time my consciousness, like an outside observer, stood terrified, and asked: What is happening? Will this go on, and am I losing my mind? . . .

THE END

APPENDICES

I

THE LETTER OF THE EXECUTIVE COMMITTEE OF THE WILL OF THE PEOPLE TO TSAR ALEXANDER III

YOUR MAJESTY:—

Fully comprehending the sorrow which you are experiencing during these present moments, the Executive Committee does not, however, feel it right to yield to the impulse of natural delicacy, which demands, perhaps, a certain interval of waiting before the following explanation should be made. There is something higher than the most legitimate emotions of a human being: that is one's duty to his native land, a duty for which every citizen is obliged to sacrifice himself and his own feelings, and even the feelings of others. In obedience to this primal duty, we have determined to address you at once, without any delay, since that historical process does not wait, which threatens us in the future with rivers of blood and the most violent convulsions.

The bloody tragedy which was played on the shores of the Ekaterininsky Canal, was not accidental, and surprised no one. After all that has passed in the course of the last decade, it was absolutely inevitable, and in this lies its profound meaning—a meaning which must be understood by the man whom fate has placed at the head of the state power. To interpret such facts as being the evil plots of separate individuals, or even of a band of criminals, would be possible only to a man who was quite incapable of analysing the life of nations. In the course of ten years we have seen how, notwithstanding the most severe persecutions, notwithstanding the fact that the government of the late Emperor sacrificed everything, freedom, the interests of all classes, the interests of industry and even its own dignity, everything, unconditionally, in its attempt to suppress the revolutionary movement, that movement has nevertheless tenaciously grown and spread, attracting to itself the best elements of the nation, the most energetic and self-denying people of Russia, and for three years now has engaged in desperate, partisan warfare with the government. You know well, your Majesty, that it is impossible to accuse the government of the late Emperor of lack of energy. They have hanged our followers, both guilty and innocent; they have filled the prisons and distant provinces with exiles. Whole dozens of our leaders have been seized and hanged. They have died with the courage and calmness of martyrs, but the movement has not been suppressed, it has grown and gained strength. Yes, your Majesty, the revolutionary movement is not such as to depend on individual personalities. It is a function of the national organism, and the gallows, erected to hang the most energetic exponents of that function, is as powerless to save this outworn order of life, as was the death of the Saviour on the cross, to save the corrupt, ancient world from the triumph of reforming Christianity.

Of course, the government may continue to arrest and hang a great multitude of separate individuals. It may destroy many revolutionary groups. Let us grant that it will destroy even the most important of the existing revolutionary organisations. This will not change the state of affairs in the least. The conditions under which we are living, the general dissatisfaction of the people, Russia's aspiration towards a new order of life, all these create revolutionists. You cannot exterminate the whole Russian people, you cannot therefore destroy its discontent by means of reprisals; on the contrary, discontent grows thereby. This is the reason that fresh individuals, still more incensed, still more energetic, are constantly arising from the ranks of the people in great numbers to take the place of those who are being destroyed. These individuals, in the interests of the conflict, will of course organise themselves, having at hand the ready experience of their predecessors, and therefore the revolutionary movement in the course of time must grow stronger, both in quality and quantity. This we have actually seen in the last ten years. What did the death of the adherents of Dolgushin, Tchaikovsky, the agitators of the year 1784, avail the government? The far more determined populists arose to take their place. The terrible reprisals of the government called forth upon the stage the terrorists of '78 and '79. In vain did the government exterminate such men as the adherents Kovalsky, Dubrovin, Osinsky, and Lizogub; in vain did it destroy dozens of revolutionary cicles. From those imperfect organisations, by the course of natural selection there developed still hardier forms. There appeared at last the Executive Committee, with which the government has not yet been able to cope.

Casting a dispassionate glance over the depressing decade through which we have lived, we can accurately foretell the future progress of the movement if the political tactics of the government do not change. The movement must go on growing, gaining strength; terroristic acts will be repeated in ever more alarming and intensified forms. A more perfect, stronger revolutionary organisation will take the place of the groups that are wiped out. In the meantime, the number of malcontents in the land will increase, popular faith in the government will lapse, and the idea of revolution, of its possibility and inevitability, will take root and grow more and more rapidly in Russia. A terrible outburst, a bloody subversion, a violent revolutionary convulsion throughout all Russia, will complete the process of the overthrow of the old order.

What evokes this terrible perspective, what is responsible for it? Yes, your Majesty, a terrible and sad perspective. Do not take this for a mere phrase. We understand better than any one else, how sad is the perishing of so much talent, such energy, in a labour of destruction, in bloody conflicts, when, under different conditions, these forces might be directly applied to creative work, to the progress of the people, the development of their minds, and the well-being of their national life. Whence comes this sad necessity for bloody strife?

From the fact, your Majesty, that there exists among us now no actual government, in the true meaning of the word. A government, according to its fundamental principle, should express only the aspirations of the people, should accomplish only the Will of the People. While in Russia, pardon us for the expression, the government has degenerated into a veritable camarilla, and deserves to be called a band of usurpers far more than does the Executive Committee.

Whatever may have been the intentions of the Sovereign, the acts of the government have had nothing in common with the popular welfare and desires. The Imperial Government has subjugated the people to the state of bondage, it has delivered the masses into the power of the nobility; and now it is openly creating a pernicious class of speculators and profiteers. All its reforms lead to but one result, that the people have sunk into ever greater slavery, into a state of more complete exploitation. It has brought Russia to such a point that at the present time the popular masses find themselves in a state of utter beggary and ruin, not free even at their own domestic firesides from the most insulting surveillance, powerless even in their own communal village affairs. Only the spoiler, the exploiter, is favoured by the protection of the law and the government. The most revolting depredations remain unpunished. But what a terrible fate awaits the man who sincerely thinks and plans for the public welfare! You know well, your Majesty, that it is not only the socialists who are exiled and persecuted. What kind of a government is this, then, which protects such an "order"? Is it not rather a band of rascals, an absolute usurpation?

This is the reason why the Russian government has no moral influence, no support in the people; this is why Russia gives birth to so many revolutionists; this is why even such a fact as regicide awakens joy and sympathetic approval in an enormous part of the population. Yes, your Majesty, do not deceive yourself with the declarations of fawners and flatterers. Regicide is very popular in Russia.

There are two possible escapes from this situation: either a revolution, quite inevitable, which cannot be averted by any number of executions, or a voluntary turning to the people on the part of the Supreme Authority. In the interests of our native land, in the desire to avoid those terrible calamities which always accompany a revolution, the Executive Committee turns to your Majesty with the advice to choose the second course. Believe us that as soon as the Supreme Authority ceases to be arbitrary, as soon as it firmly determines to accomplish only the demands of the nation's consciousness and conscience, you may boldly drive out the spies who defile your government, send your convoys into their barracks, and burn the gallows which are depraving your people. The Executive Committee itself will cease its present activity, and the forces organised around it will disperse and consecrate themselves to cultural work for the benefit of their own people. A peaceful conflict of ideas will take the place of the violence which is more repugnant to us than to your servants, and which we practise only from sad necessity.

We turn to you, casting aside all prejudices, stifling that distrust, which the age-long activity of the government has created. We forget that you are the representative of that power which has so deceived the people, and done them so much harm. We address you as a citizen and an honourable man. We hope that the feeling of personal bitterness will not suppress in you the recognition of your duties, and the desire to know the truth. We too might be embittered. You have lost your father. We have lost not only our fathers, but also our brothers, our wives, our children, our best friends. But we are ready to suppress our personal feelings if the good of Russia demands it. And we expect the same from you also.

We do not lay conditions upon you. Do not be shocked by our proposition. The conditions which are indispensable in order that the revolutionary movement shall be transformed into peaceful activity, have been created, not by us, but by history. We do not impose them, we only recall them to your mind.

In our opinion there are two such conditions:

1. A general amnesty for all political crimes committed in the past, inasmuch as these were not crimes, but the fulfilment of a civic duty.

2. The convocation of an assembly of representatives of all the Russian people, for the purpose of examining the existing forms of our state and society, and revising them in accord with the desires of the people.

We consider it necessary to mention, however, that in order that the legality of the Supreme Authority may be confirmed by popular representation, the process of selecting delegates must be absolutely unrestricted. Therefore the elections must be held under the following conditions:

1. The deputies must be sent from all ranks and classes alike, and in numbers proportionate to the population.

2. There must be no restrictions imposed upon either the electors or the deputies.

3. Electioneering, and the elections themselves, must be carried out in complete freedom, and therefore the government must grant as a temporary measure, prior to the decision of the popular assembly:

a. Complete freedom of the press,

b. Complete freedom of speech,

c. Complete freedom of assembly,

d. Complete freedom of electoral programmes.

This is the only way in which Russia can be restored to a course of normal and peaceful development. We solemnly declare before our native land and all the world, that our party will submit unconditionally to the decision of a Popular Assembly which shall have been chosen in accord with the above-mentioned conditions;

and in the future we shall offer no armed resistance whatever to a government that has been sanctioned by the Popular Assembly.

And so, your Majesty, decide. Before you are two courses. On you depends the choice; we can only ask Fate that your reason and conscience dictate to you a decision which will conform only to the good of Russia, to your own dignity, and to your duty to your native land.

(Signed)   THE EXECUTIVE COMMITTEE.

March 10 (23), 1881.

TO MY MOTHER

O comrade, if you see the light again,
The free, bright sun, if you embrace your own,
Remember then my mother in her pain—
My mother, waiting through the years alone.
And for the sake of all things dear to us,
Sacred, and pure, and tender, near to us,
I charge you, give her word of me, and say
That I am well, and live, and greet each day
With no repining, no regret, but true
To my ideals and to my country, too.
At first the days were stern and hard for me;
The burden of my longing grievously
Crushed to the earth my spirit and its song—
Ah, joy is short, but life is very long—
My face no longer pales, although I know
That weary, endless years shall come, and go,
And that I cannot ever hope to see
My mother, nor embrace her tenderly.
I ask not that she love me, for my heart
Feels that she loves me warmly, though apart
From me for many a long year.
I feel that in her breast she still holds dear
My memory. But oh, let her not weep;
Remembering me—my griefs are all asleep—
And I am happy, brave. She shall not grieve!
One little charge alone with her I leave.

Ask her to bless me in her prayers at night,
To seal my spirit with a cross of light,
So that with stouter heart her daughter may
Travel the long and rough and dreary way.